The American Revolution

The Critical Issues / Robert F. Berkhofer, Jr.

THE AMERICAN
REVOLUTION
The Critical Issues

THE AMERICAN
REVOLUTION
The Critical Issues

Edited by

ROBERT F. BERKHOFER, JR.
The University of Wisconsin

 LITTLE, BROWN AND COMPANY   BOSTON

CONTENTS

INTRODUCTION

Before a historian can explain the whys of the American Revolution, he must figure out what it was; and its nature is as perplexing and controversial a problem in historical circles as the explanation of its causes. To professional historians, the phrase "American Revolution" means more than the hostilities between England and thirteen of her colonies. It refers also to the social, economic, and political changes in the colonies that they presume caused, accompanied, or resulted from the conflict. Historians, therefore, usually have grouped their questions about the nature, causes, and consequences of the Revolution around three images:

1. A war of independence between colonies and a mother country. Who initiated the hostilities? When and where did the conflict start? What were the issues? Did the conflict result from the grievances voiced shortly before the war broke out, or did it result from long-term trends? Who were the individuals involved upon both sides and why? What was the rebels' aim? Was it independence or some accommodation within the empire? Why were just thirteen of England's North American colonies involved? Why was it a war of rebellion rather than a guerrilla war or a palace revolution?

2. A political revolution. Did the colonies revolt to preserve the basic political system they had or to establish a new kind of government? Why? Were there political innovations despite the aims of the revolutionaries, and, if so, why? What was new about the political results of the Revolution? Was it a new type of revolution at the time? Can it be compared to other revolutions at the time, such as the French Revolution? Can it be compared to the revolutions to establish new nations today?

3. A social revolution. Was the American Revolution a social revolution as well as a political revolution? If so, why; if not, why not? What is the model for the meaning of the word "revolution"? How do we judge a set of events to be a revolution? Is the American Revolution comparable to other full-scale revolutions or not? What is the relationship between the social structure of a country and a revolution in general and the social structure of the American colonies and the American Revolution in particular?

These questions suggest the whole problem of comparability as an important way of describing what the American Revolution was and explaining why it was what it was. In other words, we must try to determine

viii   INTRODUCTION

what was "American" about the American Revolution and what was revolutionary about it in order to discuss its nature, causes, and consequences.
    Answers to all these questions depend as much upon the historian's
theories about human behavior as upon the evidence he discovers about past
human actions. In fact, he cannot interpret the evidence about the past without employing his theories about the nature of man and society to make
sense of it. The credence the historian gives the multitude of pamphlets,
newspapers, and letters written by the participants in the Revolution directly reflects his belief whether professed ideals or something else better
explains why men did what they did. For example, should the rhetoric of
the Declaration of Independence be taken at face value in explaining why
the colonists went to war with England? In other words, is there a difference
between rationale and motivation, and how do we differentiate between
them? Are there deeper causes for human behavior than men of the time
say or even understand fully? How do we know whether to trust words or
deeds more in seeking to understand the American Revolution? How does
the historian know the real reasons for such a complex occurrence as the
Revolution? Ultimately each student of history must combine the evidence
from the past with his theories of how men act and societies operate in order
to derive the "facts" he says happened and that he calls history.
    The historian must use his theories of man and society to interpret
his evidence in another way also, for he asserts facts about a whole society
upon the basis of documents produced by a few of its members. How representative of the people of their time were Thomas Jefferson, Patrick
Henry, or John and Sam Adams? Were their aims also the goals of all
segments of the population? Or, did they desire some end quite different
from what they told the public? What is the role of leaders in a revolution,
and what relationship do they bear to the society of their day? Were some
groups of people quite unrepresented by any of the spokesmen for the
Revolution? Did most colonists support the war? Did they even care about
it? How do we know when so little evidence about their thoughts remains?
Should the analyst presume a societal consensus on Revolutionary goals,
excepting Tories of course, in order to interpret his evidence? Or, should he
assume agreement on goals was due to majority compromise, or public
apathy, or coerced submission, or all of these in combination? Again the
historian resorts as much to his theories of culture and society as he does to
his evidence in constructing the synthesis of facts that he calls history.
    So fundamental are these questions about theoretical orientations
and so complex the set of events called the Revolution that historians today
are no more in agreement upon the answers about the nature, causes, and
consequences of the Revolution than were contemporary observers. Now as
then some historians focus their attention on the battle of ideas and ideals

expressed in the polemical literature of the period. For them the Revolution was fought for political and constitutional ends and the society as a whole subscribed to these aims. Still other observers, then as now, picture the Revolutionary leaders as seeking only selfish political and economic ends behind their propaganda of ideals. To these analysts, the Revolution was perpetrated by an elite which sought to retain or gain political office and social status denied to them by the British imperial system. To attain their economic and political goals, according to this view, the Revolutionary leaders not only challenged English sovereignty and control but also repressed the demands of the masses for the very rights and ideals the leaders proclaimed they were denied in their polemics against England.

Although these two interpretations have existed since the Revolution, their fullest formulation has come in the twentieth century. One group of historians, led by Charles McLean Andrews in the 1920s and Lawrence Henry Gipson more recently, sought to place the colonists' aims and activities in the larger context of the British Empire. Hence, they are called the imperial school. In looking at the colonial struggle in terms of the imperial system, they generally took at face value the importance of the debates over political representation and the constitutional issues of empire. Opposing this approach were such historians as Carl Becker, Charles Beard, Arthur Schlesinger, Sr., and, more recently, Merrill Jensen. They portrayed the Revolution as a struggle among different colonial classes for economic and political hegemony in addition to the fight for independence from England. Since this interpretation arose during the Progressive period and featured an economic interpretation of people's motives, it has been named the progressive or economic interpretation school.

According to the progressive school, the Revolution became an internal or class conflict as well as a rebellion against an external power. As one of the chief formulators of this approach, Carl Becker, stated in *History of Political Parties in the Province of New York, 1760–1776* (New York: University of Wisconsin, 1909),

> The American Revolution was the result of two general movements; the contest for home-rule and independence, and the democratization of American politics and society. Of these movements, the latter was fundamental; it began before the contest for home-rule, and was not completed until after the achievement of independence. From 1765 to 1776, therefore, two questions, about equally prominent, determined party history. The first was whether essential colonial rights should be maintained; the second was by whom and by what methods they should be maintained. The first was the question of home-rule; the second was the question, if we may so put it, of who should rule at home.

Arthur M. Schlesinger, Sr., bolstered this view with *The Colonial Merchants and the American Revolution* (New York: Longmans, 1918), in which he found that merchants in all the colonies spearheaded the opposition at first against the Stamp and Trade Acts. When, however, they discovered their movement encouraged men lower in the social hierarchy to question their leadership, they drew back from such bold opposition to English control. Only the Tea and Coercive Acts in Schlesinger's opinion provided sufficient provocation to reunite the merchants with the more radical elements of society in favor of open rebellion against British rule. As the capstone of this interpretation, Charles Beard in *An Economic Interpretation of the Constitution* (New York: Macmillan, 1913) portrayed the foundation document of the federal union as the work of conservative upper-class men to foster their own economic welfare by inventing a system of government directly benefitting their own economic interests at the expense of the bulk of small farmers and tradesmen and by forcing this document through ratifying conventions before the majority of Americans understood what was happening.

According to these historians and others who followed their lead, the course of the Revolution moved from conservatives demanding colonial rights, to radicals seeking the rights of men as opposed to property in the Declaration of Independence, to a counter-revolution of the conservatives culminating in the adoption of the Constitution and the temporary repression of the lower classes. It remained for Merrill Jensen to finish this picture by showing in *Articles of Confederation* (Madison: University of Wisconsin Press, 1940) and *New Nation* (New York: Alfred A. Knopf, 1950) that the history of the whole Revolutionary era resulted from the struggle for power between two continuous and consistently opposed groups based upon socioeconomic cleavages fundamental in the American society of the time. On one side were most members of the colonial upper classes and nouveau riche of the Revolution who favored stronger central government always as means to check lower-class democracy and to regulate trade and pass taxes in their interest. In opposition to these "nationalists" were the "federalists," or the democratic radicals, who favored decentralization of government in the interests of the agrarian democratic views of the majority of the population. For Jensen, as for the others of this school, the ideals expressed in the polemics of the period determined less the actual behavior of the Founding Fathers than their economic interests, and the significant story of the Revolution was found more in the internal conflict of social classes based upon economic power than in the external struggle with England.

After World War II, the progressive version of the causes, nature, and consequences of the Revolution was denied by such writers as Daniel Boorstin, Louis Hartz, Benjamin Wright, and most important, Edmund

Morgan, who synthesized his research and their outlook in his influential little book, *Birth of the Republic, 1763–89* (Chicago: University of Chicago Press, 1956). As the title of Benjamin Wright's *Consensus and Continuity, 1776–1787* (Boston: Boston University Press, 1958) suggests, these men find neither class conflict nor swings between radical and conservative leadership during the course of the Revolution. Rather they see a consensus upon ideals and aims among the whole non-Tory population. For them, as for nineteenth-century interpreters, the fight was over constitutional principles expressed in the rhetoric of the period, and they minimize the internal divisions among the people. Robert E. Brown in *Middle-Class Democracy and the Revolution in Massachusetts, 1691–1780* (Ithaca: Cornell University Press, 1955), in fact, reversed the progressive or social conflict school by arguing that the colonists were primarily middle-class property owners, making conflict as unnecessary as it was absent. According to these historians, the revolutionaries went to war to conserve or preserve the rights and class structure they already possessed against England's efforts to change the system rather than to gain new rights and new institutions. As a result of their approach, these men have been denominated the conservative or the consensus school. Later observers think they reflect the conservative ideology of the post-war Eisenhower years.

The consensus school approach continued into the decade of the 1960s and formed the focus of much of the discussion upon the nature of the Revolution. The inclusive term, consensus school, hides the difference between those concerned about the ideas of the revolutionists and those interested in the nature of social stratification and political power. The former analyzed the ideology said to be shared by all, while the latter reconstructed the statistics of class and leadership. During the 1960s Robert E. Brown extended his research to Virginia as a crucial example of his thesis on middle-class democracy and found the Old Dominion relatively equalitarian in class structure and open in economic opportunity. Jackson Turner Main came to the same conclusion in *The Social Structure of Revolutionary America* (Princeton: Princeton University Press, 1965). However, in a study of legislative membership he found a trend toward greater democratization during the course of the Revolution. The major contributor to the analysis of ideology during the 1960s was Bernard Bailyn. By taking all of the rhetoric of the revolutionaries seriously, he reconstructed their world-view of political ideals, history, and social hierarchy. He also converted the previous static view of Revolutionary ideals and principles into one that was dynamic and evolving. Thus, he calls his introduction to *Pamphlets of the American Revolution* (Cambridge, Mass.: Harvard University Press, 1965), "The Transforming Radicalism of the American Revolution." In these ways, both he and Main subtly but nevertheless definitely shifted the emphasis upon ideas and class of the consensus school into a new path stressing change and new developments.

Although the consensus school dominated the interpretation of the Revolution during most of the 1960s, it never held the field uncontested. Not only did older men such as Merrill Jensen continue to write vigorously in refutation of the consensus view, but younger men once again found class conflict a key to Revolutionary history. Chief among these was Staughton Lynd, who employed New York State, just as Becker did, to study the effects of class division upon Revolutionary politics. Parallel to this reemphasis upon class conflict and the internal struggle for political power has been the attempt of the "New Left" school, as it is called, to determine the actual views of the inarticulate masses, or to produce the history of "The American Revolution Seen From the Bottom Up," as Jesse Lemisch, the most vociferous advocate of this approach, phrased it in Barton Bernstein, ed., *Towards a New Past: Dissenting Essays in American History* (New York: Pantheon Books, 1968).

By the end of the 1960s, a new mood was evident among historians of the Revolution. Even younger historians trained by consensus or idealist historians questioned the exclusive stress upon ideas, no matter how dynamic. Bailyn's student, Gordon Wood, in the selection reprinted below, wonders whether attention to rhetoric alone answers the question why the colonists acted as they did as opposed to what they said. Though his book, *The Creation of the American Republic, 1776–1787* (Chapel Hill: University of North Carolina Press, 1969), mainly examines the public ideology of Revolutionary leaders in the tradition of his mentor, he asserts in passing that the leaders' words were motivated by reasons other than those that appeared in their public pronouncements — by anxieties grounded in changing social realities of the time. Bailyn himself in *The Origins of American Politics* (New York: Alfred A. Knopf, 1968) moved to place the ideology he had uncovered into a political context. Other historians reassessed their own and newer work upon the nature of political factions and conflict before, during, and after the Revolution. In short, the conflict and consensus schools seem to be combining to create a new synthesis that acknowledges the existence of social classes but also points out that conflict, except in certain conspicuous cases, was confined to fights among the elites in the colonies. Similarly this emerging synthesis says the majority of the population shared the same ideology although Tories and certain radicals formed a strong minority. Thus, neither conflict nor consensus, neither ideas nor action is stressed to the exclusion of the other. Rather, further research is needed to determine the role of each element.

So far we have discussed only the ideological and other behavior of the American side of the Revolution without giving any attention to the conflict between Britain and her colonies. A discussion of when and who began the Revolution and why must include consideration of both sides in the controversy, leading directly to the problem of overall causation. Again the historian must resort to some theoretical framework of how he explains revolution or "internal wars" in the words of one analyst. Some patriot historians, inspired by the indictment in Jefferson's Declaration of Independence blamed the war on English selfishness in general and the stupidity of George III in particular. Some loyalist historians, on the other hand, condemned the stubborn colonists and the shrewd demagogues who duped the people into disloyalty to Crown and mother country. On the whole, however, observers then and historians of this century agree that the factors that produced the hostilities were diverse and the causes for independence extend beyond the battles of Lexington and Concord or even the Sugar and Stamp Acts. No matter which side the imperial school historians took on the constitutionality of the English and colonial views of the empire and sovereignty, they placed the perspective of causation where it belonged: on the changing relations between both sides in the conflict. Though many books have been published on this phase of the Revolution, the relationships were so complex that still more research is needed. The imperial school also questioned whether the imperial economic regulations were unfair to colonial capitalists. In other words, did the colonists have legitimate grievances against trade regulation, or was the English government only requesting the colonists to pay their fair share of the empire's expenses? Today we study this issue on two levels: (1) what the actors said and believed regardless of what the true balance of payments may have been, and (2) what the historian reconstructs that true balance of payments to have been using statistics and economic theory. In this debate, as in preceding ones, we see historians seeking resolution of issues through greater precision in specifying what questions the problem involves and what theories and evidence are needed to produce answers to these questions. Unfortunately, this problem of dynamics and causation is not well represented in this volume because of space limitations, but the bibliography contains suggestions for further reading in this area.

From this hasty survey of the history of the history (called historiography) of the Revolution, the student can see the importance of theory as well as evidence in seeking to understand the nature, causes, and consequences of it. Equally obvious is the need for a good set of questions about what has to be known and what we seek to and can know from the evidence. The student should therefore compare the questions historians ask and the questions that he wants to ask. Do the writers below ask and answer not only what happened, who was involved, and when did things happen, but also why it was what it was (or why it happened that way), why these particular people were involved, and why these things happened at these particular times. In short, how complete is their description and explanation of what they think is at issue? Do they include all the description and explanation needed to prove their case? Can you think of additional issues and other questions that ought to be asked and answered about the Revolution?

The student should examine what proportions of theory and of evidence the historians use to prove their cases. Is the evidence sufficient? Is the theory, explicit or implicit, applicable? Are there better theories that might raise new questions or make better use of the evidence? In all cases, how do the historians know what they say they know? Do you agree with them? Do they prove what they set out to prove? Footnotes are retained in the selections, so that the student can judge the sources of the historians' reasoning.

The American Revolution created American history by creating a new nation. Thus, Americans study the history surrounding the American Revolution for clues to American identity and character. At the same time their beliefs about themselves as a people influence what they perceive to be the nature, causes, and consequences of the Revolution. What the Revolution was, then, depends to a large extent upon what Americans think they are or ought to be. Thus, as the attitudes Americans hold about themselves change, so too does the history of the Revolution and especially the meaning of the Revolution for American history. Can this be detected in the writers below? To what extent are the historians' moral judgments about what America ought to be linked to their analyses of what the Revolution was? Do historians use morality as well as theory and evidence to produce facts? Ought this and must this be the case?

As a result of this changing compound of morality, theory, and the search for national identity, each generation interprets and reinterprets the American Revolution. Is this the ultimate, and perhaps the only, truth about the Revolution, or can we determine the facts about it independently of the mental climate of our times?

THE AMERICAN
REVOLUTION
The Critical Issues

WHAT WAS THE POLITICAL NATURE OF THE REVOLUTION?

Republicanism and Radicalism in the American Revolution

CECELIA M. KENYON

In one of the first major articles to assess the implications of post-World War II research and thinking for interpreting the overall nature of the American Revolution, Professor Cecelia Kenyon (1922–   ) of the Smith College Department of Government argues that the chief significance of the Revolution lay in its political rather than its [social or economic consequences]. She maintains further that we can only judge the question of significance if we know how the people of the time viewed the issues and the results. Thus, according to her, the Revolution produced four "principal achievements": independence from England; the feeling that republican government best served the ends of life, liberty, and happiness; the "crystallization" of a philosophy of individualism and equality into an operative form; and the development of a new kind of federal state embracing for the first time a large population spread over an extended area.

Kenyon's views place us immediately in the midst of the current controversies about the nature of the Revolution. How much real change does she see? Were the changes mainly in the realm of ideas or of deeds? In short, what does she see as the role of ideas in bringing on the Revolution and in producing its consequences? Are the espousal of ideals and actual practice closely correlated? Can you tell from her analysis whether the practice of individuality and equality followed the espousal of the ideals? Was there consensus upon the ideas she sees as crucial to the new United States? Did all the people believe to the same extent in the same

1

*ideas? For example, did everyone support radical individualism
or the new federalism of the Constitution equally? How did the
Tories react?*

*Do you agree with Kenyon's judgment that we can best under-
stand the Revolution by looking at it through the eyes of the
actors at the time? How does she know what they thought? Do
she and Bernard Bailyn in his selection below define "individualism," "liberty," "democracy," and "republicanism" in the same
way? Why do both see republican government in the eighteenth
century, as an "experiment"? Even if you agree with her criterion
of employing the actors' viewpoint to measure the meaning of
the Revolution, do you think she is right in concluding that there
was a rapid transformation of attitudes in regard to individualism? Did practices change equally rapidly? Did people abandon
as quickly as she implies the traditional ideal of men subordinat-
ing their selfish and diverse interests to the common good in
favor of glorifying in the name of individualism an ideal of a
society divided and ruled by such interests? Is she consistent on
this point? Gordon Wood in* The Creation of the American Republic, 1776–1787 *(Chapel Hill: University of North Carolina
Press, 1969), argues that only a few leaders subscribed to such an
ideal of individualism regardless of what they or others practiced,
again raising the problem of the relation of ideas to deeds.*

*Kenyon's article shows that no matter what stance we take in
writing about the nature of the Revolution, we must address ourselves to issues of conflict versus consensus, of ideas versus actions
in causing change, and to the dilemma of using the actors' versus
later observers' viewpoints in measuring change and in judging
the meaning of the events called the Revolution. She argues that
the Revolution exhibited radical change but continuity also, but
is her evidence consistent? Which "achievements" did the actors
consciously seek and which were the unanticipated consequences
of their ideas and actions?*

I

Although the American Revolution was a central and decisive phenomenon in the national life of the American people, taken comfortably
for granted by its heirs and nominally commemorated by a convenient summer holiday, its nature and significance continue to puzzle historians who

Reprinted by permission from Cecelia M. Kenyon, "Republicanism and
Radicalism in the American Revolution: An Old-Fashioned Interpretation," *William and Mary Quarterly,* XIX, 3d Ser. (April, 1962), pp.
153–154, 163–182.

seek to know it well. From the very beginning, it was believed by those who participated in it — on the western side of the Atlantic — to be a quite remarkable event, not merely because it was their revolution, but because it seemed to them to introduce a new phase in the political evolution of mankind, and therefore to be touched with universal significance. This native estimate was not entirely parochial. There was considerable interest in the American experiment among contemporary Europeans, and the volumes of commentary written by visitors in the nineteenth century indicate that this interest was not merely ephemeral. In more recent times, Americans have been reminded of their Revolutionary heritage by later rebels against colonial rule, who have sometimes seemed to find the America of 1776 more inspiring than the America of 1962. Thus the Revolution was, and continues to be, an event of enduring importance. And yet, in spite of generations of study, its essential nature remains obscure. In fact, as its two-hundredth anniversary approaches, there seems to be more uncertainty about its meaning, more diversity in interpretation, than ever before. For the last two generations, scholars have debated such questions as the relationship between the Declaration of Independence and the Constitution, what the real causes of the Revolution were, whether it was essentially a colonial revolt or an internal struggle for power, whether it was radical or conservative — indeed, whether, in fact, it was actually a revolution. Among these and other issues, a crucial one over which there has been much confusion is whether the Revolution was radical or conservative. The purpose of this article is to consider some of the intellectual forces which have contributed to this confusion, to suggest a way by which some of this confusion may be resolved, and to analyze the Revolution with respect to its radical and conservative immediate aspects and long-range implications. . . .

III

In the later years of their lives, John Adams and Thomas Jefferson both had occasion to comment on the nature of the Revolution, in which each had played a major role. Both left no doubt that after nearly fifty years they still regarded it, as they had in the beginning, as the fundamental change in the history of the American people. Adams emphasized the death of loyalty, affection, and allegiance toward the King of England and toward England itself. *"This radical change in the principles, opinions, sentiments, and affections of the people was the real American Revolution."* [1]* Jefferson expressed a hope for the universal realization of the principles of the Declaration of Independence: "May it be to the world, what I believe it will be, (to some parts sooner, to others later, but finally to all,) the signal of arousing men to burst the chains under which monkish ignorance and supersti-

* [See pp. 147–148 for notes to this article. — Ed.]

tion had persuaded them to bind themselves, and to assume the blessings and security of self-government.[2] Both men were in their eighties at the time of these remarks, and one may be tempted to make some allowance for the inclination of old men to exaggerate the importance of an event which they had helped to bring about. I am prepared to accept their opinion, and have accordingly described this article as an old-fashioned interpretation. The Revolution was radical in its four principal achievements: independence; the establishment of republican government and the identification of republicanism with political right; the crystallization of the individualism and equalitarianism of the Declaration of Independence into an operative as well as a formal political philosophy; the extension of the principle and practice of republicanism to a large and heterogeneous population by combination with a new form of federalism.

Of these four results, the first was prior to all the rest and the one most consciously and immediately felt to be radical. The decision to declare formal separation from Great Britain was a difficult one, taken only after a long period of deliberation and after the colonies had been in armed revolt against the mother country for more than a year. Nearly three-quarters of the colonists were of British descent, and the vast majority of these were accustomed to thinking of themselves as Englishmen. Their resistance to the Stamp Act and subsequent colonial regulations had not been motivated by a desire for independence, but by a desire to maintain their rights as Englishmen. Independence was a last resort, a means to secure these rights as men, and as Americans. Once accepted as the only means to get what they wanted, the decision for independence inexorably produced consequences other than the achievement of their original goal. The United States developed as an independent nation, not as British colonies nor as a constituent member of the British Commonwealth. We take this fact so much for granted today that it is difficult to conceive of what our political, economic, social, and even geographical development might have been had the colonists achieved their goals within the Empire, or had the Revolution been unsuccessful. It is tempting to speculate about the possible "might-have-beens" had the long years of protest resulted in either of these eventualities. But the facts are that we did win our independence, and that we did so with revolutionary violence. Colonial political ideas and practice had already deviated to some extent from British patterns; the institution of independent governments widened the gap and produced a markedly different political tradition.

IV

The most important, as well as the most immediate, change was the formal establishment of republican governments. Throughout most of the

period of colonial protest, there had been little criticism of the British constitution or of its aristocratic and monarchical elements as such. The main
thrust of American argument had been directed toward Parliament rather
than the King, and primarily toward the House of Commons rather than
the House of Lords. It was almost inevitable that Americans would not
carry their arguments further, given the fact that the issue of taxation was
at the heart of colonial opposition. The habitual professions of allegiance,
devotion, and loyalty to their gracious Sovereign which accompanied colonial petitions, resolutions, and acts of defiance were both formal and traditional, but they were not completely insincere. As long as Americans believed
that the crux of their problem was legislative and not administrative, they
could not but consider Parliament as the central opponent; as long as they
believed that their aims could be achieved within the Empire, there was no
reason for hostility to the institution of the Crown. The Americans were
not republicans in either a formal or an ideological sense before 1776.
Within a few months, they were, and have remained so ever since. Once the
decision for independence was made, there seems to have been no serious
question that any other form of government was either possible or desirable.
Certainly it would have been difficult for all thirteen states to agree on a
single monarch for them all, and the spectacle of thirteen separate embassies
touring Europe and interviewing prospective candidates suggests that common sense as well as *Common Sense* had something to do with the American
choice of republicanism.

This quick transition from monarchy to republic in form and belief
was accomplished with relative ease. The question whether it was a radical
change is difficult to answer. In its actual and immediate effect on the general population, it was not. Almost from the very beginning, with some
exceptions of time and place, monarchy had rested lightly upon the colonists. George III and his predecessors were weeks away by sea, and in most
of the colonies most of the time, the royal governors were effectively limited
in the exercise of their authority by the power of the purse and the difficulty of enforcing unpopular measures in the face of concerted opposition
without adequate and reliable military forces. Above all, there had been the
long years of salutary neglect. It would be too much to say that the American colonies were autonomous republics before 1776, but their governments
had been far more republican than that of the home country, and they had
long been accustomed to governing themselves with relatively little interference or assistance from the other side of the Atlantic. The transition from
monarchy to republic did not therefore bring with it pervasive and fundamental changes, either in private or public life. In this sense, the establishment of republican governments was not a radical change, and it is not
remarkable that it took place so quickly and easily.

What is more remarkable is the rapid shift in attitude and belief. Within a very short period of time, Americans developed an ideological attachment to republicanism, and this change was a radical one, with radical and far-reaching consequences. Before 1776, the prevailing opinion in America had been that the ends of government — liberty, justice, happiness, and the public good — could be secured within the framework of monarchy. To be sure, they meant a limited or mixed monarchy, and they emphasized the central importance of constitutionalism. Still, they assumed the compatibility of monarchy with good government. After 1776, they tended to associate all the characteristics of good government with republicanism, and with republicanism only. To be sure, there were dissenters, of whom Alexander Hamilton was the most illustrious. But the preponderant opinion, the genius, to use Madison's word,[3] was clear and unambiguous: good government meant republican government. Thus there emerged an element of rigidity in American political thinking which has never disappeared and scarcely, if ever, been relaxed. The idea was so central and so fixed in the public mind, and the fear and distrust of other forms of government so great (perhaps inconsistently), that a guarantee of republican government to each state was written into the Constitution of 1787. More important, the idea has continued to dominate the American attitude toward politics and has been an important element in the formation of foreign policy. This identification of republican or democratic government with political right was a change both in substance and in intellectual outlook from pre-Revolutionary thought, and its consequences have been radical and far-reaching. Americans have regarded themselves, and have been regarded, as an essentially pragmatic people, but the preference for republicanism which crystallized at the time of the Revolution has constituted an ideological, doctrinaire element in their political outlook which has rarely been questioned. It may also be suggested that the ideological habit thus acquired has been extended to other areas and has become a major factor in American political thinking. Like republicanism, socialism, imperialism, and colonialism are all terms which have become stereotypes for Americans, frequently exercising a powerful ideological force at odds with our alleged pragmatism.

Thus I would suggest that the actual establishment of republican governments in 1776–80 was not a radical change, but that its intellectual consequences were. What is puzzling is the reason for the sudden and virtually complete revolution in attitude. There was, of course, the influence of Paine's critique of monarchy in *Common Sense*. There was the fact that the potential counterinfluence of the losing Loyalists was virtually eliminated by their exodus during and after the war. There was the psychological necessity in the midst of war for an ideal that would inspire, sustain, and justify the participants and their actions. None of these reasons seems quite adequate, but the last was probably the most important. For the concept of republicanism, linked with the modified Lockeian ideals of the Declaration of Independence, provided a truly revolutionary doctrine with universal significance. Had the Revolution been merely a fight for independence, it would have remained a parochial affair of interest only to Great Britain and possibly to her continental rivals as convenient material for troublemaking. It was the genius of the Americans to see this, and once committed, to transform what might have remained a petty rebellion within the Empire into a symbol for the liberation of all mankind. Republicanism was an integral part of the symbol, and both contributed to and drew strength from it. The Revolution in its origins was a conservative movement to resist what were believed to be the pernicious innovations of George III and his Parliament. After 1776 it was, and was believed to be by its makers, truly radical.

v

The philosophy associated with republicanism and with the Revolution was also radical. It was the philosophy drawn from Locke's *Second Treatise*, but it was Lockeianism with an American gloss. A survey of Revolutionary literature both before and after 1776 reveals a number of modifications in and deviations from the original treatise which the Americans made as they used the great philosopher for their polemical purposes. The most familiar was the substitution in the Declaration of Independence of the *pursuit of happiness* for *property*. Another somewhat less familiar and certainly less clearly defined change was the American refusal to make a sharp distinction between the state of nature and civil society. These and other differences were apparent before the final break with England. The establishment of republican governments induced still other differences, of which the most important were an emphasis on equality, an intensification of individualism, and the identification of Locke with republicanism. The result was a subtle but substantial simplification and radicalization of the doctrine of the *Second Treatise*.

None of the separate changes was radical in the sense of being completely new or unrooted in the original *Treatise* or in the seventeenth-century body of thought upon which Locke drew. Nor was their sum more radical than the ideas set forth by the Levellers of the Civil War or their English heirs. Furthermore, the ideas were rooted in the colonial past and were therefore not unfamiliar. Yet the total complex was radical in implication and operation, especially when linked with the belief in, as well as the practice of, republicanism.

The most important of the changes was the American tendency to blur the differences which Locke had either stated or implied between the state of nature and the state of civil society. The concept of a state of nature was familiar to American thinkers before Locke wrote the *Second Treatise,* and, in American Puritan thought, it more closely resembled the Hobbesian version than the Lockeian. Americans emphasized the innate selfishness of man and the consequently hostile competition of a society in which men lived without the external restraints of law and government. Like Hobbes and Locke, they used the concept as a justification of government. What they did not do was to accept the idea that government could or would provide a completely impartial judge.[4] Their long experience in colonial self-government had taught them the inevitability of factious disputes and the difficulty if not the impossibility of securing impartial legislators and governors. Furthermore, the basis of their case against Parliamentary taxation and against the British theory of virtual representation had been the assumption that men in politics pursue their selfish interests and, in doing so, influence governmental policy. Accordingly, long before Madison's famous Tenth *Federalist,* Americans had questioned the likelihood, though not the ideal, of government as an impartial judge. Perhaps because their governments were already more republican than anything Locke knew, they were more acutely aware of "the people" as a collectivity of different and sometimes competitive groups and individuals than he was.

Similarly, because they expected men to behave selfishly in civil society, whether in or out of the government, they were also more rigorous than Locke was in attempting to insure that the rights men were entitled to in the state of nature were actually enjoyed in civil society. Locke had left the rights of the individual in an ambiguous if not precarious position. He stated that the consent of the majority could be taken for the consent of the individual and that, for generations other than the original contracting one, consent might be no more than tacit acceptance of the status quo. Locke also said that the original contractors might select hereditary monarchy or aristocracy as the form of government. Furthermore, the only kind of revolution Locke defined as a legitimate one was a revolution by the majority of the people. Thus, although he provided for protection of majority rights against monarchical or aristocratic infringement, he did not provide, either in the ordinary operation of government or through revolutionary means, for the protection of individual or minority rights against a majority or against a government supported by a majority. These rights would be secure only if the majority acted in accordance with the dictates of natural law. Locke seems to have assumed that it would so act, though he did not assume that individuals would always do so. The Americans were more consistent and more pessimistic. They did not assume that the behavior of groups of men, whether minorities or majorities, would be more virtuous than that of individuals. In the decade of constitutional protest before Lexington and Concord, the Americans found Locke very congenial and useful, for in the *Second Treatise* the problem of securing liberty is treated almost entirely in terms of the people against the government. Since the colonists were not represented in Parliament, their position was more or less that of Locke's "people," while Parliament's was that of Locke's "government." But the Americans did not ignore the fact that Parliament also represented the people of England and thus was, in another sense, a Lockeian "majority." James Wilson's case against Parliamentary authority over the colonies rested not only on the argument that the members of Parliament were not bound to Americans by mutual or identical interests, but on the assumption that members of Parliament *were* bound in this way to their English constituents and could therefore be held accountable by the latter.[5] It followed that the interests of Americans and of Englishmen were different. By implication, therefore, the people of England were responsible for Parliamentary oppression, not just Parliament itself. Americans constituted a minority in the Empire of which they regarded themselves members, and their demand for legislative autonomy under the Crown was, in one sense, a means to protect their minority rights and interests.

Thus, in their collective relationship to Parliament, the colonists had had some experience with governmental policies which represented, from their point of view, a self-interested and dominant faction of the Empire. Far more important in determining their political attitudes, however, was their long experience in internal colonial politics. Long before the natural rights doctrine of the *Second Treatise* was generally accepted, the existence of factions had been recognized and deplored, and eventually accepted.[6] The Americans had advanced far beyond the point where they could view the problems of liberty and its opposite *simply* in terms of the people against the government. Their political ideas reflected not only the influence of Locke, but also the lessons of their greater experience in self-government. Accordingly, while Locke was ambiguous as to how and to what extent the rights of the individual or of minorities would be protected in civil society, his avowed disciples were not. They emphasized the necessity of securing the rights derived from the state of nature against both a monarch and a legislative majority in a civil society. The fear of majority oppression, which has been so persistent and pervasive a factor in American politics, was thus firmly rooted in colonial experience and in the movement of protest which resulted in revolution and independence. When combined with another major modification in the original Locke, this position led the Revolutionists to a radical individualism.

This modification was the substitution of the *pursuit of happiness* for *property* in the Lockeian trilogy of rights. The substitution was not a mere linguistic one made in the Declaration of Independence for rhetorical effect. The colonists had included happiness as one of the natural and fundamental rights in polemical literature of the preceding decade. John Dickinson, for example, had gone so far as to suggest that the constitutionality of Parliamentary statutes be measured by their tendency to make the people of America happy.[7] So indefinite a concept was obviously impossible as a legal test, but the idea of happiness as an end of government was firmly rooted in colonial attitudes before 1776. It was, furthermore, a far more individualistic end than the protection of property.[8] Property was a tangible, objective element, while happiness was a subjective goal dependent on individual interpretation. Also, the assertion of a right to happiness had strong equalitarian implications. The concept of property as a right to be protected and fostered by government may be and has been interpreted to mean the protection of property already vested in individuals. It may therefore mean the preservation of the *status quo,* and the *status quo* may be an aristocratic one. This seems to have been Locke's intention, for there is nothing in the *Second Treatise* to suggest that he had an economic or social revolution in mind. The idea of the pursuit of happiness necessarily had both dynamic and equalitarian implications, and these have played a substantial role in American politics. The situation at the time of the Revolution was not such as to lead to an explosive implementation of these implications, but the implications were there, and to some extent recognized and acted upon. Since happiness is a subjective state, no individual can decide for another what will promote his happiness. If happiness is really an end of government, and if all men have by nature an equal right to the pursuit of it, then it follows logically that every man should have a voice in the determination of public policy. Thus the two American modifications — the emphasis on happiness rather than property, and the greater concern for the actual implementation of rights in civil society — led to a democratization of Locke as well as to an unequivocal individualism.

The relationship between the ideal of individual happiness and the recognition of factions in society was an important one. As I have indicated before, the Americans had become thoroughly familiar with the existence and operation of factious divisions in society, and they had come to accept with considerable equanimity the fact that self-interest was a primary political motive. They therefore could not, as Locke for the most part did, think and write of "the people" as a corporate whole more or less distinct from the government. Such a dichotomy was not absent from their thought, but because they had already had experience with a relatively high degree of representative government, they were aware of government as a tool of the stronger faction among the people. This realistic or pessimistic attitude toward human nature has come to be associated with conservatism, but it had a logical connection with the radical implications of the Declaration of Independence. It embodied the American view that the same defects of human nature which Locke and Hobbes had used to explain the transition from the state of nature to civil society would still be present in the latter condition and would still jeopardize the ends for which government was instituted. The connection was succinctly stated in Jefferson's First Inaugural Address: "Some times it is said that Man cannot be trusted with the government of himself. Can he then be trusted with the government of others? Or have we found angels in the form of kings to govern him?"[9] In other words, the imperfection of man was itself an argument for republican government. By logical extension, it was also an argument for a democratic republic. For if all men were equally entitled to the rights of life, liberty, and the pursuit of happiness, and if self-interest was a universal characteristic of human nature, then all men must be given the opportunity of defending their rights against encroachment by others. Thus, although the colonists had not set out with the intention of establishing republicanism, once they had done so, as a corollary of independence, the pessimistic strain in their thought provided ideological reinforcement for practical accomplishment. Similarly, the establishment of republican governments served to accentuate the equalitarian and individualistic content of their official philosophy.

This philosophy was one of radical individualism, and it was accepted, I think, by the majority of Americans at the time, including many of those who are frequently regarded as conservatives. Without abandoning completely the concept of a common good or public interest or justice, they tended to regard the pursuit of self-interest as legitimate and sought primarily to avoid an overwhelming concentration of power behind a single interest, whether it be upper or lower class, urban, rural, northern, southern, or other. It was the refusal of Thomas Paine and Alexander Hamilton to accept this individualism which made both of them alien to the prevailing political attitude. Paine was a radical democrat, but he could not stomach the rough and tumble politics of his colleagues in Pennsylvania, who pursued what he regarded as selfish interests with little restraint. Similarly, Hamilton could not recognize opposition to his policies as legitimate because he interpreted the national interest in terms of corporate greatness, while his opponents interpreted it in terms of individual satisfaction. Paine and Hamilton, therefore, were both conservative in their attitude toward the proper ends of government and the proper political behavior of individual citizens. The individualism which they rejected was not new in theory. It was clearly explicit in *The Leviathan,* present though somewhat obscured in the *Second Treatise,* and had been an increasing element in both colonial thought and practice. With the coming of the Revolution it became manifestly operative, and has continued to exert a decisive influence in American politics.

This individualism, rooted in colonial experience but transformed by the break with Britain and the establishment of republican governments, had ramifications which influenced the nature of our political tradition and served further to set it apart from that of the mother country. These ramifications, though some of them did not become apparent until much later, help to illuminate the radical effects of the Revolution.

As I have suggested in the preceding pages, the individualism of the early republic was associated with equalitarianism in civil society as well as in the state of nature. Of this, the Revolutionists were themselves aware. They were less aware of the relativistic implications of the theory summarized in the Declaration, and of the extent to which that theory gave philosophical justification to the egoism which they so frequently and habitually deplored, but which they accepted as an ordinary ingredient of politics. The relativism of the Declaration can be summarized briefly. Two of the central rights, to which all men are entitled, are not amenable to objective definition or delimitation. The *liberty* of the trilogy was to some extent defined in the specific terms of traditional procedural liberties associated with the British constitution or common law, and in the newer substantive terms of freedom of speech, press, and religion. There were also attempts, by Jefferson and Paine, for example, to classify rights into primary and secondary categories, the latter being subject to social or political regulation. Except for the allegedly absolute rights of the first order, a man's liberty was commonly said to extend so far as it did not interfere with or jeopardize the similar liberties of other men. This sounds like a good enough common-sense definition. However, the Revolutionary American conception of society as composed of selfish individuals and groups whose interests would frequently be in conflict, suggests the impossibility of using that common-sense definition in practice with any degree of precision. If, that is to say, men's interests habitually and *normally* come into conflict, then this formula is not altogether relevant or applicable. Somewhat the same thing is true of the third right in the trilogy, the pursuit of happiness. It is an even more subjective right than liberty. And unless one assumes a very harmonious society, the happinesses of different individuals are likely to come in conflict with each other. If all individuals possess these rights equally, and if they are an integral end of government, then there is no logical criterion by which such conflicts can be adjudicated. There is no way to define justice objectively, and there is great difficulty in defining the substantive common good objectively, except perhaps in some obvious crisis of national preservation. What is left is political relativism, combined with a philosophy of natural rights which tended to provide a justification of political and ethical egoism.

I do not think the men of the Revolution were fully aware of the trend of their thought. They continued to think in terms of justice and the general welfare and to deplore man's tendency toward self-interest and bias. Their hostility to parties is in itself an indication of their belief in a common good to which all men owed their allegiance. Nevertheless, the relativism implicit in natural rights doctrine had undermined the operative force of the common good by making it difficult if not impossible to define. This difficulty of defining justice or the common interest would, paradoxically and ironically, encourage the propensity to use ideological stereotypes in political debate.

Had the Americans been imbued with a strong sense of nationalism, or had their security not been so easily achieved by the happy windfall of Louisiana and the physical barrier of the Atlantic Ocean, this relativism might have been balanced by a concern for national defense or perhaps national glory. As it was, the same individualism which produced the relativism contributed to the really profound inclination toward isolation and withdrawal from international affairs. It is perhaps ironical that the Declaration of Independence, written partly for the purpose of securing foreign aid, should have had so strong an influence in the direction of concentration on domestic affairs. Yet I think it did. If the primary function of government is believed to be the protection of individual rights, and if by the grace of history and geography this can be done in the absence of serious and continuous threats from abroad, then it is natural that the people involved should be primarily occupied with immediate and domestic concerns. If, furthermore, they have another ocean to aim at, with nothing much in between but a few savages, and if they regard themselves as the world's torchbearers for a great ideal, whatever ambitions they may have for national and imperial greatness may be satisfied with a minimum awareness of or involvement in the affairs of other nations. There was very little to keep Americans constantly aware of one of the traditional functions of statehood—defense against external danger. This fact, plus the nature of our federal system, inhibited the emergence of a sense of national interest transcendent of individual, group, and sectional interests which would supply content for the concept of the common good. There was thus no strong compensatory factor, such as the mystique of the British Empire, to offset the relativism and individualism implicit in Revolutionary doctrine.

These factors, combined with the Revolutionary acceptance of egoism, gradually brought about a major divergence in the American attitude toward politics from the heritage which the colonists had shared with the home country. At the time of the Revolution, in America as in Britain, politics was an occupation regarded with respect and engaged in by men of distinguished qualities. It was, to use modern sociological terminology, a prestige occupation. To be sure, this condition was due in part to the property qualifications for officeholding, in some colonies and states considerably stiffer than those for voting. But far more important, both ambition and a sense of responsibility drew men of wealth and learning into colonial, state, and federal office. It was Jefferson's intention and hope that his scheme of education would, among other things, provide a reservoir of political leaders — a kind of aristocracy of talent. This concept of aristocratic leadership was undermined in a number of ways. Historically as well as philosophically, it had been linked with belief in an objective good, and it was this link which the idea of happiness as an end of government tended to negate. For if individual happiness — or self-interest — is an end of government, then one man's opinion is as good as another. Thus, though the concept of the public good as a composite of individual and group interests does not require the rejection of wisdom and virtue as a qualification for the exercise of political authority, it does promote a powerful alternative — identity of opinion and interest, or the willingness to give the voter what he wants. To be sure, this was not a peculiarly American phenomenon, as Burke's experience with the electors of Bristol indicates. Furthermore, there was a touch of the Burkeian theory of representation in that of the authors of the Constitution, especially in their attitude toward the Senate. Nevertheless, the realism concerning political motivation and behavior which characterized the American attitude, as it was summarized in the Tenth *Federalist,* expressed something very close to a theory of pressure group politics. And it is this kind of politics which, by and large, has dominated the American tradition. However, Americans have never been completely comfortable with it, and their uneasiness has produced a reliable scapegoat. At the time of the Revolution, dissatisfaction found expression and release in the almost universal dislike and distrust of parties, a tribute to the lost ideal of a transcendent public good. Gradually, this antipathy was extended to the men who manned and ran the parties, the politicians. There has thus been a peculiar schizophrenia in the American political mind. On the one hand, we have engaged in pressure and partisan politics continuously and with vigor; on the other, we despise the men who act as brokers to carry out our demands, whether honestly or corruptly. Even now, a sure way of winning popular approval is to create the image that one is not a politician. Something of the same attitude is involved in the American reaction to the word and the fact of bipartisanship; it gives a comfortable sense of satisfied virtue. This distrust and contempt for politicians is no doubt partially attributable to the personal corruption of individuals, but it has more profound causes, and one of these is the somewhat obscurely felt dissatisfaction with the relativism and its consequent pressure group politics which have as their basis the radical individualism of the Declaration of Independence.

VI

Equally radical was the Revolution's culmination, the creation and adoption of the Constitution of 1787. There had been federations of states before, both in ancient and modern times, and the idea of a central government had become familiar in America with the Albany Plan, the first two Continental Congresses, and the Articles of Confederation. What was new was the direct control over the central government exercised by the electorate, the relative independence of that government with respect to the governments of the constituent states, and its direct authority over the individual citizens of those states. This was a government so new that, as its critics gibed, it lacked a name. It was, in the strict meaning of the word, radical.

Its opponents perceived this fact from the very beginning, and both the spirit and substance of their polemics provide evidence of a typically conservative stance. They argued that the Philadelphia Convention had gone too far, that they had exceeded their instructions, that there was no necessity for an entirely new frame of government, and that a little patching up of the Articles of Confederation would have been sufficient. They pointed out that what was proposed had never been done before and bewailed the loss of resistance to innovation which the Revolution itself had induced in the people. They paraded a succession of imaginary horribles, and they said that the authors of the Constitution had based their scheme of government on too optimistic a view of human nature. Furthermore, they saw quite clearly that the Constitution, if adopted, would bring about a new kind of politics in which large-scale organization would be a major factor, and they identified the old, familiar, personal politics with liberty and responsible government. Most important and most significant, they denied that the principle and practice of republicanism could be made operative over the area and population then embraced by the thirteen separate states. Their position, both with respect to the *status quo* of 1776–87 and with that of the pre-Revolutionary experience of self-government, was the conservative one in the great debate over ratification.[10]

It was the Founding Fathers who were the true radicals. In the very first number of *The Federalist,* Hamilton struck a radical stance when he stated that the question for decision was whether mankind could determine its government by deliberate choice or must continue to be subject to the forces of accident and chance.[11] Indeed, the whole idea of drafting a constitution for an entire nation and then submitting it to conventions chosen by the people for ratification or rejection was radical in the extreme, though the example of Massachusetts had provided a precedent for a similar procedure on a much smaller scale. Scholars may argue until doomsday as to whether the Constitution was democratic or not, but they are less likely to argue as to whether it was a new departure in political institutions It must rank with the establishment of republican government and the philosophy of the Declaration of Independence as one of the great and radical achievements of the Revolution.

VII

The establishment of a new nation, the initiation of the first great modern experiment in republican government, the combination of this experiment with an entirely new kind of federalism, the crystallization in operative form of a political philosophy of individualism and equality — these were the results of the American Revolution. Together with the Revolutionary experience itself, they gave decisive shape to the American political tradition and, in particular, operated to differentiate it from that of the mother country and from those of the older British Commonwealths which won their independence in a later period and without revolution. The relatively short period of intensive opposition and resistance to imperial impositions, the realistic recognition of egoism as a general cause of these, the emphasis in the Declaration on the rights of the individual combined to fix in the American mind an ineradicable fear and distrust of government and government officials, even when popularly elected. This general fear was more profound and more enduring than the specific fear of the executive which stemmed from colonial experience with nonelective governors, and helped to sustain the system of separation of powers, which was also rooted in colonial institutions. Later, the individualist relativism implicit in the Declaration, added to this recognition of egoism, accentuated the distrust of politicians, and reduced the prestige of government as a career. To fear and distrust of government, there was thus added contempt. The American attitude toward government as a necessary evil (and probably more evil than necessary) goes back to the Revolution. It has, perhaps paradoxically, continued to find expression in the strong localist conservatism which helped precipitate the Revolution and later provided much of the opposition to the Constitution. Our Revolutionary experience also both embodied and encouraged that peculiar combination of pragmatism and appeal to ideological principles which has characterized American political thinking. The men of 1776 did not set out to establish republicanism, but once they had done so as a means of securing the rights of life, liberty, and the pursuit of happiness, republicanism itself became a principle of political right. So it has been with later concepts. We have not asked only whether policies would or would not contribute to the realization of these rights; we have asked whether the policies were democratic or antidemocratic, socialist or laissez-faire. Our political tradition has involved the interaction of pragmatic and ideological attitudes and thus has reflected the spirit of 1776.

That spirit was not a particularly radical one, certainly not when compared with that of the French Revolution, the Soviet Revolution of 1917, or the nationalist revolutions of the present time. It had a profoundly conservative aspect, and the radicalism it involved was of a very sober variety. Apart from the recent revival of conservatism and the consequent desire to establish its roots in the political foundation of the nation, there are excellent reasons for regarding the American Revolution as conservative — at least in some respects.

It was a limited revolution, and it was primarily a political movement. There were some social and economic repercussions, but there was no concerted, deliberate attempt at wholesale reconstruction of society or of the habits and everyday lives of the people. There was no American Robespierre or Lenin; Thomas Paine, who looked like a radical in the American context, was imprisoned in France because of the moderate position he took there. The American leaders, even while initiating radical changes, acted with sobriety and, with some exceptions, exhibited a political sophistication based on experience in politics other than as revolutionists.

Most important of all, the Revolution began as a movement of conservative protest, and none of its results represented a total break with the colonial past. Independence had been preceded by a long enjoyment of considerable autonomy; long before Paul Revere ordered lanterns hung in the Old North Church, John Winthrop had mounted a cannon on Beacon Hill to repel any British attempt to seize the Charter of the Colony. Before Thomas Paine ridiculed the British Monarchy in *Common Sense,* the colonists had put a bridle on their governors. The ideas expressed in the second paragraph of the Declaration of Independence were not quite so firmly rooted in colonial experience, and the fact of their formal acceptance gave them an operative force they had previously lacked. But if we are to believe Thomas Jefferson, even they had become embedded in the American mind. The one thing which was most truly radical was the new federalism of the Constitution of 1787. Even it had been preceded by the lesser authority of the Empire and the experience of intercolonial co-operation preceding the war and under the Articles of Confederation. And it was combined with a structure of government, many of whose elements were familiar, because they, too, were rooted in colonial institutions.

So it seems to me that we must conclude that the American Revolution was partly radical and partly conservative. If I may borrow a figure from the great Greek so despised by the author of the Declaration of Independence, the character of the Revolution was the character of the men who made it writ large.[12] Their attitude toward the past was selective. Part of it they wished to preserve, part of it they wished to abandon. They were quite self-conscious about the newness of their enterprise and referred to it frequently as an experiment, but they never had the slightest inclination to repudiate the whole of their British heritage or of their colonial past. They had some fine old bricks to start with, and they knew it. Nevertheless, what they designed and partly built from these bricks was not Georgian. It was American, and they knew that too.

The American Revolution as a Colonial War for Independence

THOMAS C. BARROW

Comparative analysis of the American Revolution with other revolutions is not new, but comparison of it with the experience of newly emerging nations is. Crane Brinton long ago in Anatomy of Revolution (*New York: W. W. Norton, 1938*) *studied the English, American, French, and Russian revolutions as processes, but only recently did social scientist Seymour Lipset make the similarity between our war for independence and struggles of the emerging nations the basis of his book,* The First New Nation (*New York: Basis Books, 1963*). *Even more recently, Thomas C. Barrow (1929–   ), associate professor of history at Clark University, has turned his attention to the same comparison. Using the findings of contemporary analyses of political development, he asserts that we can explain the American Revolution better by referring to current colonial wars for independence than by comparing it to past social revolutions such as Brinton did. Thus, he finds an "inner logic" to the course of the war when we compare it to colonial wars for liberation. The divisions among leaders, their actions, and their search for some form of unity all become explicable in his opinion through such a comparison. Of great importance in any such comparison is the definition of revolution. Not only will a definition emerge from comparative study, but the prior definition determines the very entity studied.*

Such a view of the Revolution is as controversial among historians as it is difficult to accomplish. Robert R. Palmer, author of

The Age of Democratic Revolution (*Princeton: Princeton University Press, 1959–1964*), *denies the validity of such comparison, but the real question would seem to be just what is comparative and what is not about the Revolution? In many ways, the answer to this question would depend upon the state of knowledge in the social sciences rather than upon a priori rejection of the approach. Do we know enough now about political development to assert that such an "inner logic" exists? Are the findings Barrow uses correct? Even if they are correct, are they illuminating?*

To say that the Revolution was a colonial war of independence does not negate necessarily the other interpretations of the Revolution. In many ways such a view seems an up-to-date version of the imperial school of historians, and Barrow's book, Trade and Empire: The British Customs Service in Colonial America, 1660–1775 (*Cambridge, Mass.: Harvard University Press, 1967*), *is in this tradition. Does his article really deny the social revolution school of interpretation? Though he admits there was conflict of thought in the colonies, he does not explain its sources.*

The current historiographical controversies over the American Revolution owe much to Carl Becker. From Becker's day to the present, historians have debated the question of the existence or non-existence of an "internal revolution" in American society. Some historians, following Becker's lead, search for traces of internal social or political turmoil. Others, disagreeing with Becker, stress the continuity of institutions and traditions during the Revolution. At issue is the basic question of just "how revolutionary was the American Revolution," and in the failure of historians to agree on an answer to that question lies the source of controversy. And so the great debate continues.[1]*

Unfortunately, there is no adequate definition of a "revolution." The dictionary description of a revolution as a "total or radical change" certainly provides no effective guideline. Since history is the study of change in human society, locating a revolution according to that formula becomes a matter of appraising just how much change is involved in a given event, which inevitably comes down to a question of where one wants to place the emphasis. In any case, precise definitions are somewhat beside the point. When the word *revolution* is used today in connection with a political

Reprinted by permission from Thomas C. Barrow, "The American Revolution as a Colonial War for Independence," *William and Mary Quarterly*, XXV, 3d Ser. (July, 1968), pp. 452–464.
* [See pp. 148–150 for notes to this article. — Ed.]

system, its meaning, if not its precise definition, is abundantly clear. The image called to mind is inescapably that of the French and Russian revolutions, which have provided us with our classic formulas for revolutionary re-structurings of society. A revolution in these terms represents the replacement of an archaic, repressive regime or regimes with something new, something more open, more flexible, more adaptable. In effect, in the interests of "progress," within the political system stability is replaced by instability until some new synthesis is achieved. Only then is stability restored, at which point the revolutionary drama is closed.

For generations now American historians have struggled to fit their "revolution" into this classic mold.[2] The difficulties they have encountered in doing so are reflected in the present historiographical impasse. It is a problem that might have been avoided had we remembered that the American people were, until 1776, colonials. By its very nature, a colonial society must be, in certain vital ways, unstable. Unable to exercise complete political control, subject to continual external intervention and negative interference, a colonial society cannot achieve effective "maturity" — that is, cannot create and control a political system that will be suited to the requirements of the interests indigenous to that society. A colonial society is an "incomplete" society, and consequently an inherently unstable society. This was as true of American society prior to 1776 as it is today of the colonial societies left in our world.[3] And, consequently, if instability is the given fact in American society at the beginning of the imperial crisis, it is hard to see how the classic pattern of "stability replaced by instability" can be imposed upon it. The answer, of course, is that it cannot, that in fact colonial wars for independence or "liberation" are generically different from revolutions of the French or Russian variety. And, after all, the American Revolution was just that — a colonial war of liberation. Given the widespread existence of such wars in today's world, it is odd that for so long a time we have overlooked the full implications of this fact.

Colonial wars for independence have an inner logic of their own. The first problem is to achieve self-determination. Once that is accomplished, it then becomes a matter of organization, about which, naturally, there always will be fundamental disagreement. What course this disagreement will take, and how bitter it will be, will be determined by the nature of the particular society. In former colonies which have emerged into nationhood in this century, the determining factor has largely been the heterogeneous nature of their societies; with little internal unity or coherence, these new nations generally have fallen back at first on authoritarian centralism. When this has proved incapable of solving the complex problems confronting the society, it has been replaced usually by some kind of collective leadership, often based on the only effective national organization in existence, the military.[4] It is at this point that many of the emergent nations of today find themselves.

Americans were more fortunate in their escape from colonialism. Thanks to the nature of the First British Empire, with its emphasis on commercial growth rather than on imperial efficiency, its loose organization, and the high degree of self-government allowed to the colonists, Americans had developed effective political units which commanded the allegiance of most inhabitants and served as adequate vehicles for the transition from colonial status to nationhood. Given a common English inheritance and a common struggle against British "tyranny," these states made the transition with a minimum of disagreement and dissension. In effect, by 1760 self-government in America, while still incomplete, had gone far. A tightening of English imperial authority after the last war with France brought about a reaction within the colonies toward complete self-determination, which was achieved finally through military success.

Yet, whatever the difference of the American experience from other colonial wars of liberation, certain elements were of necessity shared in common. Within any colonial society there exists an establishment, a group of men whose interests and situation tie them to the existing structure and whose orientation is towards the preservation of the colonial status. When the issue of independence or self-determination begins to be debated, these men are caught in powerful crosscurrents. As natives to the society, they identify to some degree with its problems. At the same time, as beneficiaries of their privileged position within the existing colonial structure, they are not enthusiastic for change. Such men fall back on arguments of moderation, particularly stressing the economic benefits of association with the dominant country and also emphasizing the immaturity of their own society. The gains associated with independence are outweighed for them by the prospects of social and political disorganization. So these men cast their lot with their colonial rulers. Such a man was Thomas Hutchinson. So, too, were many of his Tory associates.

And men like Hutchinson found much to disturb them within American society. Actually, not only was American colonial society subjected to the instability normally inherent in colonial status but there were certain peculiar circumstances which complicated matters further. The melting-pot aspects of American society, the diversity of ethnic, religious, and cultural backgrounds to be found within it, created problems of communication.[5] And, of equal importance, American colonial society was, after all, an artificial creation. Unlike most other historic colonial episodes, the American case was not a matter of an indigenous native society being expropriated and exploited by outsiders. In such instances, the pre-existing patterns of such native societies provide a degree of internal continuity and stability. But the

English colonies in North America had at their disposal no such pre-exis-
tence. They were created specifically and artificially to perform certain functions in relation to the mother country. Most particularly, from the very
beginning their economy was geared to production for distant markets over
which they had no control and little influence.

At the same time, while there were sizeable non-English elements
within the colonial population which created special problems, nevertheless
the majority of the colonists were of the same national origin as their
"rulers." It was not an instance of a conquered native population forced to
bow fatalistically before the superior skills and power of an alien culture.
Rather, it was a case in large part of Englishmen being governed and exploited by Englishmen. The result was a high degree of friction between
governed and governors — an insistence by the colonists on their rights as
Englishmen — that gave a special flavor and complexity to colonial politics.

Thoughtful colonials were well aware of and influenced by these
problems. Thomas Hutchinson and John Adams — Tory and Whig — disagreed not so much on the question of the eventual independence of the
American colonies as on the question of timing. Hutchinson's toryism sprang
in part from his conviction that American society was too immature, too
unstable, to stand alone. External force and authority, it seemed to him,
would be required for many years to maintain internal order and stability in
America. Realistically, he understood that eventually independence was
probable: "It is not likely that the American Colonies will remain part of
the Dominions of Great Britain another century." [6] But, Hutchinson added,
until then, "as we cannot otherwise subsist I am consulting the best interest
of my country when I propose measures for maintaining this subjection
[to England]." [7] What particularly disturbed Hutchinson about the changes
in English policy after 1760 was that they tended to increase the instability
and disorder inherent within American society: "Sieur Montesquieu is right
in supposing men good or bad according to the Climate where they live.
In less than two centuries Englishmen by change of country are become
more barbarous and fierce than the Savages who inhabited the country before they extirpated them, the Indians themselves." [8]

John Adams viewed American development in a different way. Contrasting the New World with the Old, he found the former far superior.
The settlement of America had produced men who "knew that government
was a plain, simple, intelligible thing, founded in nature and reason, and
quite comprehensible by common sense. They detested all the base services
and servile dependencies of the feudal system . . . and they thought all
such slavish subordinations were equally inconsistent with the constitution
of human nature and that religious liberty with which Jesus had made them
free." [9] The problem was that this purity of mind and behavior was always

threatened by contact with the corruption of the Old World. Specifically, subordination of Americans to a distant Parliament which knew little of their needs and desires was not only frustrating but dangerous to the American experiment: "A legislature that has so often discovered a want of information concerning us and our country; a legislature interested to lay burdens upon us; a legislature, two branches of which, I mean the lords and commons, neither love nor fear us! Every American of fortune and common sense, must look upon his property to be sunk downright one half of its value, the moment such an absolute subjection to parliament is established." [10] Independence was a logical capstone to such reasoning, although it took Adams some time to take that final step.

The differences between Hutchinson and Adams suggest that the divisions in American society between conservatives and radicals on the question of separation from Great Britain were related in part to a disagreement over the means to achieve coherence or stability within American society. For one side, continued tutelage under English authority was a necessity until such a time as maturity was achieved. For the other, it seemed that the major roadblock to maturity, to internal harmony and unity, was that self-same English authority. In effect, it was a disagreement on means, not ends. And disagreements similar to that between Hutchinson and Adams can be found within any society — whether in the eighteenth or twentieth century — which is in the process of tearing itself loose from its colonial ties.

It is possible, too, to suggest certain similarities between American intellectual development in these years and the experience of other colonial peoples. From his study of politics in eighteenth-century America, and particularly from his analysis of the pamphlet literature of the Revolutionary years, Bernard Bailyn has concluded that the "configuration of ideas and attitudes" which comprised the "Revolutionary ideology could be found intact — completely formed — as far back as the 1730's" and that these ideas had their origin in the "transmission from England to America of the literature of political opposition that furnished the substance of the ideology of the Revolution." [11] Colonial societies are both fascinated and yet antagonized by the culture of the dominant exploiting nation. They tend to borrow much from their rulers. The English background of a majority of the American colonists in their case made such borrowing a natural and easy process, particularly for those who, for one reason or another, identified themselves with British rule.

However, in colonial societies even many of those who are anxious to assert, or preserve, their native interests or culture cannot resist that fascination exerted by the dominant "mother country." These "patriots" borrow, too, but they are likely to borrow from the dissenting tradition within the dominant culture, from the literature of "opposition," to utilize in their own defense the language and literature of those elements within the ruling society which are critical, or subversive, of the governing traditions. In this way the prestige of the "superior" society can be used against that society itself. On the evidence of Bailyn's research, it seems that the Americans followed just such a line of development, fitting the "opposition" tradition into the framework of their own evolving institutions and traditions — a process which was facilitated by the natural connections between the American religious dissenting traditions and the "opposition" traditions of eighteenth-century English society.

Again, once the movement for independence enters its final phase within a colonial society and becomes an open contest of strength, other divisions tend to become obscured. The most determined supporters of the colonial rule are silenced or forced to rely increasingly on the military strength of their rulers to maintain their position. On the other side, the advocates of independence submerge momentarily whatever differences they may have and present a common front. It is a time of common effort, of mutual support within the forces interested in achieving self-determination. At the same time the "patriot" groups develop special organizations capable of coercing those elements within society, often a majority of the population, which are inclined towards neutrality or moderation. Such were the Sons of Liberty in the American Revolution, and the evidence suggests that they performed their work effectively. Partly because of their efforts, and more generally because of the peculiar character of American colonial society and the nature of the imperial conflict, American society weathered the crisis with relative stability and harmony. As John Adams put it, "The zeal and ardor of the people during the revolutionary war, supplying the place of government, commanded a degree of order, sufficient at least for the temporary preservation of society."[12]

With independence come altered circumstances for a former colonial society. Victorious patriots, confronted with the task of creating a permanent political structure, gradually begin to disagree among themselves as to how it can best be done. Since the only effective central direction came previously from the colonial rulers, the problem in each newly independent society is to fit the surviving local units into some coherent national structure. Here the forces of localism and centralism come into conflict. Those men or interests firmly entrenched in their positions at the local level see in increased centralism a threat to their existence and power. On the other hand, those men or interests of a more cosmopolitan nature, geared to extra-local activities and contacts, can see the benefits that would accrue to them through the introduction of the smoother flow of communications and transactions that effective centralization would bring.[13] The disagreement pits the particularism of the entrenched local interests and individuals against the nationalism of the cosmopolitan interests and individuals. In most contemporary emergent societies these latter groups are by far the weaker. Fortunately, in America the cosmopolitan groups were stronger and more effective, partly again because of the unusual origin and nature of American colonial society. From the beginning the English colonies had been geared to production for European markets; it was the reason for their existence. The result was the development of an economy which had geographical variations but a common external orientation. Merchants and large-scale producers of items for export dominated this society. In the period after independence was achieved, these men provided a firm base for the construction of an effective national political system. Their success came with the substitution of the Constitution of 1787 for the Articles of Confederation.

Historians following the Becker-Beard approach put a different interpretation on the period following the achievement of de facto independence. For them, it was the moment of the triumph of radical democratic elements within American society. The wording of the Declaration of Independence, the constitutions of the new state governments, and particularly the drawing up of the Articles of Confederation represent for these historians the influence of a form of "radicalism." Yet, as Elisha Douglass has noted, in the formation of the governments for the new states, rather puzzlingly the one political reorganization that was subjected to the most democratic method of discussion and adoption — that of Massachusetts — turned out to be not only the most conservative of all the state constitutions but more conservative, in fact, than the previous system.[14] Somehow in Massachusetts, at least, an excess of democracy seems to have led to an enthronement of conservatism. And, indeed, the new constitutions or systems adopted in all the states were remarkable generally for their adherence to known and familiar forms and institutions.

Obviously, given the disruption of the traditional ties to England, the interruption of the natural economic dependence on English markets, the division of American society into opposing Whig and Tory camps, and the presence on American soil of enemy troops (which occupied at different moments the most important commercial centers), some confusion and dissension was inevitable within American society. What is remarkable is how little upheaval and disagreement there actually was. Had American society been ripe for a social upheaval, had it been comprised of oppressing and oppressed classes, no better opportunity could have been offered. The conservative nature of the American response suggests that something other than a radical re-structuring of society was what was debated or desired.

Again, some historians have interpreted the decentralized political system created under the Articles of Confederation as a "triumph" of radi-

cal democracy. However⌈ if instability, associated with colonial status and
with the peculiar character of American colonial society, was a recurrent
problem, and if inability to achieve positive control of their own political
system was a major irritant, then the decentralization of the Articles was a
logical development.⌋In effect, if home rule was the issue and the cure, it
was only natural that each local unit should seek as much autonomy within
the national framework as possible. Seemingly, decentralization was the best
method to bring coherence and stability, or maturity, to American society.
Each local unit could look to its own needs, could arrange for the effective
solution of its own special problems, could work to create that internal balance and harmony of conflicting interests that are the earmark of stability
and maturity.

The problem with the Articles was not an excess of democracy. What
brought about an effective opposition to them was their failure to achieve
their purpose. The history of the states under the Articles, at least in the
eyes of many contemporaries, suggested that decentralization, rather than
being a source of stability, was a source of confusion and turmoil. James
Madison explained the nature of the mistake in his Tenth Federalist. In
spite of independence, under the system created by the Articles, wrote Madison, "complaints are everywhere heard from our most considerate and virtuous citizens . . . that our governments are too unstable." The problem,
for Madison, was to control faction within society, and the most dangerous
type of faction is that which includes a majority. Unfortunately, the "smaller
the society, the fewer probably will be the distinct parties and interests composing it; the fewer the distinct parties and interests, the more frequently
will a majority be found of the same party; and the smaller the number of
individuals composing a majority, and the smaller the compass within which
they are placed, the more easily will they concert and execute their plans of
oppression." The solution is to enlarge the sphere, because if "you take in a
greater variety of parties and interests," then "you make it less probable that
a majority of the whole will have a common motive to invade the rights of
other citizens . . . The influence of factious leaders may kindle a flame
within their particular States, but will be unable to spread a general con-
flagration through the other States." [15]

Nor was the opposition to the Constitution less concerned than
Madison about order and stability within society. Again, disagreement was
fundamentally over means, not ends. The anti-Federalists clung to the former ideas of local autonomy. They were, in fact, not more democratic than
their opponents but more conservative. They were afraid of change: "If it
were not for the stability and attachment which time and habit gives to
forms of government, it would be in the power of the enlightened and aspir-
ing few, if they should combine, at any time to destroy the best establish-

ments, and even make the people the instruments of their own subjugation." The trouble was that the system created under the Articles was not yet sanctified by time: "The late revolution having effaced in a great measure all former habits, and the present institutions are so recent, that there exists not that great reluctance to innovation, so remarkable in old communities . . . it is the genius of the common law to resist innovation." [16] George Clinton agreed with Madison on the dangers of faction: "The people, when wearied with their distresses, will in the moment of frenzy, be guilty of the most imprudent and desperate measures. . . . I know the people are too apt to vibrate from one extreme to another. The effects of this disposition are what I wish to guard against." [17] It was on the solution to the problem, not on the nature of the problem, that Clinton differed from Madison. For Clinton, the powerful central government created by the Constitution might too easily become a vehicle for popular tyranny. It was this same sentiment which led eventually to the adoption of the first ten amendments, the Bill of Rights, with their reservations of basic rights and powers to local units and individuals.

It would not do to carry the comparison between the American Revolution and other colonial wars of liberation, particularly those of the twentieth century, too far. But there is enough evidence to suggest certain basic similarities between the American experience and that of other emergent colonial peoples — enough evidence, at least, to suggest that the efforts of historians to impose on the American Revolution the classic pattern of the French and Russian revolutions have led to a distorted view of our national beginnings. A French Revolution is the product of unbearable tensions within a society. The purpose of such a revolution is to destroy society as it exists, or at least to destroy its most objectional aspects, and to replace the old with something new. In contrast, a colonial "revolution" or war of liberation has as its purpose the achievement of self-determination, the "completion" or fulfillment of an existing society, rather than its destruction. A French Revolution is first of all destructive; a colonial revolution, first of all constructive. In either case the process may not be completed. In the instance of the French Revolution, the re-constructed society may contain more of the old than the original revolutionaries desired. And in the case of the colonial revolution, the process of winning independence and the difficulties of organizing an effective national political structure may open the gates to change, may create a radicalism that carries the original society far from its former course; the result may be more destruction than was originally envisaged. Yet, the goals of these two revolutions are fundamentally different, and their different goals determine a different process of fulfillment. The unfolding of the revolutionary drama, the "stages" of revolution, will be quite different, if not opposite.

[For John Adams, the American Revolution was an epochal event, a moment of wonder for the world to behold and consider. At times his rhetoric carried him beyond the confines of his innate caution, and he sounded like a typical revolutionary: "The progress of society will be accelerated by centuries by this revolution . . . Light spreads from the dayspring in the west, and may it shine more and more until the perfect day."]8 But, as Edward Handler has noted, "The truth is that if Adams was a revolutionary, he was so in a sense very different than that produced by the other great modern revolutions." 19 Adams did indeed feel that his revolution had a meaning for the world but it was not related to the violent re-structurings of society. Rather[its message, for Adams, was that free men can decide voluntarily to limit their freedom in the interests of mutual association, that rational men can devise a system that can at once create order and preserve liberty.]The American success was in contrast to the traditional authoritarian systems of the Old World: "Can authority be more amiable or respectable, when it descends from accidents or institutions established in remote antiquity, than when it springs fresh from the hearts and judgments of an honest and enlightened people?" 20

Most wars of liberation are not so orderly as that of the American Revolution. Most, at least in this century, have led to increasing radicalism and division within the liberated society. National unity has not been easily achieved. That the American emergence from colonialism had a different ending is significant. A firm basis for unity obviously existed within American society, which, naturally, suggests that the reverse, too, was true — that such tensions and divisions as did exist within American society were relatively minor and harmless. It is no wonder that historians determined to find an internal social or political revolution of the French variety within the American Revolution have encountered such difficulties. Nor is it a wonder that the Revolution has become so beclouded with historiographical debates and arguments. The problem has been in our approach. We have been studying, it would seem, the wrong revolution.

WAS IT ALSO A SOCIAL REVOLUTION?

The Preservation of Colonial Democracy through Revolution

ROBERT E. BROWN

Robert E. Brown (1907–   ), professor of history at Michigan State University, is the leading opponent of the class conflict interpretation of the Revolution founded by Carl Becker and Charles Beard at the beginning of this century. Instead of seeing the Revolution as the result of internal conflict among social classes as well as a struggle for independence from the mother country, Brown argues that the Revolution occurred because of the efforts of the colonists to preserve the democratic society they already possessed against the efforts of England to change it. Far from seeking to reshape their society along more democratic lines, the colonists only went to war to conserve the open and free society England wanted to change. According to Brown's view, class conflict was as impossible as it was unnecessary because colonial American society was relatively classless, or middle class, and therefore politically and economically democratic already. Since Brown's analysis stresses the colonists' attempts to conserve what they had rather than their innovations, historians call it the conservative interpretation. Some think it is conservative politically as well for it stresses consensus more than conflict and internal power struggles.

Crucial to Brown's whole thesis is his argument that since colonial society was primarily composed of middle-class property owners no internal conflict occurred or was even necessary. In the following selection, Brown summarizes his findings from his two major books on this theme, Middle-Class Democracy *and the*

Revolution in Massachusetts, 1691–1780 (*Ithaca: Cornell University Press, 1955*) *and* Virginia, 1705–1786: Democracy or Aristocracy? (*East Lansing, Mich.: Michigan State University Press, 1964*). *Though here he focuses on the forces behind the Constitution, his argument really concerns the nature and causes of the Revolution. Do you believe he establishes his case? What is his method of proof? What is his evidence? Would a statistical reconstruction of the class structure be more convincing? Compare the writings of other historians on the nature of colonial society, particularly the article by Kenneth Lockridge listed in the bibliography. Likewise compare Brown's use of the word "democracy" with the way the people at the time defined it according to Bernard Bailyn in the section below. Does Brown view the scene through the eyes of the actors or from his own perspective? How did the revolutionists see their plight? What was England trying to accomplish? Does Brown's thesis bolster or hurt the arguments of Kenyon and Barrow?*

John Adams once remarked that if we would understand the American Revolution, we must study the previous two hundred years of experience by the American people, especially the treatment they received at the hands of the British.* Those two hundred years were also the formative years of the American Constitution as well as the incubation period of the American Revolution. The Constitution did not spring full-blown from the pens of the Founding Fathers as something completely new in government. Since it was not a document that was imposed upon the American people by force, we must consider it as the product of a long evolutionary process.

Before we can fully appreciate the Constitution, however, we must first understand the structure of the society which produced it. We have become especially sensitive to class structure in recent years because of the threat of communism in undeveloped areas. We know that this factor has a direct bearing on the type of government that these undeveloped areas are apt to adopt. Economic and social class structure, the extent of political democracy, educational opportunity, and religious toleration or its absence are fundamental aspects of any society, and it is with these various aspects of colonial life that we shall concern ourselves here.

Reprinted by permission of the publishers from *Reinterpretation of the Formation of the American Constitution* by Robert E. Brown, Boston, Mass.: Boston University Press. © Copyright 1963 by the Trustees of Boston University.
* [See pp. 150–155 for notes to this article. — Ed.]

When we consider the class structure of the colonies, we encounter the first of our major points of reinterpretation.

For the past half-century or more, historians have interpreted the economic life of colonial times in terms of class divisions and class conflicts. They have assumed that the sharp class lines of Europe were transplanted to this country, where, in spite of the economic opportunity offered by the frontier, they not only took root but grew sharper as the Revolution approached. The emphasis has varied from writer to writer, but most historians have assumed that colonial society was divided horizontally into two classes, the rich and the poor, the haves and the have-nots, the upper and lower classes, the conservatives and the radicals. Occasionally a writer mentioned a middle class, but there has been no great emphasis placed on this class.[2] THE

Recent research would seem to indicate that we have been mistaken about the class structure of colonial society and that we need to take a hard second look at some of our assumptions. Instead of a society of the few rich and the many poor, we are coming to believe that the great mass of the American people before the Revolution were what we would now call "middle class." There were a few wealthy men, although they were not wealthy by European standards then or our own standards now, and a few poor people. But the bulk of the people, lying between these two extremes, were neither rich enough to live off their property without some gainful employment nor poor enough to be considered a "proletariat" or working class. Most men either owned property or were in the process of acquiring it — property which was capitalistic in nature, such as a farm or a shop, which aided them in making a living.[3]

The use of the term "middle class" probably calls for some kind of definition. Classes are difficult to define because they include not only economic but also psychological factors. Webster defines the middle class economically as "the social class between the aristocracy or very wealthy and the working class or proletariat." Psychologically, we would also probably have to include in the middle class those who considered themselves to be in this class, or aspired to be in it, or expected that their children would become members of it. Among my students I seldom find any who will admit to being of the upper or lower classes — they are all middle class. And since people act on the basis of what they believe, not just what is, we must consider psychological as well as economic factors in determining colonial class structure.

When we ask the question, what did contemporaries think of American class structure, the answer is that they considered it fundamentally middle class. Almost to a man, those who were acquainted with European and American conditions were struck by their differences, not their similarities, and in the comparison, American society fared very well indeed. A few examples must suffice.

The well-known French observer of the American scene, St. John de Crèvecoeur, was especially impressed by the middle-class nature of American society. This was not a country of a few great lords who possessed everything and a herd of people who had nothing, he declared. The gulf between rich and poor was not what it was in Europe. There the haughty mansion was in contrast with the clay hut where man and beast lived together in mutual misery. Here were fair cities, extensive fields, and decent houses. From Nova Scotia to west Florida, said Crèvecoeur, this was a country inhabited chiefly by independent farmers who were motivated by a spirit of industry because they worked for themselves. There was a pleasing uniformity of decent competence throughout the country — the most perfect society then in existence, a predominantly middle-class, equalitarian society.

The reason for this middle-class society, according to Crèvecoeur, was the great amount of economic opportunity available for the common man. Crèvecoeur obviously did not look on colonial America as a place where a few rich men dominated the economic lives of the masses. Immigrant laborers were well paid and their compensation enabled them to buy land. Here the poor became rich — not rich in gold and silver, but in cleared land, cattle, good houses, and good clothing. Wages were several times the wages of Europe, and thousands of acres were available at cheap prices. America, Crèvecoeur concluded, was a land of opportunity for the middle and lower classes of Europe.[4]

Benjamin Franklin was another observer who stressed the contrast between Europe and America and also depicted the latter as primarily middle class. In Europe, men remained poor because they had to work for others, he declared, but in America a laboring man could soon save enough to buy a farm, raise a family, and be assured that his children would also have an opportunity to get ahead. It was a middle-class society, he said, where few were either as poor or as rich as their counterparts in Europe. America was a "land of labor" in which an "almost general mediocrity of fortune" prevailed among the people.[5]

After a trip through Scotland and Ireland, Franklin wrote the following:

"I often thought of the happiness of New England, where every man is a freeholder, has a vote in public affairs, lives in a tidy, warm house, has plenty of good food and fewel, with whole clothes from head to foot. . . ." It seemed to Franklin that the poor of Europe lived in misery only that the rich might live in luxury. If this were civilization, he would advise the Indians to remain as savages, for to Franklin, in the possession and enjoyments of the various comforts of life, every Indian was a gentleman compared with the poor of Europe.[6]

If we think of Crèvecoeur and Franklin as unreliable observers because they were too liberal, we can turn to conservative contemporaries only to find them saying the same things. Thomas Hutchinson, Governor of Massachusetts and certainly not what we would now call a liberal, wrote as follows:

"Property is more equally distributed in the colonies, especially those to the northward of Maryland, than in any nation in Europe. In some towns you see scarce a man destitute of a competency to make him easy." [7]

On another occasion Hutchinson had this to say about land-owning and tenantry:

> I must observe to you that but few farms in the colonies are in the hands of tenants. . . . In all the colonies upon the continent but the northermost more especially the inhabitants are generally freeholders. [W]here there is one farm in the hands of a tenant I suppose there are fifty occupied by him who has the fee of it. This is the ruling passion to be a freeholder.[8]

In other words, the people in general were middle class because they either were freeholders or aspired to be freeholders.

Other observers merely footnoted the above ideas. A customs officer, Comptroller Weare, spoke of the opportunity for labor in this country and the fact that all mortifying distinctions of rank were lost in common equality.[9] And a traveling officer wrote that the "levelling principle here, everywhere operates strongly, and takes the lead, everybody has property, & everybody knows it." [10]

Even Virginia, which has often been considered one of the most aristocratic of the colonies, possessed a population that was either mainly middle class or in the process of joining the middle class. Observers pointed out that poor men, rather than work for others, could easily procure land, become their own masters, and provide small estates for themselves and their families.[11] A tutor, William Proctor, said that "a poor man, if diligent, may in a short time (less than seven years) become able to purchase & set upon perhaps a mile square of land." [12] Skilled artisans soon joined the ranks of independent property-owning farmers. Peter Fontaine declared on one occasion that "every Virginia tradesman must be at least half a planter," and on another he said there were "no tradesmen or artificers of any sort but what become planters in a short time." [13] And another observer commented that the town of Port Royal was inhabited by merchants and factors and the country around the town "by planters, in general in middling circumstances." [14]

Virginia governors had trouble raising troops because the people were mostly property-owning farmers who were not attracted by the dubious advantages of army life as lower-class Europeans were. William Gooch attributed his failure to the fact that white men in Virginia were "all planters, and such as have their plantations under their own management." [15] And Governor Francis Fauquier, experiencing similar difficulties in raising men, declared that "every man in this colony has land and none but Negroes are laborers." [16]

In the past we have been led to believe that upper-class land specu-lators monopolized the land so that poor people could not procure it except at great sacrifice, but this was not true in Virginia. Cheap land was avail-able there through the headright system whereby each imported person was entitled to fifty acres of land, and these headrights were easily purchased from people who did not want land. The government also adopted the policy of selling a right to fifty acres, called a treasury right, for five shillings.[17]

Land speculators, far from monopolizing land, often served as the means whereby poor people could get land easier than in any other way. Because land was plentiful and easily secured from the government, specu-lators had to sell at reasonable prices, usually £3 or less for a hundred acres. This was not much more than the price of government land when the charges of surveying and patenting were added to the original 10 s. cost of treasury rights for 100 acres.[18] The Beverley family, for example, sold 71,541 acres over the thirty-two years from 1741 to 1773 for a total price of only £3,602, the Borden family sold 84,666 acres during the same years for £4,328, and other Virginia speculators, such as Hites, Pattons, and Byrds, sold at similar prices.[19] As one governor said, it was easier for a poor man from another colony to get land from a speculator than from the govern-ment, and another observer claimed that many speculators never realized any profit on their land speculations.[20]

The cost of speculative land, when compared with colonial prices and wages, tell us to some extent why society was heavily middle class. The £3 for 100 acres amounted to the price of one good cow, half of a fair horse, three sheep, or fifteen bushels of wheat, the produce of about one acre of land.[21] Skilled workers, and most workers classified themselves as skilled, re-ceived four to six shillings a day. Robert Carter paid a shipcarpenter £6 a month for himself, £4 for his apprentice, and £2.12.0 for his slave. Wash-ington paid carpenters from £25 to £50 a year to manage slave carpenters, plus a house, 300–400 pounds of meat, and fifteen to twenty bushels of corn.[22] In short, a hundred acres could be purchased for less than a month's wages, and to make it even easier, much land was acquired with a small down payment.

There was virtually no labor class in the colonies as we now think of a labor class. This was true even in "aristocratic" Virginia, except for slaves. Washington complained that labor was not to be hired in the country and others spoke of Virginia as a place "where labourers are few, and those chiefly slaves." [23] Peter Fontaine claimed that a man could not live in Virginia without a slave, unless he was willing to do menial labor, for labor could not be hired "for love or money." [24] So if all those above the class of laborers were middle class or better, most Virginians were middle class.

In the past we have assumed that tenants were part of the lower classes, but this was not necessarily true. In the first place, as Hutchinson said, there were not many tenants compared with the freeholding farmers. But even in Virginia, where there were some tenants, these tenants were often in the middle class. There a man could procure land on a life lease, most leases were for life or lives, and for legal purposes such a lease was considered the same as a freehold. Often the tenant was given from two to six years to improve the land before he had to pay any rent. It was not unusual for a man to sell his lease with the improvements he had made for as much as £100, and sometimes he sold the lease even before he started to pay rent. Tenants also bought other land of their own as well as slaves, so we would have to be very careful in relegating tenants to the lower classes.[25]

The county records — deeds, wills, rent rolls, and tax lists — confirm in great detail the statements that most men were property owners. Overseers, servants, and apprentices soon acquired property, sometimes to a considerable extent, both in land and slaves.[26] As one traveller said, rather than engage in hard work which was both contrary to their dispositions and considered the special province of slaves, Virginians preferred to settle on fresh western lands where they could enjoy "an easy and indolent independency" on the labor of a slave or two.[27] Perhaps this attitude is not middle class, but neither is it the attitude of a confirmed proletarian.

In the world of practical affairs, it is not necessary that a man rise from the bottom of the social ladder to the top rung in order to be satisfied with the existing social order. All that is usually essential is that he be able to better himself to an extent somewhat commensurate with his own evaluation of his ability. C students seldom start academic revolutions because they fail to get A's. Colonial society offered men the opportunity of improving their station, and this, I think, is the important consideration.

In the realm of economics, also, we have been led in the past to believe that entail and primogeniture were strong bulwarks of an aristocratic society. But as with other aspects of economic life, this assumption fails to stand the test of evidence.

Entail and primogeniture were relatively unimportant before the Revolution, Jefferson's well-known statement to the contrary notwithstanding. In some colonies entail was not used. John Adams said that land was divided among the common people in this country in such a way that nineteen-twentieths of the property was in their hands. On another occasion, Adams declared that the law for the distribution of intestate estates resulted in frequent divisions of landed property and prevented monopolies of land.[28] In Virginia, the amount of entailed land was minor compared with that held in fee simple. Entails were easily broken, and if they were not broken, a man could leave an entailed estate so burdened with debts or bequests to younger children that the estate became a liability rather than an asset to the person who inherited it.[29]

There were two other reasons why entail and primogeniture did not have the effects that we have attributed to them. One was that a man could and often did procure other land to leave to his younger children so that the eldest son did not get everything. Secondly, in some colonies, primogeniture did not apply to intestate estates, but even when it did, as in Virginia, the younger children had frequently received their share of the property during the life of their father.[30] As a result of these factors, entail and primogeniture were really of minor importance.

A final point in the economic class structure concerns the position of the upper class in colonial society. In the past the assumption has prevailed that there was great antagonism between classes, and the implication has been that the lower classes wanted to annihilate the upper classes. The facts seem to point to a different conclusion, however. To the extent that there were class differences, it would appear that the upper class was something to be emulated rather than extinguished. One finds numerous statements that if the better sort set the example, the others would follow.[31] Then, as now, men engaged in name-dropping, a process by which the name-dropper vicariously associates himself with people of a higher status.[32] One also finds statements that the best way to discredit a man in the eyes of the people was to call him poor.[33] And finally, perhaps the most convincing evidence of the absence of class conflict is the fact that the sources simply do not show any significant conflict.

Until we have better evidence to the contrary, we must accept the fact that colonial America was predominantly middle class rather than class-ridden. It offered great opportunities for the common man, and because most men owned property, there was a widespread belief in the rights of property. We should not be surprised, therefore, that colonists looked upon property as one of man's natural rights along with life and liberty.

When we turn from the economic to the political structure of colonial America, we again find an equally significant change of interpretation.

For many years we have believed that colonial politics were aristocratically dominated by an upper class of merchants or planters or both, who naturally ran the political machine in the interests of the upper classes. Two political devices served to maintain upper-class domination — a restricted electorate and inequitable representation. The voting franchise was limited to men who possessed adequate property, which presumably meant the upper economic group. In addition, the upper classes, located mainly in seaport towns and in the tidewater, refused to allot adequate representation to the poorer piedmont and frontier regions.[34]

Recent research seems to indicate that we have been mistaken on both points.

While it is quite true that the colonies imposed property restrictions on voting, it is not true, as we have believed, that these property requirements excluded a large portion of the population from the franchise. Colonists held a "stake in society" philosophy of politics, believing that if a man participated in government involving taxes and men's property, he should himself pay taxes and possess property. In the past, historians have jumped from the factual premise that there were property qualifications for voting to the fanciful conclusion that most men were disfranchised.

It is also true that women, children, slaves, and indentured servants could not vote, and of course this was undemocratic. But if we must include these groups before we can call American society democratic, we are still not a democracy. The fact is, however, that the historians who have considered colonial society undemocratic have also believed that democracy arrived with Andrew Jackson and "Jacksonian Democracy," yet these same groups were still disfranchised at the time of Jackson. Some historians and political scientists are not sure that the enfranchisement of women has affected democracy more than merely doubling the vote. We must remember that Grant was elected when men only could vote and Harding was elected when the women had the ballot, and one would be hard-pressed in deciding which choice was worse.

The amount of property required for voting in the colonies was not sufficient to exclude any but the very poorest men, if those. In the section under economic opportunity, I have already mentioned property values in terms of wages and commodity prices. The 40 s. freehold required for the vote in some colonies meant real estate that would rent for 40 s. a year, the equivalent of ten day's wages for a carpenter. By comparison, ten day's wages for a carpenter today would not even pay a year's rent on a single room. In Virginia, a half acre of land carried the vote until 1736, then the requirement was raised to 100 acres of wild land, twenty-five acres of improved land, or a house and lot in town. In the boroughs of Norfolk and Williamsburg, men with £50 of property could vote, as could also anyone who had served a five-year apprenticeship to a trade.[35]

A few examples must suffice to show that contemporaries did not look upon the prevailing franchise requirements as very restrictive. Speaking of the Massachusetts Land Bank of 1740, Thomas Hutchinson said that "the needy part of the province in general favored the scheme," then added,

"One of their votes will go as far in popular elections as one of the most opulent." [36] After his defeat in 1749 for an unpopular stand on paper money, Hutchinson wrote plaintively: "You have heard my fate. I could make but 200 votes in near 700. They were the principal inhabitants but you know we are governed not by weight but by numbers." [37] Calling every town in Massachusetts a democracy and Boston an "absolute democracy," Hutchinson gave this description of voting restrictions: "By the constitution forty pounds sterl. — which they say may be in cloaths household furniture or any sort of property is a qualification and even into that there is scarce ever any inquiry and anything with the appearance of a man is admitted without scrutiny." [38] If Boston was dominated by a merchant aristocracy, Hutchinson was completely oblivious of this fact.

Thomas Paine, as liberal as Hutchinson was conservative, gave about the same interpretation of the franchise in Pennsylvania:

> By a former law of Pennsylvania, prior to the forming the Constitution, it was enjoined that a man is [if?] required, should swear or affirm himself worth fifty pounds currency before he should be entitled to vote. The only end this answered was, that of tempting men to forswear themselves. Every man with a chest of tools, a few implements of husbandry, a few spare clothes, a bed and a few household utensils, a few articles for sale in a window, or almost anything else he could call or even think his own, supposed himself within the pale of an oath, and made no hesitation of taking it; and to serve the particular purpose of an election day the money has even been lent.[39]

An extant account of a Philadelphia election substantiates Paine's estimate of the voters. The poll was open all day, all night, and until three the next afternoon. Both sides combed the political bushes to bring in the halt and the lame on litters and in carriages. In the past we have been told that only about two per cent of the people of Philadephia could vote, but over 3,900 men participated in this particular election.[40] So in a city where the total population was only about 25,000, which would have meant less than 5,000 adult men, 3,900 voters was a large majority — nearer eighty per cent than two per cent.

The same voting situation prevailed in Virginia. Before the voting qualifications were raised in 1736, Governor Alexander Spotswood declared that "half an acre of land here makes a man as sufficient a voter, and as lawful a burgess as he that is possess'd of 10,000 acres & 100 Negroes." Spotswood referred to the body of the electorate as "the meaner sort of people," the "lowest mob," the "lower class," and the "common people." [41] After voting requirements were raised in 1736, Governor William Gooch claimed that the "better sort" seldom carried a Virginia election.[42] And in 1756 Governor Dinwiddie said that "most of the people are freeholders in course have votes for choosing assembly men, on which they strenuously insist on their privileges." [43]

A check of the deeds, wills, election polls, quitrent rolls, and tithable lists shows that almost anything with the appearance of a man voted in the Old Dominion as well as in Massachusetts and Pennsylvania. This included Catholics, tenants with life leases, which included most leases, apprentices often the same year that they ended their apprenticeship or within a year or two thereafter, overseers, men too poor to pay taxes, and former servants. A man with a house and lot in any of the 85 or 90 Virginia towns could vote, and the House of Burgesses ruled that a "house" 8 ft. × 10 ft. moved onto the lot just prior to the election fulfilled the requirements.[44]

In representation, contrary to the old interpretation, it was often the backcountry, not the seaports or tidewater, that was over-represented. In Massachusetts, the seaports could send only fourteen of an estimated 338 possible representatives in 1763. In addition, towns attempted to get their representation reduced and seldom sent as many delegates as they were entitled to send.[45] In Virginia, the House established new counties as fast as people moved west, and passed a bill to allow representation for towns only to have the bill disallowed in England. For example, the area that was Prince George County in 1714 was cut up into ten additional counties by 1770, all ten in the piedmont.[46] Frontier Frederick County petitioned in 1772 to be divided into two or three counties, and the House established three when it could have set up only two or rejected the petition altogether.[47] Opposition to new counties in Virginia usually came from within the counties involved, either from men who did not want to pay additional taxes or from dissenters who did not relish supporting another Church of England minister.[48] The British government attempted to stop the growth of powerful and democratic assemblies by restricting representation, but this is not the same thing as restrictions by a local aristocracy.[49]

Since recent research has dispelled the notions of a restricted electorate and inequitable representation, supporters of the old interpretation have come up with a new generalization to bolster their contention that colonial society was undemocratic. This is the argument that even if the people could vote, they still did not have democracy because aristocrats rigged elections so that only aristocrats were elected. The people, they say, had no real choice of candidates, and supposedly these aristocratic delegates functioned in the interests of their class.[50]

Unfortunately, however, this assumption also fails the test of evidence. Candidates for office had to meet the approval of a sufficient number of the electorate either to get into, or stay in, office. In a democracy, this almost never means unanimous approval, for "the people" usually have opposing views on almost every issue. But since most of the voters were com-

mon people, a large number of "common men" had to approve before a man
could win office. In effect, Thomas Hutchinson was saying this very thing
when he declared that he could get only 200 of 700 votes, even if the votes
he received came from the "better sort." Governor William Shirley said that
the people in general opposed a fixed salary for the governor and that even
those representatives who favored it dared not vote for it because they were
so dependent on their constituents.[51]

The political careers of Landon Carter and his son Robert Wormeley Carter of Virginia tell us much about the power of the voters in what
we have previously considered an aristocratic colony. Landon Carter, the
son of Robert "King" Carter, ran for office for at least seventeen years before
he could even get elected, in spite of his family name. After serving some
years in the House, he complained bitterly that he was "turned out" because
he did not familiarize himself "among the people." His son Robert Wormeley learned the political lesson, cultivated the people, and with Francis
Lightfoot Lee, who used the same tactics, was elected to the House. Lee's
father-in-law, council member John Tayloe, predicted that these methods
would keep both Carter and Lee in office. But what happened? Young Carter, as his father so graphically recorded in his Diary, had "kissed the arses
of the people and very servilely accommodated himself to others," but he
was "shamefully turned out." Out, also, went Francis Lightfoot Lee in spite
of the best efforts of his father-in-law and the political prestige of the Lee
name. Landon Carter cursed fickle popularity as an adulteress of the first
order, particularly complaining that in this key election, "even relations as
well as tenants" voted the wrong way.[52]

As is true today, most of the elected representatives came from the
upper bands of the income spectrum, although the voters usually had a
choice of candidates with very modest property holdings. This should not
surprise us, given a middle-class society which believed emphatically in
property. In fact, it would have been most unusual had such people elected
poor farmers or mechanics to represent them.[53] Even today, when we presumably have an industrial proletariat, it has been reliably reported to me
that a certain well-known industrial state has elected proletarians by the
name of Lodge, Saltonstall, and Kennedy to represent them.

While the economic and political structures of colonial society are
doubtless paramount in any study of the background of the Constitution,
there are also other aspects of the society that should be mentioned at least
briefly.

Education, long considered the prerogative of the upper classes in
line with the general class interpretation, now appears quite the opposite
to us. The colonies, in fact, probably afforded the best opportunity in the
world at that time for the common man to acquire some measure of educa-

tion. The comparison of colonial education should not be with our own educational system geared to a highly industrial and professional society, but with what other countries at the time were doing to educate their common people.

According to John Adams, who admitted a possible prejudice, New England had the best educational system in the world. "The public institutions in New England for the education of youth, supporting colleges at public expense, and obliging towns to maintain grammar schools, are not equaled, and never were, in any part of the world," Adams contended.[54]

Historians who adhere to the aristocratic interpretation of colonial education are confronted with the contradiction of aristocratically dominated legislatures fining towns for failure to provide public education for the common people.

The results of American educational opportunity for the common people were evident for all to see. Said Adams:

> A native of America who cannot read or write is as rare an appearance as a Jacobite or a Roman Catholic, that is as rare as a camel or an earthquake. It has been observed, that we are all of us lawyers, divines, politicians, and philosophers. And I have good authorities to say, that all candid foreigners who have passed through this country, and conversed freely with all sorts of people here, will allow that they have never seen so much knowledge and civility among the common people in any part of the world.[55]

Adams, who has often mistakenly been considered an extreme conservative, believed that education for the common people was of the utmost importance. Men who could read would find in their Bible, almanacs, newspapers, and other available materials the principles by which to guide their lives. Liberty, he said, "cannot be preserved without a general knowledge among the people." And he declared that "the preservation of the means of knowledge among the lowest ranks, is of more importance to the public than all the property of all the rich men in the country." [56]

Benjamin Franklin, speaking for all the colonies, had about the same view of American education as that expressed by John Adams. He said that all good books published in England were soon found in the colonies, "where there is not a man or woman born in the country but what can read." Later Franklin described the American people as follows: "We are a more thoroughly enlightened people, with respect to our political interest, than perhaps any other under heaven. Every man among us reads, and is so easy in his circumstances as to have leisure for conversations of improvement and for acquiring information." [57] Franklin, whose father was too poor to send him to college, is the prime example of the fact that one did not need to be wealthy to get an education.

Educational facilities varied from colony to colony, but all offered some means of education. There were charity schools and free schools for those who could not pay, and among the poorer people, apprenticeships furnished an opportunity for what was probably an adequate education at that time for boys who expected to be farmers or skilled artisans.[58] It would be an interesting problem to determine whether the poorer people demanded more educational opportunity for their children from a reluctant upper class or whether it was the upper class who provided the impetus for colonial education.

Religion, declining in importance as the 18th century wore on, does not now appear to have been the class issue that it was once considered. Much emphasis has been placed on the established church as a conservative upper-class instrument, and the statement has even been made that the upper classes used the terrors of religion to keep the masses in order.[59]

Religion was an influence in colonial politics, just as the recent education bill shows that it is still an influence with us today, but nowhere in the colonies did the church exert its power as it had in the 17th century. The Massachusetts Charter of 1691 cut the formal ties between church and state in that colony by providing for a property rather than a religious qualification for voting. The Congregational Church became a semi-established church, but non-Congregationalists did not pay taxes to support Congregational ministers, and the church was definitely subordinate to the state. Religious intolerance could not have been a great problem in the Bay Colony, for according to the Reverend Jonathan Mayhew, Congregationalists outnumbered others by fifty to one.[60]

Some of the colonies went virtually all the way toward religious toleration. New York had all kinds of churches, including even a Jewish synagogue. There were complaints that colonies such as New Jersey and North Carolina had all religions and that many of the people had no religion whatever.[61]

In Virginia, where the Church of England was established, there was a notable decline in religious influence and certainly religion was not a class issue in the Old Dominion. Churchmen complained that William and Mary College, established to train Anglican ministers, not only had no professors of divinity where the charter required two, but also would soon have no ministers on its board of trustees.[62] Thomas Hutchinson once said that both church and state in Massachusetts were as "popular as could be conceived," [63] a statement which applied to the churches in Virginia as well. There, instead of ministers appointed by a bishop or the governor, appointment was in the hands of each parish vestry. But in actual practice, according to the ministers, it was the church congregation which made the decisions. The church was often at odds with the Virginia Assembly, particularly in the two-penny act controversy, when the ministers accused the Assembly of trying to starve them.[64]

There eventually was considerable religious controversy in the Old Dominion but it was not along class lines. After 1750, dissenting groups gained tremendously in the colony, bringing a demand for more toleration and equal treatment of all religions. Some of the dissenters came from groups imported to settle the frontier, others came from Pennsylvania, but a large number were converts from the Church of England. But these dissenters were not from the lower classes only, as we have believed. Important men in every community, including even Robert Carter, were dissenters. And it was common for a parish to petition for the dissolution of a vestry on the ground that its members had gone over to a dissenting church but still retained their offices as Church of England vestrymen.[65] Religious changes that came in Virginia as a result of the Revolution were of long preparation, and as we shall see later in dealing with the Revolution, were not the product of class conflict.

In the realm of justice, colonists were accustomed to rule by law, to trial by jury of jurors selected in the area where the crime was committed, and in some colonies, to the election of jurors. The penal code was undoubtedly harsher than our present code, but it was spelled out so that a man knew what to expect by way of punishment. Judges and justices of the peace, like representatives, naturally came from the upper strata of society, just as they do today. But an accused man could always demand a trial by jury, he could challenge jurors that he considered biased or unfriendly, and he could not be convicted by a high-handed aristocracy.[66]

Court records indicate that jurors were more apt to be men of very moderate means, not members of the upper class. Often during a court session the same men sat as jurors on several cases, probably indicating that they were known to be fair in their decisions. Most of the extant complaints that we have about juries come from members of the upper class. In the Parsons' Cause in Virginia, the Reverend James Maury claimed that the sheriff had picked a jury from among the plebeians instead of the gentlemen. And Archibald Cary, merchant and representative, feared that he would not receive justice because the plaintiff, a tavern-keeper, knew the kind of men who were apt to be on the jury.[67]

In conclusion, then, our concepts of the colonial society which produced the American Revolution and Constitution are in the process of undergoing some rather drastic revisions. Some of us no longer believe that colonial America was an aristocratic, class-ridden America, with limited opportunities for the common man and sharp class conflict between upper and lower classes. Instead, we are coming to an interpretation of colonial society as predominantly middle class, with much economic opportunity, a broad franchise, representation that favored the agricultural areas, educational facilities for the common man, and much religious freedom. Colonial America, so some of us think, was much more liberal than we have previously believed.

As a background for the Constitution, it matters a great deal whether it was one or the other — aristocratic and class-ridden or democratic and middle class. Perhaps another ten years of historical research will do much to resolve the controversy.

The second topic in our general subject of the reinterpretation of the formation of the American Constitution involves the nature of the American Revolution. If the structure of colonial society is of concern in the background of the Constitution, certain it is that the Revolution is equally so. If we can say "No evidence — no history," we can also say "No Revolution — no Constitution."

Given the differences between the old and new interpretations of colonial society, one might suspect that there would be comparable differences over interpretation of the Revolution. Such suspicions would be well-grounded. So our problem is to discover what our views have been in the past, what we now believe, and of what significance our changing interpretation has on our understanding of the Constitution.

The late Carl Becker, professor of history at Cornell University, was one of the earliest of the historians to interpret the American Revolution in terms of class conflict. Writing more than half a century ago, Becker said: "The American Revolution was the result of two general movements: the contest for home rule and independence, and the democratization of American politics and society. Of these movements, the latter was fundamental; it began before the contest for home rule, and was not completed until after the achievement of home rule." Later in the same work Becker characterized the two movements of the Revolution in this way: "The first was the question of home rule; the second was the question, if we may so put it, of who should rule at home." [68]

Becker's injection of the class struggle into the American Revolution caught on quickly with other historians whose immediate background was the liberal Progressive Movement in this country — a movement to improve the lot of the common man. To these historians, colonial society was undemocratic and class-ridden: there were rich and poor, enfranchised and disfranchised, privileged and under-privileged. Thus the Revolution became in large part a movement to improve the lot of the common man, just as was the Progressive Era.[69]

From that day to this, Becker's statement of home rule and who should rule at home has found its way into countless books dealing with the American Revolution. We have come to call this the "dual revolution" — the war for independence against Britain and the internal class struggle within the colonies over which class should dominate. And as with Becker, the internal conflict between classes of Americans has assumed greater significance than has the war with Britain.[70]

But just as our interpretation of colonial society has undergone sharp scrutiny and drastic revision in recent years, so also has our view of the Revolution as a "dual revolution." It would follow naturally that if colonial society was middle class, democratic, and offered much opportunity for the common man, the ingredients for a class revolution would be largely absent. There had to be some other explanation.

With the new interpretation, we are coming to look upon the American Revolution as one that was fought on the part of Americans to preserve an already democratic social order rather than to achieve democracy. This aim to *preserve* rather than to *change* made our revolution somewhat unique in world history. Most revolutions occur because men become dissatisfied with the *status quo* and desire to change it. The American Revolution occurred because Americans were reasonably satisfied with the *status quo* and did not want the British to change it. Democracy was involved, but it was a democracy that had already been achieved, not something to be gained from a class conflict between upper and lower classes.

Briefly, the evidence points to the following interpretation: British imperial policies, designed to benefit the Mother Country, had long been ineffective because they could not be enforced, and one of the main reasons for the failure of enforcement was the action of democratic assemblies in the colonies. Fearing colonial growth and the unpleasant prospect of future colonial independence, the British attempted to reform their colonial system after 1760. Since these reforms involved the curtailment of American democracy, Americans objected to British reforms. When objections failed, Revolution resulted, and while American democracy gained a great deal by the elimination of Great Britain, it was not a gain that resulted from internal class war between upper and lower classes.[71]

The Mechanics in New York Politics, 1774–1788

STAUGHTON LYND

Reaction to the conservative interpretation of the Revolution took two forms. On one hand, historians of the older internal conflict school, led by Merrill Jensen, continued to write a refined version of the economic interpretation. On the other hand, some young historians thought they had found a "new past," which would stress the story of the inarticulate lower classes as much as that of rival elites struggling for power. Christened the "New Left" school, the latter shared the former's emphasis on class conflict but tried to view it according to the radical criteria of today rather than those of the 1930s. To them a conspiracy of values is as oppressive as crude economic exploitation.

One of the more widely read of these new left historians is Staughton C. Lynd, who is well known for his commitment to radical ideals for American society. His main area of historical research (for his doctorate at Columbia and subsequently) has been the era of the Revolution. Like Carl Becker, Lynd uses the local history of New York State for a case study of internal conflict among classes. In the selection below, he focuses on the New York City mechanics immediately before, during, and after the war. His analysis of the mechanics moves beyond the simple economic interpretation of correlating ideology, social class, and radical action according to the latter day observer's values. In place of assuming such correlation, he carefully ascertains the social status, economic rank, and political privileges of the mechanics. In addition, he compares the actual causes they espoused to the traditional assumptions about their affiliation and attitudes.

The very complexity of Lynd's account raises questions about his stated and implied conclusions. Do you agree with his description of the mechanics' social class, particularly that of the leaders? Does he prove class consciousness as well as class standing? Did the mechanics assert an ideology peculiar to their class and separate from the ideas expressed by other classes? Did this result in actions and aims different from other classes? In other words, what effect did the ideas and actions of the mechanics have upon such political outcomes as independence and the adoption of the Constitution? How do we judge how radical the mechanics were? Should we assume that the views and actions of the leaders of the mechanics reflected accurately the attitudes of the majority of mechanics? How much evidence does Lynd possess about the views of the majority of the mechanics? How typical were the mechanics of the entire lower class?

For Carl Becker, the mechanic was the revolutionary democrat *par excellence*. When Becker spoke of the American Revolution as not only a struggle for home rule, but also a struggle over who should rule at home, he saw the city artisan as the principal protagonist in the internal struggle. Becker's teacher Frederick Jackson Turner believed that the democratization of American politics and society began on the frontier. Becker, in contrast, relegated protest among upstate tenants to the wings and brought the urban workingman front and center. He called the extra-legal committees of the American Revolution the "open door" through which the politically excluded "pushed their way into the political arena," and it was above all "the unfranchised mechanic and artisan" whom Becker saw striding through the door. He discerned in their demands "the germs of those opposing tendencies which, after the war was over," would divide the patriot party into radical and conservative wings. The rivalry of Federalist and Republican parties in the 1790's, Becker suggested, was "merely the revival, in a slightly different form, of the fundamental party divisions which had existed from the time of the stamp act." [1]*

Becker's portrait of the mechanic as a young democrat was accepted by scholars as late as World War II.[2] More recently it has been severely criticized, on the ground that the Revolutionary "mechanic" was a small businessman, not a laborer, as well as on the ground that the mechanic, contrary to Becker, could vote and, insofar as he exercised this right, staunchly supported upper-class leaders.[3] Meantime, however, interest has grown as to the part played by the inarticulate in the politics of late eighteenth-century Europe. George Rudé, Albert Soboul, Robert R. Palmer and others suggest that the "mobs" who supported John Wilkes in England and formed the revolutionary clubs in Jacobin Paris were extremely heterogeneous in their social and economic composition, but nevertheless (particularly in the case of France) played a genuinely autonomous role in pushing middle-class reformers toward radical acts.[4]

Reprinted by permission from Staughton Lynd, "The Mechanics in New York Politics, 1774–1788," *Labor History*, V (Fall, 1964), pp. 215–246. This version is taken from the revised version which appeared in Staughton Lynd, *Class Conflict, Slavery, and the United States Constitution* (Indianapolis: Bobbs-Merrill, 1968), pp. 79–108.
* [See pp. 155–160 for notes to this article. — Ed.]

There is a further circumstance which lends special interest to reexamination of the Revolutionary mechanics. While Becker regarded the city mechanics as the most revolutionary and democratic of social groups in the years before the Revolution, his fellow Progressive, Charles Beard, wrote of the mechanics after the Revolution that they had not "developed a consciousness of a separate interest or an organization that commanded the attention of the politicians of the time." In the dramatic struggle over ratification of the Constitution which occupied a key position in his classic work, *An Economic Interpretation of the Constitution,* the mechanics to Beard were "politically non-existent." [5]

I

"Contemporary Englishmen," writes Carl Bridenbaugh, "defined the mechanic arts 'as such Arts wherein the Hand and Body are more concerned than the Mind.' " [6] The term "mechanic" was used to refer not only to skilled artisans, but to all groups below the rank of merchants and lawyers. This included, at one end of the occupational spectrum, the unskilled laborer on the docks and, at the other extreme, the master craftsman who owned his shop, employed a dozen journeymen and apprentices, was taxed more than many merchants, and might do some general retailing on the side.[7] In between were a numerous body of cartmen or draymen (some 300 in 1788, 1,000 in 1800), petty retail tradesmen, and stallkeepers. Contemporaries also were careful to draw distinctions within the working population as is suggested by such phrases in common usage as "mechanics, laborers and cartmen," or "the substantial mechanics" and "the lowest order of mechanics." Taken together, the mechanics were a large group; by Bridenbaugh's estimate, about one-half the population of Revolutionary Charleston, and two-thirds the population of Boston, Newport, New York City, and Philadelphia belonged to the mechanic class. Benjamin Labaree's figures for Newburyport, where over half the adult males (in 1773) were artisans and laborers, suggests that mechanics were a majority in smaller cities, too.[8] We may conclude that the mechanics of the American Revolution were — as Robert Palmer describes the Parisian *sans culottes* — "the people . . . without the frosting." [9]

The best known of Revolutionary mechanics, Paul Revere, illustrates the diversity of the group. Revere had a brother and a cousin who were silversmiths, two sons-in-law who were house carpenters, a nephew who was a tailor, and another cousin who built ships. Besides his skilled and lucrative metal work, Revere imported hardware, cloth, and paper. Himself the employer of many workmen and (to use his own words) "very well off for a tradesman," Revere permitted his daughter to marry an apprentice.[10] There can be little doubt that most of those known as "mechanics" were below the level of master craftsmen. The prevailing mode of production in colonial towns was a small workshop in which a master employed one to four journeymen and apprentices.[11] Many enterprises were even larger. The New York City printer Rivington employed sixteen men, and one master carpenter employed twenty-three.[12] Shipyards and ropewalks, Richard Morris estimates, employed at least five and sometimes as many as twenty-five workmen; distilleries, breweries, and candle works were also substantial enterprises.[13] Some indication of the relative strength of different types of mechanics emerges from the figures reported for two trades in a New York City parade of 1788. Among the cabinet-makers there were sixteen master workmen, twenty journeymen, and thirty apprentices; among the coopers 138 master workmen and journeymen, and fifty-five apprentices.[14]

The term "mechanic" does not imply unanimity on all issues, since clearly it was a diverse grouping. Witness, for instance, the existence of economic action of journeymen against employers. Such action was rare, but not unknown in large trades such as printing, shoemaking, and house carpentry.[15] Post-war economic trends — the shift from custom-made to wholesale order work, the decline of apprenticeship and indentured servitude, the emergence of a factory district in the suburb which is now New York's lower east side [16] — coincided with the influx of poor immigrants to intensify the conflict between employer and employee, as well as between the mechanics *en masse* and the city's merchants.

The mechanic of the American Revolution was well-paid when compared to his European counterpart [17]; "nearly all craftsmen were literate" [18]; and, as we shall see in a moment, more than half of the mechanic class could vote. Yet the mechanic was hardly a first-class citizen. Before 1776, Noah Webster noted, the "principal families" of New York City "by associating, in their public amusements, with the middling class of well-bred citizens, render[ed] their rank subservient to the happiness of society." But the war, Webster continued, "operated to diminish the sociability of the citizen of New York." [19] The Reverend Manasseh Cutler, passing through the city in the mid-1780's, observed likewise that "the several classes of people mix very little."[20] A decade later the French traveler, La Rochefoucauld, very aptly sketched the paradox of quasi-equality in the midst of hierarchy:

> In balls, concerts, and public amusements, these classes do not mix; and yet, except the laborer in ports, and the common sailor, everyone calls himself, and is called by others, a *gentleman;* a small fortune is sufficient for the assumption of this title, as it carries men from one class to another. They deceive themselves very much who think that pure Republican manners prevail in America.[21]

There was economic exclusion, too. In eighteenth-century America, as in seventeenth-century England, the "provision of capital" was "the fundamental question" on which the craftsman's status depended.[22] Mechanics, like merchants, required access to capital, and the bank wars of the 1780's and 1790's were as important to the mechanic as was the issue of political recognition.

Carl Becker and the scholars who followed him took it for granted that mechanics, lacking social and economic recognition, also lacked the vote. So far as New York City is concerned, this was too sweeping a conclusion. The mechanics, said a New York pamphleteer in 1783, had ever had it in their power to carry an election; and a newspaper correspondent in 1785 confirmed this testimony, remarking that the mechanics "undoubtedly constitute a great majority of the citizens." [23] On the other hand, comparison of the electoral statistics in a rich and poor ward suggests that among the poorer class of mechanics less than half could vote for state Assemblymen (see Table). In the East ward, where most of the great merchants lived, assessed property valuation per head of family in 1790 was more than five times the comparable figure for the Out ward, known as a factory district and a residential area for the poor. In 1790 the proportion of voters among free white males over twenty-one was 74 per cent in the East ward and only 42 per cent in the Out ward.[24] The suffrage bottle thus may be viewed as half full or half empty [25]; any generalization that all or most mechanics could not vote or that virtually all mechanics could vote [26] is inadmissible.

PROPERTY VALUATION AND VOTERS, NEW YORK CITY, 1790

Ward	Heads of families	Assessed valuation	Valuation per head of family	Free white males over 21	Voters	Voters as % of free white males
East	582	£630,000	£1083	773	575	74%
Out	1089	£186,000	£171	1189	504	42%

(For the sources of these statistics, see note 24.)

In Becker's presentation, then, it would appear that the suffrage question was too much emphasized. He was not wholly wrong in suggesting that mechanics were kept from voting: many were. But the sense of political exclusion embraced many more issues than the suffrage. The suitability of mechanics for elective office, the voter's ability to instruct and control his representatives once they were elected, the administration of justice, the ability to elect officers who had traditionally been appointed, were as important in the period considered as the right to vote.

In Philadelphia, the largest American city, such grievances were agitated well before the War for Independence. Thus, for example, Philadelphia mechanics complained in 1770 that

> it has been customary for a certain company of leading men to nominate persons and *settle the ticket* for assemblymen, commissioners, assessors, etc., without even permitting the affirmative or negative voice of a mechanic to interefere, and, when they have concluded, to expect the Tradesmen to give a sanction thereto by passing the ticket; this we have tamely submitted to so long that those gentlemen make no scruples to say that the Mechanics (though by far the most numerous, especially in this country) have no right to be consulted, that is, in fact have no right to speak or think for themselves.[27]

In New York, it was 1774 before such grievances, expressed by mechanic organizations, began to be heard. And though interrupted by the wartime British occupation, they rose to a crescendo through the decade which followed.

II

The mechanics appeared as an independent and organized force in New York politics in the spring of 1774. During the previous decade "one group, the mechanics, was uniformly identified with the Sons of Liberty." [28] But the Sons of Liberty in New York were always controlled by merchants, and it was not until 1774, apparently, that the General Committee of Mechanics was formed.

Carl Becker himself believed that this Committee "was virtually a continuation of the organization of the *Sons of Liberty*," and that "ostensibly representing the mechanics only, this committee was in fact the chief instrument through which the radical leaders" continued their agitation.[29] Evidence for this assertion is lacking. On the contrary, one finds that of six chairmen of the pre-Revolutionary Committee of Mechanics, those whose occupations can readily be identified were a sailmaker and a cooper [30]; that the Committee of Mechanics was regularly distinguished by contemporaries from the organizations of merchants; and that, in the spring of 1776, when the principal radical merchants had left the city or become politically inactive, the Committee of Mechanics operated more vigorously than ever.[31]

When early in May 1774, the Boston Port Bill reached New York City, "a number of merchants and the Body of Mechanics" of the city nominated a committee of correspondence.[32] In a famous letter of May 20, the young conservative Governeur Morris described the public meeting at which the list of fifty-one nominees was presented to the general populace for its approval. "I stood in the balcony," Morris wrote,

and on my right hand were ranged all the people of property, with some
few poor dependents, and on the other all the tradesmen, etc., who
thought it worth their while to leave daily labour for the good of the
country. . . . The mob begin to think and reason. Poor reptiles! it is
with them a vernal morning; they are struggling to cast off their winter's
slough, they bask in the sunshine, and ere noon they will bite, depend
upon it. The gentry begin to fear this. . . . I see, and I see it with fear
and trembling, that if the disputes with *Great Britain* continue, we shall
be under the worst of all possible dominions; we shall be under the domination of a riotous mob.

Like Becker, Morris believed that one issue between the "people of property" and the "mob" was domestic: "they fairly contended about the future
forms of our Government, whether it should be founded upon aristocratic
or democratic principles." [33]

"Most if not all" of the committee of fifty-one were merchants or
lawyers,[34] and from its inception this committee was under pressure from
the Committee of Mechanics. In May 1774, the mechanics decided that "they
would try the committee of 51 and if they misbehaved they would be removed." [35] In June 1774, a radical commentator wrote from Boston:

Those worthy members of society, the tradesmen, we depend on, under
God, to form the resolution of the other ranks of citizens, in Philadelphia
and New York. They are certainly carrying all before them here. . . . This
will insure a non-importation in this province, whether messieurs les
marchands, will be graciously pleased to come into it or not.[36]

In July 1774, when the committee of fifty-one nominated delegates to attend
the first Continental Congress, the Committee of Mechanics complained
that "the Committee of Merchants did refuse the Mechanics a representative on their body, or to consult with their committee, or offer the names
of the persons nominated to them for their concurrence." [37] In the end,
however, the committee of fifty-one agreed that the election in each ward
should be supervised by two of its own members and two members of the
Committee of Mechanics. For a time it seemed, too, that the committees
would offer rival slates of delegates, but the Committee of Mechanics finally
withdrew its own list when the merchants' nominees pledged themselves to
press for complete non-importation at the forthcoming Congress.[38]

Whether (as Becker thought) the idea of a Continental Congress
originated with the conservative merchants or whether (as Roger Champagne, Becker's reviser, argues) the idea came from radicals Sears, Lamb, and
McDougall,[39] when the first Continental Congress adopted the radical program of non-importation and non-exportation in the fall of 1774 the mechanics at once became identified with the embryo federal government. As
Arthur M. Schlesinger, Sr., put it, radicals at the first Continental Congress

had defined — nationalized — the issue at stake in such a manner as to afford prestige to radical groups, wherever they were to be found, and to weaken the hold of the moderate elements, on the ground that the latter were at variance with the Continental Congress.[40]

Becker makes the same point. After this first Congress, he writes:

the old factions, based upon differences of opinion as to how and by whom the resistance to English measures should be conducted, gradually gave place to parties asserting allegiance to different authorities. . . . The ultra-radicals, although asserting in words their allegiance to Great Britain, were more and more inclined to regard any refusal to submit to the decrees of Congress as a treasonable desertion of the American cause.[41]

The New York mechanics were prominent in welcoming the work of the Congress, and in enforcing its authority by obstructing the movement of supplies and workingmen to the British troops in Boston.[42] Thus fourteen years before the adoption of the United States Constitution the mechanics were acting on the premise that strong national government and democracy were complementary, not in conflict.

An important result of the first Continental Congress was that the committee of fifty-one was dissolved by agreement between itself and the Committee of Mechanics, and a new Committee of Inspection was created to carry out Congress' non-intercourse policy. The sixty members of the Committee of Inspection were chosen from two lists of 100 names separately proposed by the committee of fifty-one and the Committee of Mechanics.[43] In April 1775, the Committee of Inspection was enlarged to 100, including Daniel Dunscomb, chairman of the Committee of Mechanics, and three other members of the mechanics' committee.[44] Yet the officers of the Committee of Inspection remained merchants, albeit radical merchants,[45] and the Committee of Mechanics stayed in existence to needle its mercantile counterpart.

In the climactic spring of 1776 the Committee of Mechanics functioned as the most popular link in the chain of *ad hoc* bodies which had taken over government from the British. Ultimate authority rested with the Committee of Safety of the New York Provincial Congress. In New York City the Committee of Inspection held power. The Committee of Mechanics suggested new measures to the higher bodies, ran its own candidates for elections, insisted on the sovereignty of the "people at large," and attempted to clear a direct channel of communication between the general populace and the Continental Congress. Like its European counterparts as described by Robert Palmer, the mechanics' committee laid more emphasis upon democracy, in the sense of "the delegation of authority and the removability of officials," than upon the extension of the suffrage.[46] Indeed, in addressing the Provincial Congress and the Committee of Inspection the Committee of Mechanics described itself as "part of your constituents," "part of the Electors for this city and county" [47]; and asked, not that its members be given the ballot, but that the mandate of their votes be heeded.

On occasion the Committee of Mechanics simply registered assent to actions taken at higher levels. Thus on March 14, 1776, "about 6 or 700 of the Mechanicks of this city" escorted their Committee to the Exchange, where an address was delivered thanking the Committee of Inspection for regulating the prices of articles of general consumption imported from the West Indies.[48] More often, however, the mechanics urged the merchants to new action. On April 1, the Committee of Mechanics memorialized the Committee of Inspection regarding the "unwarrantable stretch of power" by the Provincial Congress in asserting that it, rather than "the people at large," should elect New York's delegates to the Continental Congress. The memorial thanked the Committee of Inspection for appointing deputies to attend a public meeting on this issue called by the mechanics. Then it concluded: "Gentlemen, if you agree with us, we make no doubt but every necessary step will be taken, and that letters of advice will be sent to each county." [49]

Again on April 6, the General Committee of Mechanics informed the General Committee of Inspection that the mechanics had resolved to accept the paper money of Massachusetts and Rhode Island so as to strengthen national unity. This address ended by saying: "[We] call on you, Gentlemen of the General Committee of Inspection, and pray that you will be pleased, as soon as convenient, to resolve and order that same may take place throughout your jurisdiction." [50]

The mechanics were ever-ready to back up their good advice with direct action. On March 18, the printer Samuel Loudon advertised for sale a pamphlet criticizing Tom Paine's *Common Sense,* which had been published two months earlier. Loudon was at once summoned before the Committee of Mechanics by its chairman, Christopher Duyckinck. Loudon asked that the matter be referred to the Committee of Safety of the Provincial Congress. The mechanics agreed, but only after locking up the printed sheets of Loudon's pamphlets. Loudon appeared before the Committee of Safety on March 19 and agreed to stop printing the offending pamphlet; but at ten that night Duyckinck, with a "large company" of "unauthorized men," broke into Loudon's home, took the printed sheets, and burned them on the Common.[51]

The defense of *Common Sense* was a congenial task for the mechanics because Paine, himself a former staymaker, voiced a political philosophy which the mechanics of New York City shared. As Paine sought to push America toward independence, so on May 29 the "General Committee of Mechanics in Union," meeting in "Mechanicks Hall," asked the Provincial Congress to instruct New York's delegates in the Continental Congress to press for immediate independence.[52] As Paine recommended a Continental Conference, a majority of whose delegates should be elected by the "people at large," so the New York mechanics employed the same phrase in asking that the state's delegates to the Continental Congress should be popularly elected.[53]

Paine's ideas were everywhere that spring of 1776. Between January and July almost every issue of the city's three weekly newspapers carried some lengthy discussion on "the different kinds of government." Universal adult suffrage, annual elections, rotation of office, equal apportionment, the secret ballot, popular election of all local officials, complete religious tolerance, and the abolition of slavery, were repeatedly discussed.[54]

The mechanics' request that the Provincial Congress instruct the state delegates (in Philadelphia) for independence was carried to the Congress by Lewis Thibon, Committee of Mechanics chairman. The Provincial Congress coldly rebuked the messenger. "We consider the mechanics in union as a voluntary association," ran the Congress reply. "[We believe] that neither that association, nor their committee, will claim any authority whatsoever in the public transactions of the present time." The Provincial Congress letter ended by refusing to instruct its delegates to the Continental Congress.[55]

Ten days after this rebuff the mechanics again addressed the Congress, this time turning the logic of republicanism from the question of home rule to the question of who should rule at home. Independence was imminent. It would mean the formation of a new state government. The language of the June 14 memorial signed by Malcolm McEwen, as Committee of Mechanics chairman, recalled the phrases of *Common Sense* and anticipated those of the Declaration of Independence. The mechanics' address demanded that the people ratify the new state constitution. "Inhabitants at large," it said, "exercise the right which God has given them, in common with all men, to judge whether it be consistent with their interest to accept, or reject, a Constitution framed for that State of which they are members. This is the birthright of every man [who] is, or ought to be, by inalienable right, a co-legislator with all the other members of that community." Not all men were qualified to draft constitutions, the letter continued,

> but that share of common sense which the Almighty has bountifully distributed amongst mankind in general, is sufficient to quicken every one's feeling, and enable him to judge rightly, what degree of safety, and what

advantages he is likely to enjoy or be deprived of, under any Constitution proposed to him. For this reason, should a preposterous confidence in the abilities and integrity of our future Delegates, delude us into measures which might imply a renunciation of our inalienable right to ratify our laws?

Warning against either "foreign or domestic oligarchy," the mechanic memorial went on to insist that the people must also have power to amend their Constitution with ease. "This power necessarily involves that of every district, occasionally to renew their deputies to committees and congresses, when the majority of such district shall think fit; and therefore, without the intervention of the executive, or any other power, foreign to the body of the respective electors." [56]

The Declaration of Independence, when it appeared, voiced apprehension of "convulsions within" and "domestic insurrections amongst us." It would seem that the government-from-below evident in the ideas and actions of the New York Committee of Mechanics in the spring of 1776 was a sample of just what the drafters of the Declaration feared. Roger Champagne, the most recent scholar to survey New York City politics in these months, concludes that "only the timely invasion of Long Island by the British saved the aristocrats from a political crisis of an explosive character." [57]

III

Something like half of New York City's population of almost 25,000 fled the city in the summer and fall of 1776. These refugees faced seven lean years of exile between September 1776, when the British occupied New York City, and November 1783, when General Washington and his army led the returning natives down Broadway.

We see little of the mechanics during the war, but those few glimpses are significant. Cooper Daniel Dunscomb and silversmith Abraham Brasher were among the nine men appointed by the Provincial Convention to represent the New York City refugees in the new state Assembly. Blacksmith Robert Boyd, chairman of the General Society of Mechanics and Tradesmen after the war, made axes for the Continental Army [58] and also served two years in the Assembly as a representative for Ulster County. Ropemaker Thomas Ivers, active in the Sons of Liberty since the Stamp Act crisis and a controversial candidate for alderman after the return to New York City, was prominent in a 1770 petition campaign.[59] The votes and activities of these mechanic leaders are suggestive as to the thinking of the larger body of mechanics during the war years.

"Radicalism" during and after the War for Independence is commonly associated with the confiscation of Loyalist lands, renunciation of debts to Loyalists, and the emission of paper money. Mechanic legislators opposed all these measures. When in the spring of 1779 the Council of Revision vetoed a bill for the confiscation of Loyalist lands, Brasher and Dunscomb were among the handful of Assemblymen who voted to sustain the veto. A year later Brasher, Boyd, and Dunscomb all voted against speedy sale of confiscated lands, and Brasher and Dunscomb were two of the five members of the Assembly who voted to uphold the Council of Revision's veto of this bill. In 1782, Dunscomb opposed a bill to permit persons owing debts to Tories to discharge their obligation by paying one-fortieth of the sum into the state treasury: he moved that the law be entitled, "An Act for the Payment of one fortieth Part of the Debts due to Persons within the Power of the Enemy." Boyd was again a member of the Assembly in 1786, when a bill for the emission of bills of credit (paper money) passed the New York legislature, and he was one of seven persons who opposed this law.[60]

Yet, to borrow a phrase from Eric Williams, there was method in their badness. The difference between rural extremists like Brinckerhoff of Dutchess [61] and the refugee legislators from New York City was not that one group was "radical" and the other not, but that they espoused different kinds of radicalism. Rural radicals favored a syndrome of measures designed to avoid taxation by means of confiscation. City radicals, during and after the war, favored heavy taxation to enable the state to meet its obligations to Congress.[62] Thus Boyd, as a member of the Assembly's paper currency committee in 1779, recommended heavy taxes and price-fixing rather than new emissions, and in that same session sponsored an act "to prevent monopoly and extortion, and to regulate trade." [63] A rural member, Thomas Palmer, charged in the press that

> a wicked party, with the Refugee Members, and Boyd at their head, determine to ruin the State by tax and otherwise. They had brought in a bill for seizing all the wheat for the army, except one bushel per head per month to each family.

Palmer went on to assert that Boyd "with those of his opinion, has made up a majority against" confiscating lands and taxing appropriated lands of persons outside the state. Boyd replied, stressing the importance of fulfilling the state's obligations to Congress.[64]

There were other refugees who favored confiscation, however. In October 1779 five petitions with 143 signatures were presented to the Assembly by refugees from New York City. The name of mechanic Thomas Ivers was at the head of two of the petitions. The petitions asked that elections be held to replace the Senators and Assemblymen appointed to represent New York City; that a confiscation law be passed immediately; that New York's delegates to the Continental Congress be changed each year;

that a school be established in Dutchess County for the instruction of the refugees' children, under the direction of trustees chosen annually by ballot.[65] The political demands of these petitions, as well as the suggested manner for governing the refugees' school, were entirely congruent with the demands of the Committee of Mechanics in the spring of 1776. The petitions were no doubt formulated in meetings of the refugees from New York City and from Long and Staten islands in the summer of 1779. According to Alexander Hamilton, these meetings had as their "ostensible object to choose representatives for those places in Assembly," but he expected they might also plant "the seeds of a future reformation" of the New York state government.[66]

Again in the summer of 1783, with independence secure but New York City still occupied by the British, the city refugees met several times and produced two fiery memorials threatening revenge and confiscation to the Tories in the city.[67] The refugees set up a committee of arrangements to plan their triumphal parade into the city which included upholsterer Henry Kipp, silversmiths William Gilbert and Ephraim Brasher, and hatters Thomas LeFoy and Henry Bicker, with the latter as chairman.[68] Mechanic influence was evident in New York City's first postwar election in December 1783. After a spirited exchange of broadsides — in which "Juvenis" recommended the election of merchants since "the prosperity of the Mechanic depends on that of the Merchant," and "A Citizen" replied by advising "that the various Classes should as far as is practicable, be immediately represented" — the entire slate of Assemblymen nominated by a "general meeting of the Committee of Mechanicks" was elected by a four-to-one landslide.[69]

As in the spring of 1776, so in the spring of 1784 it was the Committee of Mechanics not the Sons of Liberty which met most frequently.[70] After 1784 the Sons of Liberty are no longer heard from but the Committee of Mechanics continues, nominating its own ticket in each annual election.[71]

In January 1784 a committee of "late exiled Mechanics, Grocers, Retailers and Innholders" was formed to instruct the city's Assemblymen. Hatter Henry Bicker was chairman, and among the members were tallow chandler Hugh Walsh, saddler John Young, and pewterer William Ellsworth. The committee's instructions began with payment of the public debt, one more indication of the mechanics' concern that the national government fulfill its obligations. The program recommended by the committee also included duties on imported manufactures, especially luxuries, to encourage native industries; denial to England of all commercial privileges not accorded by England to the United States, with a recommendation that Congress make such regulations general; support for public education; easy naturalization; and a variety of restrictions against Loyalists who had spent the war in New York City.[72] The same concern for strengthening the Federal government appears in an Address to the Continental Congress by "the Artificers, Tradesmen and Mechanics" of New York City in February 1785. The address was signed by prominent mechanics, including blacksmiths Robert Boyd and Edward Meeks, silversmith John Burger, and hatter Henry Bicker. "We sincerely hope," said the address, "our Representatives will coincide with the other States, in augmenting your power to every exigency of the Union." [73]

Although they agreed in desiring a stronger national government, on other issues New York City's mechanics and merchants were as much at odds after the war as before it. The importer of English goods who flooded the American market with products which destroyed the American mechanic's livelihood was already half a Tory in the mechanic's eyes. When in addition the merchants' Chamber of Commerce met in January 1784 with three of the five officers elected under British rule in attendance, when later that spring the Bank of New York was created with one Tory merchant as Treasurer and two others on the Board of Directors, the city mechanics found it easy to identify merchants with Loyalism, to view the refugee artisan as Whiggery's sole defender, and to pronounce particular anathemas on Alexander Hamilton for giving legal aid to Tory merchants who had "fattened" on the "spoils" of war.[74] "A Battered Soldier" penned a broadside to "the Whig Mechanicks" that ran:

> on your Union, depends the future Fate of the Whig Interest in this City and County. And if you fail herein, you may depend on it, that you and your Children, will soon become Hewers of Wood, and Drawers of Water, to the Tories in this State.[75]

During the early months of 1784 the "late exiled Mechanics, Grocers, Retailers and Innholders" protested the licensing of Tory businessmen; and the Sons of Liberty (including the chairman of the Committee of Mechanics, Henry Bicker) called on their Assembly representatives not only for political disfranchisement of Tories, but also for their exclusion from "advantages of trade and commerce." [76]

An economic issue of particular importance to the mechanics was that of access to capital. Here again the New York City mechanic found himself at odds with the city's merchants, whether Whig or Tory. All agreed that credit should be expanded: the President, Director, and Stockholders of the Bank of New York, for example, petitioned the New York legislature that "a Scarcity of Specie for a long time to come may be expected. This defect must be supplied by an Artificial Medium." [77] The question was how credit should be expanded, and by whom. The Whig merchants of New York City — including the old radical leaders Lamb,

Sears, and Willett, and the future Antifederalist Melancton Smith — joined in petitioning the legislature for Alexander Hamilton's Bank of New York.[78] No prominent mechanics signed that petition, nor were any among the Bank's first customers.[79] Artisans repeatedly expressed their distrust of private banks.[80] Instead, the mechanics sought to create a modest loan fund of £3,000 by incorporating their old Committee of Mechanics as the General Society of Mechanics and Tradesmen.[81] Mercantile opinion hovered between the fear that incorporation would enable the mechanics to raise their wages and give them governmental power, "in this city at least," and the thought that "it is less dangerous to incorporate a body of men by law, than suffer them to *cement* with an idea of having received injustice." [82] The Council of Revision vetoed the incorporation bill, and one old Son of Liberty wrote to another:

> I should like to know whether these gentlemen . . . would consider themselves endanger'd by a Combination of the Mechanicks to extinguish the Flames of their Houses, were they on fire, or if any one of the Faith was drowning whether he would reject a Mechanick's hand to save him? — And are not those honest Men, the very Persons, who *principally* extinguish all Fires, and, in Conjunction with the Country, have saved the State? [83]

As the mechanics saw the matter, equal economic opportunity was an integral part of the larger vision of equality suggested by the emblem of the General Society of Mechanics and Tradesmen: "An aged woman, with a pair of scales in one hand, and a nest of swallows in the other, fed by the old one." [84] Along with their economic concerns went the demand, social and political at the same time, that mechanics be elected to office.

"An exiled Mechanic" suggested in April 1785 the importance of choosing representatives who would favor incorporation of the General Society of Mechanics and Tradesmen: "we have a powerful mercantile interest to struggle with, and we should be extremely careful of adopting a single measure that will tend to support it." [85] Why not mechanics, then? another newspaper correspondent asked. "Being of the opinion that the pedantic lawyer, the wealthy merchant, and the lordly landholder, have already had their interests sufficiently attended to, and think[ing] the respectable mechanics and carmen are not only adequate, but entitled to the reins of government," this author concluded by naming twenty-six mechanics whom he thought suitable timber for Assemblymen.[86] In the ensuing election two mechanics, Robert Boyd and William Goforth, were in fact successful.[87] The next year, correspondents to the merchants' newspaper, *The New York Daily Advertiser,* unleashed a pre-election barrage against the idea of class representation. "Nobody" opined:

We ought to invest no man at this critical period with that important trust, but such whose firmness, integrity and ability are sufficiently ascertained. I am very sensible that the application of reasoning of this nature will have little avail, if the mechanics of the city are solely allowed to fill up the appointments of statesmen. That they are a respectable body of men I willingly grant, and ought to have their due weight, but it is unreasonable for them to ask more.[88]

"Somebody" took up the same theme four days later:

Men who have spent the prime and vigour of their days in reading and contemplating the rise, progress and declension of states and empires; — men who study Grotius, Puffendorf, Montesquieu and Blackstone. . . . Away with such legislators! we will neither be able to comprehend the laws they may make, nor to practice them when they are made. But the laws of the mechanics, like the makers of them, will be simple and unperplexed. . . . Therefore let us have mechanics, and mechanics only for our legislature.[89]

In 1774 the Loyalist Miles Cooper had asked in vain "whether it be not time for our farmers and mechanics and laborers to return to their business, and the care of their families"; now in 1786 "Two Shoes" suggested: "Let the mechanics tarry at home, and follow their different employments, as I think they will not be able to do both at once." [90] And "Censor" denounced

those narrow, contracted, self-taught politicians who are for selecting out of each class of citizens a person to represent them, whether he is to be found competent or not, and think none would serve them honestly but those of their own body. . . . How can they expect that men, such as the laborious mechanic, whose whole study and progress in life has been to secure a maintenance for himself and family . . . are calculated to frame laws for a large and commercial community? [91]

As it turned out no mechanics were elected in 1786. The Committee of Mechanics "with a Committee from a number of Merchants and other Citizens" put forward a slate of assemblymen including William Goforth. Newspaper correspondents suggested Boyd and carpenter Anthony Post.[92] But none of the three were chosen, while the mechanics' erstwhile *bête noire*, Alexander Hamilton, was elected with support from "some of the Mechanics" to mount the campaign which led to the Annapolis Convention, the Constitutional Convention, and the New York ratifying convention of 1788.[93]

IV

Becker was right, then, in his contention that mechanic radicalism began before the War for Independence and continued after it. Economically disadvantaged, socially excluded, only partially enfranchised, the mechanics sought by a variety of methods to influence the making of political and economic policy; by the mid-1780's, they were insisting on the election of men of their own "class."

But Becker was wrong in supposing that the mechanics were hostile to centralization. The distinctive feature of the political demands of the mechanics throughout the period 1774–1785 was to combine a concern for democracy with unwavering support for a policy of arming the central government with sufficient power to combat the British enemy. To this end the Committee of Mechanics would join with the city merchants after 1785 to seek more power for Congress.

The American Revolution and the
Democratization of the Legislatures

JACKSON TURNER MAIN

Jackson T. Main (1917–   ), professor of history and director of the Institute of Colonial Studies at the State University of New York at Stony Brook, uses statistics to study social change during the Revolution. Research upon his two books, The Social Structure of Revolutionary America *(Princeton: Princeton University Press, 1965) and* The Upper House in Revolutionary America *(Madison: University of Wisconsin Press, 1967), provided the groundwork for this article on the changing social status and economic worth of the members of lower houses during the Revolution. Instead of using traditional evidence found in statements from newspapers and letters, Main reconstructs statistically the changing class composition of the lower houses. Thus he illustrates the current tendency toward quantification in historical writing in order to determine the actual practices of people as opposed to their verbal expressions of ideals or ideas of what occurred and to more precisely describe what happened. In this way, he is able to present the social changes during the Revolution in a dynamic manner as a trend to elect people of increasingly lower socio-economic status to the legislatures.*

The validity of Main's article rests upon his attribution of class and upon the accuracy of his statistical method. Are his measurements of status accurate enough to prove his contention about the change? Does he deny that an elite still existed? Is it proper to equate the differing social class structures of the various states? Are the variations among states more important than the similarities? What do Main's statistics show about the typicality of Lynd's choice of New York State and City politics to demonstrate the class conflict interpretation?

This article is as suggestive for what it implies as it is for what it proves. What is the role of ideas in action? What implications does Main's article have for the relation between the espousal of social and political ideals and the actual behavior of people during the Revolution? Was the change sought by the actors consciously, or was it the unintended consequences of other ideals and actions? Is a change in the social status of leaders a significant index of a more general alteration in the social structure? How much does an analysis of political elites prove about the desires and attitudes of the population as a whole? Do overall trends prove specific cases about the nature of power in the legislatures? Do trends in the state legislatures influence the founding of a new federal legislature? Was the federal system perhaps evolved to counter the trend toward democracy on the lower levels of government?

An article with "democracy" in its title, these days, must account for itself. This essay holds that few colonials in British North America believed in a government by the people, and that they were content to be ruled by local elites; but that during the Revolution two interacting developments occurred simultaneously: ordinary citizens increasingly took part in politics, and American political theorists began to defend popular government. The ideological shift can be traced most easily in the newspapers, while evidence for the change in the structure of power will be found in the make-up of the lower houses during the revolutionary years.

Truly democratic ideas, defending a concentration of power in the hands of the people, are difficult to find prior to about 1774. Most articulate colonials accepted the Whig theory in which a modicum of democracy was balanced by equal parts of aristocracy and monarchy. An unchecked democ-

Reprinted by permission from Jackson T. Main, "Government by the People: The American Revolution and the Democratization of the Legislatures," *William and Mary Quarterly*, XXIII, 3d Ser. (July, 1966), pp. 391–407.

racy was uniformly condemned.[1]* For example, a contributor to the *Newport Mercury* in 1764 felt that when a state was in its infancy, "when its members are few and virtuous, and united together by some peculiar ideas of freedom or religion; the whole power may be lodged with the people, and the government be purely democratical"; but when the state had matured, power must be removed from popular control because history demonstrated that the people "have been incapable, collectively, of acting with any degree of moderation or wisdom." [2] Therefore while colonial theorists recognized the need for some democratic element in the government, they did not intend that the ordinary people — the *demos* — should participate. The poorer men were not allowed to vote at all, and that part of the populace which did vote was expected to elect the better sort of people to represent them. "Fabricus" defended the "democratic principle," warned that "liberty, when once lost, is scarce ever recovered," and declared that laws were "made for the people, and not people for the laws." But he did not propose that ordinary citizens should govern. Rather, "it is right that men of *birth and fortune,* in every government that is free, should be invested with power, and enjoy higher honours than the people." [3] According to William Smith of New York, offices should be held by "the better Class of People" in order that they might introduce that "Spirit of Subordination essential to good Government." [4] A Marylander urged that members of the Assembly should be "ABLE in ESTATE, ABLE in KNOWLEDGE AND LEARNING," and mourned that so many "little upstart insignificant Pretenders" tried to obtain an office. "The *Creature* that is able to keep a little Shop, rate the Price of an Ell of Osnabrigs, or, at most, to judge of the Quality of a Leaf of Tobacco" was not a fit statesman, regardless of his own opinion.[5] So also in South Carolina, where William Henry Drayton warned the artisans that mechanical ability did not entitle them to hold office.[6] This conviction that most men were incompetent to rule, and that the elite should govern for them, proved a vital element in Whig thought and was its most antidemocratic quality. The assumption was almost never openly challenged during the colonial period.

Whether the majority whose capacity was thus maligned accepted the insulting assumption is another question. They were not asked, and as they were unable to speak or write on the subject, their opinions are uncertain. But the voters themselves seem to have adhered, in practice at least, to the traditional view, for when the people were asked to choose their representatives they seldom elected common farmers and artisans. Instead they put their trust in men of the upper class. In the colonies as a whole, about 30 per cent of the adult white men owned property worth £500 or

* [See pp. 160–162 for notes to this article. — Ed.]

more. About two thirds of these colonials of means had property worth £500 to £2,000; their economic status is here called *moderate*. The other third were worth over £2,000. Those worth £2,000 to £5,000 are called *well-to-do*, and those whose property was valued at more than £5,000 are called *wealthy*.[7] The overwhelming majority of the representatives belonged to that ten per cent who were well-to-do or wealthy. Government may have been for the people, but it was not administered by them. For evidence we turn to the legislatures of New Hampshire, New York, New Jersey, Maryland, Virginia, and South Carolina.

In 1765 New Hampshire elected thirty-four men to its House of Representatives.[8] Practically all of them lived within a few miles of the coast; the frontier settlements could not yet send deputies, and the Merrimack Valley towns in the south-central part of the colony, though populous, were allotted only seven. New Hampshire was not a rich colony. Most of its inhabitants were small farmers with property enough for an adequate living but no more. There were a few large agricultural estates, and the Portsmouth area had developed a prosperous commerce which supported some wealthy merchants and professional men; but judging from probate records not more than one man in forty was well-to-do, and true wealth was very rare. Merchants, professional men, and the like comprised about one tenth of the total population, though in Portsmouth, obviously, the proportion was much larger. Probably at least two thirds of the inhabitants were farmers or farm laborers and one in ten was an artisan. But New Hampshire voters did not call on farmers or men of average property to represent them. Only about one third of the representatives in the 1765 House were yeomen. Merchants and lawyers were just as numerous, and the rest followed a variety of occupations: there were four doctors and several millers and manufacturers. One third of the delegates were wealthy men and more than two thirds were at least well-to-do. The relatively small upper class of the colony, concentrated in the southeast, furnished ten of the members. They did not, of course, constitute a majority, and the family background of most of the representatives, like that of most colonials, was undistinguished. Probably nearly one half had acquired more property and prestige than their parents. In another age New Hampshire's lower house would have been considered democratic — compared with England's House of Commons it certainly was — but this was a new society, and the voters preferred the prosperous urban upper class and the more substantial farmers.

New York was a much richer colony than New Hampshire. Although most of its population were small farmers and tenants, there were many large landed estates and New York City was incomparably wealthier than Portsmouth. In general the west bank of the Hudson and the northern frontier were usually controlled by the yeomanry, as was Suffolk County on

Long Island, but the east bank from Albany to the City was dominated by great "manor lords" and merchants. The great landowners and the merchants held almost all of the twenty-eight seats in the Assembly.[9] In 1769 the voters elected only seven farmers. Five others including Frederick Philipse and Pierre Van Cortland, the wealthy manor lords from Westchester, were owners of large tenanted estates. But a majority of New York's legislators were townspeople. Merchants were almost as numerous as farmers, and together with lawyers they furnished one half of the membership. The legislators were no more representative in their property than in their occupation. At most, five men, and probably fewer, belonged to the middle class of moderate means. At least 43 per cent were wealthy and an equal number were well-to-do. The members' social background was also exceptional. Ten came from the colony's foremost families who had, for the times, a distinguished ancestry, and two thirds or more were born of well-to-do parents. Taken as a whole the legislators, far from reflecting New York's social structure, had either always belonged to or had successfully entered the colony's economic and social upper class.

New Jersey's Assembly was even smaller than that of New York. The body chosen in 1761, and which sat until 1769, contained but twenty men.[10] Half of these represented the East Jersey counties (near New York City) which were in general occupied by small farmers, but only three of the ten members came from that class. The others were merchants, lawyers, and large proprietors. Although several of these had started as yeomen they had all acquired large properties. West Jersey, which had a greater number of sizable landed estates, especially in the Delaware Valley region, sent the same sort of men as did East Jersey: three farmers, an equal number of large landowners, and an even larger number of prosperous townsmen, some of whom also owned valuable real estate. Merchants and lawyers made up one half of the membership. As usual, a considerable proportion — perhaps 40 per cent — were self-made men, but the colony's prominent old families furnished at least 30 per cent of the representatives. Four out of five members were either well-to-do or wealthy.

In contrast to the legislatures of New Hampshire, New York, and New Jersey, Maryland's House of Delegates was a large body and one dominated by the agricultural interest. Like its northern equivalents, however, its members belonged to the upper class of the colony — in Maryland, the planter aristocracy. The 1765 House supposedly contained over sixty members, but only fifty-four appear in the records.[11] About one half of these came from the Eastern Shore, an almost entirely rural area. Except for Col. Thomas Cresap who lived on Maryland's small frontier, the remainder came from the Potomac River and western Chesapeake Bay counties, where agriculture was the principal occupation but where a number of towns also existed. About one sixth of the Delegates belonged to the yeoman farmer class. Most of these lived on the Eastern Shore. Incidentally they did not vote with the antiproprietary, or "popular," party, but rather followed some of the great planters in the conservative "court" party. As in the northern colonies, a number of the Delegates were *nouveaux riches,* but in Maryland's stable and primarily "Tidewater" society, fewer than one fifth had surpassed their parents in wealth. The overwhelming majority came from the lesser or the great planter class, and probably one third belonged to the colony's elite families. Four fifths were well-to-do or wealthy. Lawyers and merchants (among whom were several of the self-made men) furnished about one sixth of the principally rural membership.

Virginia's Burgesses resembled Maryland's Delegates, but they were even richer and of even more distinguished ancestry. The Old Dominion's much larger west helped to make the House of Burgesses twice as large a body, with 122 members in 1773.[12] Small property holders, though they formed a great majority of the voters, held only one out of six seats. Half of the Burgesses were wealthy and four fifths were at least well-to-do. Merchants and lawyers contributed one fifth of the members, much more than their proper share, but most of them were also large landholders and the legislature was firmly in control of the great planters. Indeed the median property owned was 1,800 acres and 40 slaves. Virginia's social structure was quite fluid, especially in the newly settled areas, but between five sixths and seven eighths of the delegates had inherited their property. A roll call of the Burgesses would recite the names of most of the colony's elite families, who held nearly one half of the seats.

The planters of South Carolina, unlike the Virginians, were unwilling to grant representation to the upcountry, and its House of Commons was an exclusively eastern body.[13] The colony was newer and its society may have been more fluid, for in 1765 between 20 and 40 per cent of the representatives were self-made men. The legislature also differed from its southern equivalents in Maryland and Virginia in that nearly half of its members were merchants, lawyers, or doctors. But these figures are deceptive, for in reality most of these men were also great landowners, as were almost all of the representatives; and prominent old families contributed one half of the members of the House. All were at least well-to-do and over two thirds were wealthy. The rich planters of South Carolina's coastal parishes held a monopoly of power in the Assembly.

These six legislatures, from New Hampshire to South Carolina, shared the same qualities. Although farmers and artisans comprised probably between two thirds and three fourths of the voters in the six colonies, they seldom selected men from their own ranks to represent them. Not more than one out of five representatives were of that class. Fully one third were merchants and lawyers or other professionals, and most of the rest were large landowners. Although only about 10 per cent of the colonials were well-to-do or wealthy, this economic elite furnished at least 85 per cent of the assemblymen. The mobile character of colonial society meant that perhaps 30 per cent had achieved their high status by their own efforts; but an even larger percentage were from prominent, long-established families.

Collectively these "representatives of the people" comprised not a cross section of the electorate but a segment of the upper class. Although the colonials cherished the democratic branch of their governments, and although a majority may have hoped to make the lower house all powerful, they did not yet conceive that the *demos* should actually govern. The idea of a government by as well as for the people was a product of the Revolution. It should be noted here that Rhode Island and Connecticut are exceptions to this general pattern, though the upper house of Connecticut was composed entirely of well-to-do men. As for Massachusetts, the number of representatives with moderate properties exceeded that in the royal and proprietary colonies; but the Massachusetts legislature was still controlled by the well-to-do. Of the 117 men in the House in 1765, at least fifty-six were not farmers and thirteen were large landowners; of the remaining forty-eight, thirty-seven were ordinary farmers and the occupations of eleven are unknown. Among those representatives whose economic status can be discovered (about nine tenths), well over one half were well-to-do or wealthy and two fifths of these had inherited their property.

Widespread popular participation in politics began during 1774 with the various provincial congresses and other extralegal organizations. Although the majority of these bodies seem to have been made up of men of standing, both artisans and farmers appeared in greater numbers than they had in the colonial legislatures. There were several reasons for this. Whereas heretofore the more recently settled areas of most colonies had been underrepresented — at times seriously so — the legal prohibitions on their sending representatives to the colonial assemblies did not apply to the extralegal congresses, and they chose delegates when they wished. Moreover the congresses were much larger than the colonial assemblies, and consequently the over-all number of men who could be elected was greatly increased. For instance, South Carolina's House of Commons contained forty-eight men in 1772, but almost twice that number attended the first Provincial Congress in December 1774 and four times as many were present in January 1775. By 1775 the western districts were sending about one third of the members. Similarly, nothing now prevented New Hampshire's country villages from choosing representatives, and they seized the opportunity. By the time the fourth Provincial Congress met in New Hampshire, four times as many men attended as had been admitted to the 1773 legislature, and nearly one half of them came from the inland counties.

Perhaps an even more important reason for the greater participation in politics by men of moderate means than simply the enlarged and broadened membership of the Provincial Congresses was that the interior areas often contained no real upper class. They had no choice but to send men of moderate property. Furthermore, many men of the upper classes who had previously held political power were not sympathetic with the resistance movement and either withdrew from politics or did not participate in the extralegal Congresses. At the same time events thrust new men forward, as for example in Charleston where the artisans became increasingly active. As the Revolution ran its course, many new men came to fill the much larger number of civil offices, and new men won fame in battle. These developments were quickly reflected in the composition of the legislatures, and by the time the war ended the legislatures were far different bodies from what they had been in colonial days. At the same time democratic ideas spread rapidly, justifying and encouraging the new order.[14]

With the overthrow of royal government, the previously unrepresented New Hampshire villages hastened to choose representatives to the state legislature. The number of men present in the lower house varied considerably, for some smaller communities were too poor to send a man every year, while others combined to finance the sending of a single delegate; but during the 1780's between two and three times as many attended as before the war. The House chosen in 1786 had eighty-eight members. The balance of power had shifted into the Merrimack Valley, for fewer than half of the delegates came from the two counties near the coast, and even these included frontier settlements.[15]

The socio-economic composition of the New Hampshire legislature also changed. All but four of the 1765 legislators can be identified, but more than one fifth of the post-war representatives are obscure, and the parentage of very few can be established despite the existence of many town histories, genealogies, and published records. Before the war fewer than one third were farmers, exclusive of large landowners but including the men whose occupation is doubtful; by 1786 at least 50 per cent were yeomen and if those whose occupations are unknown are added, as most of them should be, the proportion rises to over 70 per cent. Merchants and lawyers, who had furnished about one third of the members of the 1765 legislature, now comprised only one tenth of the membership. Similarly men of wealth totalled one third of the former legislature but less than one tenth of the latter. The well-to-do element who had dominated the prewar Assembly with 70 per cent of the seats were now reduced to a minority of about 30 per cent.

Thus a very large majority of the new legislature consisted of ordinary farmers who had only moderate properties. Ten members of the prominent old
families had seats in the 1765 house; by 1786 there were only four in a body
two and one half times as large. Even if the newly represented towns are
eliminated, the trend toward the election of less wealthy and less distinguished representatives remains the same, though the degree of change was
less. If only the towns which sent men to both legislatures are considered,
one finds that whereas farmers formed between 20 and 30 per cent in 1765,
they accounted for 55 to 67 per cent twenty years later. Similarly, in these
towns the proportion of representatives having moderate properties rose
from 30 per cent to more than twice that. Thus the economic and social
character of the members in the lower house had been radically changed.

The pattern of change was much the same in other states. New
York's society was fundamentally less egalitarian than that of New Hampshire, having more men with large estates and proportionately fewer areas
dominated by small farmers. The agricultural upcountry had not yet extended much beyond Albany to the north and Schenectady to the west, so
that most New Yorkers still lived in the older counties. As might be expected
the changes which occurred in New York were not as striking as in New
Hampshire but they were still obvious. By 1785 the counties west of the
Hudson, together with those north of Westchester, increased their representation from about one third to nearly two thirds of the total. That fact
alone might not have guaranteed a social or economic change in the composition of the Assembly, for every county had its upper class, but the new
legislature differed from the old in many respects. The voters selected far
fewer townspeople. In the 1769 Assembly some 57 per cent of the members
had been engaged primarily in a nonagricultural occupation; by 1785 the
proportion had been halved. Farmers, exclusive of large landowners, had
made up 25 per cent of the total in 1769; now they furnished about 42
per cent.[16] In contrast, one half of the 1769 legislators had been merchants
and lawyers, but now such men held less than one third of the seats. Similarly the proportion of wealthy members dropped from 43 per cent to 15
per cent, whereas the ratio of men of moderate means increased from probably one seventh to nearly one half. New York's elite families, which had
contributed ten out of twenty-eight Assemblymen in 1769, contributed the
same number in 1785, but in a House twice as large. Meanwhile the number
of men who had started without any local family background, newcomers
to New York, increased from two to twenty-three. In general, the yeoman-
artisan "middle class," which in colonial days had furnished a half-dozen
members, now actually had a majority in the legislature. Under the leadership of George Clinton and others of higher economic and social rank, they
controlled the state during the entire decade of the eighties.[17] In New York,

as in New Hampshire, the trend was the same even within those counties which had been represented before the Revolution. If Washington and Montgomery counties are eliminated, the proportion of delegates who were well-to-do declines from 86 per cent to 60 per cent.

New Jersey's lower house, the size of which had increased in stages from twenty members to thirty-nine after the Revolution, retained equal distribution of seats between East and West Jersey. As in New Hampshire and New York, the economic upper class of well-to-do men, which in New Jersey had held three fourths of the seats before the war, saw its control vanish; indeed two thirds of the states' representatives in 1785 had only moderate properties. The typical legislator before the war held at least 1,000 acres; in 1785 the median was about 300 acres. Merchants and lawyers were all but eliminated from the legislature, retaining only a half-dozen seats. The colonial elite, once controlling one third of the votes of the house, now had one eighth; the overwhelming majority of the new legislators were men who had been unknown before the war and whose ancestry, where ascertainable, was uniformly undistinguished. Fully two thirds of the representatives were ordinary farmers, presumably men of more than average ability and sometimes with military experience, but clearly part of the common people. Again these changes occurred not just because new areas were represented but because the counties which had sent delegates in the prewar years now chose different sorts of men. In New Jersey, the counties of Cumberland, Salem, Hunterdon, Morris, and Sussex had previously been underrepresented. If these are eliminated, we find that the proportion of men of moderate property rose from 20 per cent to 73 per cent and of farmers (exclusive of large landowners) from 23.5 per cent to 60 per cent.[18]

Southern legislatures were also democratized. Maryland's House of Delegates expanded to seventy-four by 1785, with the addition of a few members from the western counties. As had been true before the war, most of the representatives were engaged in agriculture, the proportion of those with a nonfarm occupation remaining constant at about 20 per cent. The most obvious change in economic composition was the replacement of planters by farmers, of large property owners by men with moderate estates. If the planter is defined as one who held at least twenty slaves or 500 acres, then they formed 57 per cent of the House in 1765 and only 36.5 per cent in 1785, while the farmers increased from 18.5 to 28 per cent. Wealthy men occupied about two fifths of the seats in the pre-Revolutionary period, one sixth after the war, while delegates with moderate property, who had previously formed only one fifth of the total, now comprised one third. The yeoman farmer class, though still lacking a majority, had doubled in numbers while members of the old ruling families, in turn, saw their strength halved.[19] By comparison with the northern states the shift of power was decidedly less radical, but the change was considerable. It was made more obvious, incidentally, by the great contrast between the postwar House of Delegates and the postwar Senate, for the large majority of the Senators were wealthy merchants, lawyers, and planters, who fought bitterly with the popular branch.

The planter class of Virginia, like that of Maryland, did not intend that the Revolution should encourage democracy, but it was unable to prevent some erosion of its power. The great landowners still controlled the lower house, though their strength was reduced from 60 per cent to 50 per cent, while that of ordinary farmers rose from perhaps 13 per cent in 1773 to 26 per cent in 1785. An important change was the decline in the number of wealthy members, who now held one quarter instead of one half of the seats. Power thus shifted into the hands of the lesser planters, the well-to-do rather than the wealthy. Meanwhile men with moderate properties doubled their share, almost equaling in number the wealthy Burgesses. Similarly the sons of the First Families lost their commanding position, while an even larger fraction of delegates were of humble origins. The general magnitude of the change is suggested by the decline in the median property held from 1,800 acres to about 1,100, and from forty slaves to twenty.[20]

Thus, although the planter class retained control of the Burgesses, the people were now sending well-to-do rather than wealthy men, and at least one out of four representatives was an ordinary citizen. A roll call of the House would still recite the familiar names of many elite families, but it would also pronounce some never heard before. The alteration in the composition of the Virginia legislature undoubtedly sprang in part from the growing influence of westerners, for counties beyond the Blue Ridge sent many more representatives in 1785 than before the war, while the representation from the Piedmont also increased in size. However, the same shift downward also occurred within the older counties, those which had been represented in 1773. If we eliminate from consideration all of the newly formed counties, we find that delegates with moderate property increased from 13.5 per cent to 23 per cent, and that wealthy ones declined from 48 to 30 per cent, while the proportion of farmers rose from 13 to about 25 per cent.

The South Carolina constitution of 1778 is noted as an expression of conservatism. Its conservatism, however, was much more evident with respect to the Senate than to the House of Representatives, which was now nearly four times as large. Although the eastern upper class refused to grant westerners as many seats in the House as were warranted by their population, the upcountry did increase its share from not more than 6 or 8 per cent (depending on one's definition of where the upcountry started) to nearly 40 per cent. The urban upper class of merchants, lawyers, and doctors dropped to 20 per cent of the total membership in 1785, as compared to 36 per cent in 1765. The agricultural interest greatly increased its influence, the principal gain being made by farmers rather than by planters. A significant change was a reduction in the strength of wealthy representatives, who made up four fifths of those whose property is known in 1765 and but one third twenty years later. The pre-Revolutionary House of Commons seems to have contained not a single man of moderate property, but the postwar representatives included more than fifty such — probably over 30 per cent of the membership. The median acreage held by the 1765 members was certainly over 2,000 and probably a majority owned over 100 slaves each. The lack of tax records makes it impossible to determine what land the 1785 representatives held, but they obviously owned much less; while the median number of slaves was about twenty-five. The scarcity of such records as well as of genealogies and other historical materials also makes it exceedingly difficult to identify any but fairly prominent men. This situation in itself lends significance to the fact that whereas before the Revolution the desired information is available for seven out of eight representatives and even for over two thirds of their parents, data are incomplete concerning 30 per cent of the postwar delegates and most of their parents. Equally significant is the different social make-up of the two bodies. The long-established upper class of the province controlled half of the 1765 house, but less than one fourth of the 1785 legislature. Although most of the representatives were well-to-do, the house was no longer an exclusively aristocratic body, but contained a sizable element of democracy. It should be pointed out that South Carolina was peculiar in that the change in the House was due almost entirely to the admission of new delegates from the west. In those parishes which elected representatives both before and after the war, the proportion of wealthy delegates decreased very slightly, while that of men with moderate property rose from zero to between 7 and 14 per cent.

All of the six legislatures had been greatly changed as a result of the Revolution. The extent of that change varied from moderate in Virginia and Maryland to radical in New Hampshire and New Jersey, but everywhere the same process occurred. Voters were choosing many more representatives than before the war, and the newly settled areas gained considerably in representatives. The locus of power had shifted from the coast into the interior. Voters were ceasing to elect only men of wealth and family. The proportion of the wealthy in these legislatures dropped from 46 per cent to 22 per cent; members of the prominent old families declined from 40 per cent to 16 per cent. Most of these came from the long-established towns or commercial farm areas. Of course many men who were well-to-do or better continued to gain office, but their share decreased from four fifths to just one half. Even in Massachusetts the percentage of legislators who were wealthy or well-to-do dropped from 50 per cent in 1765 to 21.5 per cent in 1784.[21]

Significantly, the people more and more often chose ordinary yeomen or artisans. Before the Revolution fewer than one out of five legislators had been men of that sort; after independence they more than doubled their strength, achieving in fact a majority in the northern houses and constituting over 40 per cent generally. The magnitude of the change is suggested by the fact that the legislators of the postwar South owned only about one half as much property as their predecessors. Also suggestive is the great increase in the proportion of men of humble origin, which seems to have more than doubled. Therefore men who were or had once been a part of the *demos* totalled about two thirds of the whole number of representatives. Clearly the voters had ceased to confine themselves to an elite, but were selecting instead men like themselves. The tendency to do so had started during the colonial period, especially in the North, and had now increased so dramatically as almost to revolutionize the legislatures. The process occurred also in those areas which were represented both before and after the Revolution, as compared with those which were allowed to choose delegates

TABLE 1   ECONOMIC STATUS OF THE REPRESENTATIVES [22]

| | N.H., N.Y., and N.J. | | Md., Va., and S.C. | |
	Prewar (percentages)	Postwar (percentages)	Prewar (percentages)	Postwar (percentages)
Wealthy	36	12	52	28
Well-to-do	47	26	36	42
Moderate	17	62	12	30
Merchants & lawyers	43	18	22.5	17
Farmers	23	55	12	26

TABLE 2   ECONOMIC STATUS OF THE REPRESENTATIVES
FROM PRE-REVOLUTIONARY DISTRICTS

| | N.H., N.Y., and N.J. | | Md., Va., and S.C. | |
	Prewar	Postwar	Prewar	Postwar
Wealthy	35	18	50	38
Well-to-do	45	37	38	42
Moderate	20	45	12	20
Merchants & lawyers	41	24	22	18.5
Farmers	25	50	12	22

for the first time after the war. Although a similar change may not have taken place in Connecticut or Rhode Island, it surely did so in the states of Pennsylvania, Delaware, North Carolina, and Georgia, which have not been analyzed here.

The significance of the change may be more obvious to historians than it was to men of the Revolutionary era. Adherents of the Whig philosophy deplored the trend. They continued to demand a government run by the elite in which the democratic element, while admitted, was carefully checked. Such men were basically conservatives who conceived themselves as struggling for liberty against British tyranny, and who did not propose to substitute a democratical tyranny for a monarchical one.[23] The states, observed a philosophical New Englander in 1786, were "worse governed" than they had been because "men of sense and property have lost much of their influence by the popular spirit of the war." The people had once respected and obeyed their governors, senators, judges, and clergy. But "since the war, blustering ignorant men, who started into notice during the troubles and confusion of that critical period, have been attempting to push themselves into office." [24]

On the other hand democratic spokesmen now rose to defend this new government by the people. A writer in a Georgia newspaper rejoiced in 1789 that the state's representatives were "taken from a class of citizens who hitherto have thought it more for their interest to be contented with a humbler walk in life," and hoped that men of large property would not enter the state, for Georgia had "perhaps the most *compleat* democracy in the known world," which could be preserved only by economic equality.[25] In Massachusetts as early as 1775 "Democritus" urged the voters to "choose men that have learnt to get their living by honest industry, and that will be content with as small an income as the generality of those who pay them for their service. If you would be well represented," he continued, "choose a man in middling circumstances as to worldly estate, if he has got it by his industry so much the better, he knows the wants of the poor, and can judge pretty well what the community can bear of public burdens, if he be a man of good common understanding." [26] "A Farmer" in Connecticut boldly declared it a maxim that the people usually judged rightly, insisted that politics was not so difficult but that common sense could comprehend it, and argued that every freeman could be a legislator.[27]

The change in men might be deprecated or applauded, but it could not be denied, and some found it good. To Jedidiah Morse the government of Virginia still seemed to be "oligarchical or aristocratical," [28] but to a Virginian a revolution had taken place. The newly chosen House of Burgesses, wrote Roger Atkinson in 1776, was admirable. It was "composed of men not quite so well dressed, nor so politely educated, nor so highly born as some

Assemblies I have formerly seen," yet on the whole he liked it better. "They are the People's men (and the People in general are right). They are plain and of consequence less disguised, but I believe to the full as honest, less intriguing, more sincere. I wish the People may always have Virtue enough and Wisdom enough to chuse such plain men." [29] Democracy, for a moment at least, seemed to have come to Virginia.

WHY DID THE COLONISTS GO TO WAR?

A Fear of Conspiracy against Liberty

BERNARD BAILYN

Bernard Bailyn (1922–   ), Winthrop Professor of History at Harvard University, is the foremost representative of the intellectual interpretation of the Revolution. In the long introduction to Pamphlets of the American Revolution, 1750–1776 *(Cambridge, Mass.: Harvard University Press, 1965–   ), and in the expanded version of this introduction, the Pulitzer Prize winning* Ideological Origins of the American Revolution *(Cambridge, Mass.: Harvard University Press, 1967), he examines the semantics and logic of the revolutionists' polemics for clues to how and why the colonists thought as they did. In the selections reprinted below, he considers colonial definitions of such words as "liberty," "democracy," and "republicanism," and the fear of an English conspiracy against colonial liberties. Bailyn essentially relates the history of events from 1765 to the outbreak of fighting from the point of view of the colonists. In* Ideological Origins of the American Revolution, *he traces the concepts behind the colonial outlook back to the dissenters of the seventeenth century. By placing the basic source of revolutionary ideology in the seventeenth century however, Bailyn is faced with the question of timing: why did the Revolution occur when it did if the ideas behind it were so old? He directs his attention to this problem in his latest book,* The Origins of American Politics *(New York: Alfred A. Knopf, 1968).*

While few historians doubt Bailyn's findings, many wonder just how significant his work is in explaining the causes of the Revolution. While knowledge of the conceptual world of the colonists

may be necessary to any discussion of the causes of the Revolu-
tion, how sufficient is it in the overall determination of causes?
Some historians believe Bailyn overemphasizes ideas in general
and the fear of conspiracy in particular as causes of the revolt. In
other words, they wonder how real a cause such a colonial fear
was? Do thoughts really explain why people act as they do, or do
ideas act merely as rationalizations for deeper motivation? Per-
haps an equally important question is whether there was a real
conspiracy or not. Remember, we are not told in these selections
what the English leaders and people really thought or how they
really acted. Surely the imperial school is correct in stressing that
it takes two sides to fight.

Such questions point to larger problems of analyzing historical
causation. Again we are faced with the relation of ideas to action.
To what extent do the espousal of ideals and the conceptions of
people explain their actual behavior? Does Bailyn presume con-
flict or consensus in colonial society? Is his interpretation more
consistent with that of Brown or Lynd, with Kenyon or Main?
Last, is the actors' view of reality sufficient to explain historical
events, or must the historian also juxtapose his view of the situa-
tion to explain why events occurred as they did?

⌐. . . The colonists' attitude to the whole world of politics and government was fundamentally shaped by the root assumption that they, as
Britishers, shared in a unique inheritance of liberty. The English people,
they believed, though often threatened by despots who had risen in their
midst, had managed to maintain, to a greater degree and for a longer period
of time than any other people, a tradition of the successful control of power
and of those evil tendencies of human nature that would prevent its
proper uses. ⌐

In view of the natural obstacles that stood in the way of such a success and in view of the dismal history of other nations, this, as the colonists
saw it, had been an extraordinary achievement. But it was not a miraculous
one. It could be explained historically. The ordinary people of England,
they believed, were descended from simple, sturdy Saxons who had known
liberty in the very childhood of the race and who, through the centuries,
had retained the desire to preserve it. But it had taken more than desire.

Reprinted by permission of the author and the publishers from Ber-
nard Bailyn, ed., *Pamphlets of the American Revolution 1750–1776*,
Vol. I, Cambridge, Mass.: The Belknap Press of Harvard University
Press, Copyright 1965, by the President and Fellows of Harvard College.

Reinforcing, structuring, expressing the liberty-loving temper of the people, there was England's peculiar "constitution," described by John Adams, in words almost every American agreed with before 1763, as "the most perfect combination of human powers in society which finite wisdom has yet contrived and reduced to practice for the preservation of liberty and the production of happiness." 1*

The word "constitution" and the concept behind it was of central importance to the colonists' political thought; their entire understanding of the crisis in Anglo-American relations rested upon it. So strategically located was this idea in the minds of both English and Americans, and so great was the pressure placed upon it in the course of a decade of pounding debate that in the end it was forced apart, along the seam of a basic ambiguity, to form the two contrasting concepts of constitutionalism that have remained characteristic of England and America ever since.

At the start of the controversy, however, the most distinguishing feature of the colonists' view of the constitution was its apparent traditionalism. Like their contemporaries in England and like their predecessors for centuries before, the colonists at the beginning of the Revolutionary controversy understood by the word "constitution" not, as we would have it, a written document or even an unwritten but deliberately contrived design of government and a specification of rights beyond the power of ordinary legislation to alter; they thought of it, rather, as the constituted — that is, existing — arrangement of governmental institutions, laws, and customs together with the principles and goals that animated them. So John Adams wrote that a political constitution is like "the constitution of the human body"; "certain contextures of the nerves, fibres, and muscles, or certain qualities of the blood and juices" some of which "may properly be called *stamina vitae,* or essentials and fundamentals of the constitution; parts without which life itself cannot be preserved a moment." A constitution of government, analogously, Adams wrote, is "a frame, a scheme, a system, a combination of powers for a certain end, namely, — the good of the whole community." 2

The elements of this definition were traditional, but it was nevertheless distinctive in its emphasis on the animating principles, the *stamina vitae,* those "fundamental laws and rules of the constitution, which ought never to be infringed." Belief that a proper system of laws and institutions should be suffused with, should express, essences and fundamentals — moral rights, reason, justice — had never been absent from English notions of the constitution. But not since the Levellers had protested against Parliament's supremacy in the mid-seventeenth century had these considerations seemed so important as they did to the Americans of the 1760's. Nor could they ever

* [See pp. 163–167 for notes to this article. — Ed.]

have appeared more distinct in their content. For if the ostensible purpose of all government was the good of the people, the particular goal of the English constitution — "its end, its use, its designation, drift, and scope" — was known to all, and declared by all, to be the attainment of liberty. This was its peculiar "grandeur" and excellence; it was for this that it should be prized "next to our Bibles, above the privileges of this world." It was for this that it should be blessed, supported and maintained, and transmitted "in full, to posterity." [3]

But how had this been achieved? What was the secret of this success of the British constitution? It lay in its peculiar capacity to balance and check the basic forces within society. It was common knowledge, expressed in such familiar clichés, a Virginian complained, "that the merest sciolist, the veriest smatterer in politics must long since have had them all by rote," [4] that English society consisted of three social orders, or estates, each with its own rights and privileges, and each embodying within it the principles of a certain form of government: royalty, whose natural form of government was monarchy; the nobility, whose natural form was aristocracy; and the commons, whose form was democracy. In the best of worlds, it had been known since Aristotle, each of these forms independently was capable of creating the conditions for human happiness; in actuality all of them, if unchecked, tended to degenerate into oppressive types of government — tyranny, oligarchy, or mob rule — by enlarging their own rights at the expense of the others' and hence generating not liberty and happiness for all but misery for most. In England, however, these elements of society, each independently dangerous, entered into government in such a way as to eliminate the dangers inherent in each. They entered simultaneously, so to speak, in a balanced sharing of power. The functions, the powers, of government were so distributed among these components of society that no one of them could dominate the others and strip them of their rights. Each pressed competitively against the other two, and the result was a stable equilibrium of poised forces each of which, in protecting its own rights against the encroachments of the others, contributed to the preservation of the rights of all.

Such was the theoretical explanation, universally accepted in the eighteenth century, of the famous "mixed" constitution of England.[5] It was an arrangement of power that appeared to the colonists as it did to most of Europe as " a system of consummate wisdom and policy." But if the theory was evident and unanimously agreed on, the mechanics of its operation were not. It was not clear how the three social orders were related to the functioning branches of government. The modern assumption of a tripartite division of the functions of government into legislative, executive, and judicial powers did not exist for the colonists; even the terminology was vague:

the term "legislative" was used to mean the whole of government as well as the lawmaking branch. And in any case the balance of the constitution was not expected to be the result of the symmetrical matching of social orders with powers of government: it was not assumed that each estate would singly dominate one of the branches or functions of government.[6] What was agreed on primarily and most significantly was that all three social orders did and should enter into and share, by representation or otherwise, the legislative branch. In the legislative functioning of government, Moses Mather explained in terms that commanded universal assent, power was

> so judiciously placed as to connect the force and to preserve the rights of all; each estate, armed with a power of self-defense against the encroachments of the other two, by being enabled to put a negative upon any or all of their resolves, neither the King, Lords, or Commons could be deprived of their rights or properties but by their own consent in Parliament and no laws could be made or taxes imposed but such as were necessary and in the judgment of the three estates in Parliament, for the common good and the interest of the realm.[7]

It was also agreed that the executive function was largely if not completely the proper responsibility of the first order of society, the crown. The rights exercised there were understood to be the rights of power: prerogative rights, privileges properly enjoyed by the monarch and his servants. But there the agreement stopped. There were several explanations of how the balance of social forces worked to check the undue exercise of prerogative power. Some writers found a sufficient balance and check in the fact that executive action was confined to bounds laid down by laws in the making of which all three powers had shared. But others were able to perceive a subtler kind of check upon prerogative power. For John Adams an essential point was that the commons, or the democracy, of society shared too in the execution of laws through the institution of trial by jury. This ancient device was critical, as Adams saw it, in establishing the equipoise of the English constitution in that it introduced into the "executive branch of the constitution . . . a mixture of popular power" and as a consequence "the subject is guarded in the execution of the laws."[8] Most writers, however, turned for explanation not so much to the popular recruitment of juries and hence to a social balance within the executive branch as to the pressure exerted against the executive from outside, by an independent judiciary. It was taken as a maxim by all, whether or not they used the point to explain how the executive branch entered into the separation of powers, that it was the function of the judges "to settle the contests between prerogative and liberty, . . . to ascertain the bounds of sovereign power, and to determine the rights of the subject," and that in order for them to perform this duty

properly they must be "perfectly free from the influence of either." The
threat to this independence — liberty being passive and power active — came
most commonly from prerogative because of the effect of "its natural weight
and authority" working upon the almost universal "love of promotion and
private advantage." Unless the judiciary could stand upon its own firm and
independent foundations — unless, that is, judges held their positions by a
permanent tenure in no way dependent upon the will and pleasure of the
executive — it would be ridiculous "to look for strict impartiality and a pure
administration of justice, to expect that power should be confined within its
legal limits, and right and justice done to the subject . . ." 9

The difficulty of explaining how, precisely, the natural divisions of
society expressed themselves in the English government so as to pit power
against power for the mutual benefit of all was compounded when the unit
involved was seen to be not the single community of Britain but an empire
of communities each with its own separate social groupings and governmental institutions yet each part of a greater society and government as
well. But until the Revolutionary crisis was well under way no one sought
to settle this complicated constitutional problem.10 The colonists were content to celebrate the wonderful balance of forces they understood to exist in
England, and to assume that in some effective way the same principles operated both in epitome within each colony and in the over-all world of the
empire as well.

The result of this balanced counterpoise of social and governmental
forces in the British constitution was the confinement of social and political
powers to specified, limited spheres. So long as the crown, the nobility, and
the democracy remained in their designated places in government and performed their designated political tasks liberty would continue to be safe in
England and its dominions. But if any of them reached beyond the set
boundaries of their rightful jurisdictions; if, particularly, the agencies of
power — the prerogative, administration — managed, by corrupt practices,
to insinuate their will into the assembly of the commons and to manipulate
it at pleasure, liberty would be endangered.

The very idea of liberty was bound up with the preservation of this
balance of forces. For political liberty, as opposed to the theoretical liberty
that existed in a state of nature, "doth not consist in a freedom from all
laws and government, but in a freedom from unjust law and tyrannical government." Liberty was "a power of acting agreeable to the laws which are
made and enacted by the consent of the PEOPLE, and in no ways inconsistent
with the natural rights of a single person, or the good of the society." Liberty, that is, was the capacity to exercise "natural rights" within limits set
not by the mere will or desire of men in power but by non-arbitrary law —

law enacted by legislatures containing within them the proper balance of forces.[11]

But what were these all-important "natural rights"? They were defined in a significantly ambiguous way. They were understood to be at one and the same time the inalienable, indefeasible rights inherent in people as such, and the concrete specifications of English law. Rights, John Dickinson wrote,

> are created in us by the decrees of Providence, which establish the laws of our nature. They are born with us; exist with us; and cannot be taken from us by any human power without taking our lives. In short, they are founded on the immutable maxims of reason and justice.

Such God-given, natural, inalienable rights, distilled from reason and justice through the social and governmental compacts, were expressed in the common law of England, in the statutory enactments of Parliament, and in the charters of privileges promulgated by the crown. The great corpus of common law decisions and the pronouncements of King and Commons were but expressions of "God and nature . . . The natural absolute personal rights of individuals are . . . the very basis of all municipal laws of any great value." Indeed, "Magna Carta itself is in substance but a constrained declaration, or proclamation and promulgation in the name of King, Lords, and Commons of the sense the latter had of their original, inherent, indefeasible, natural rights." [12]

But this relationship between human rights and English law — so simple sounding when expressed in casual phrases like Daniel Dulany's "unalienable rights of the subject" — was in fact complicated even before the events of the 1760's and seventies placed the whole issue under severe pressure. Even then the identification between the two was known to be necessarily incomplete, for the provision of English law did not and properly could not wholly exhaust the great treasury of human rights. No documentary specification ever could. Laws, grants, and charters merely stated the essentials (which everyone summarized, with minor variations in phrasing, as "personal security, personal liberty, and private property") insofar, and only insofar, as they had come under attack in the course of English history. They marked out the minimum not the maximum boundaries of right. To claim more, to assert that all rights might be written into a comprehensive bill or code was surely, James Otis declared, "the insolence of a haughty and imperious minister . . . the flutter of a coxcomb, the pedantry of a quack, and the nonsense of a pettifogger." The "strange gallimaufry" of "codes, pandects, novels, decretals of popes, and the inventions of the d——l" may be suitable for "the cold bleak regions [of] Brandenburg and

Prussia or the scorching heats of Jamaica or Gambia," but not for Britain's more temperate climate.[13]

Conceiving of liberty, then, as the exercise, within the boundaries of the law, of natural rights whose essences were minimally stated in English law and custom, the colonists saw in the balance of powers of the British constitution "a system of consummate wisdom" that provided an effective "check upon the power to oppress." [14] Yet they were far from optimistic about the future of liberty under the constitution. They looked ahead with anxiety rather than with confidence, for they knew from Rapin and from other historians in the same tradition how embattled liberty had been throughout English history and by how small a margin it had been retrieved in its last, recent period of trial; and they knew too from the radical writings and from direct observation the dangers it faced in their own time. . . .

It is the meaning imparted to the events after 1763 by this integrated group of attitudes and ideas that lies behind the colonists' rebellion. In the context of these ideas, the controversial issues centering on the question of Parliament's jurisdiction in America acquired as a group new and overwhelming significance. The colonists believed they saw emerging from the welter of events during the decade after the Stamp Act a pattern whose meaning was unmistakable. They saw in the measures taken by the British government and in the actions of officials in the colonies something for which their peculiar inheritance of thought had prepared them only too well, something they had long conceived to be a possibility in view of the known tendencies of history and of the present state of affairs in England. They saw about them, with increasing clarity, not merely mistaken, or even evil, policies violating the principles upon which freedom rested, but what appeared to be evidence of nothing less than a deliberate assault launched surreptitiously by plotters against liberty both in England and in America. The danger to America, it was believed, was in fact only the small, immediately visible part of the greater whole whose ultimate manifestation would be nothing less than the destruction of the English constitution with all the rights and privileges embedded in it.

This belief transformed the meaning of the colonists' struggle, and it added an inner accelerator to the movement of opposition. For, once assumed, it could not be easily dispelled: denial only confirmed it, since conspirators profess is not what they believe; the ostensible, for them, is not the real; and the real is deliberately malign.

It was this — the overwhelming evidence, as they saw it, that they were faced with conspirators against liberty determined at all costs to gain ends which their words dissembled — that was signaled to the colonists after

1763, and it was this above all else that in the end propelled them into Revolution.

Suspicion that an active conspiracy of power against liberty existed and involved the colonies directly was deeply rooted in the consciousness of a large segment of the American population; it had assumed specific form before any of the famous political events of the struggle with England took place. No adherent of a nonconformist church or sect in the eighteenth century was free from suspicion that the Church of England, an arm of the English state, was working to bring all subjects of the crown into the community of the Church; and since toleration was official and nonconformist influence in English politics formidable, it was doing so by stealth, disguising its efforts, turning to improper uses devices that had been created for benign purposes. In particular, the Society for the Propagation of the Gospel in Foreign Parts, an arm of the Church created in 1701 to aid in bringing the Gospel to the pagan Indians, was said by 1763 to have "long had a formal design to root out Presbyterianism, etc., and to establishing both episcopacy and bishops." [15]

This suspicion, which had smoldered in the breasts of New Englanders and nonconformists throughout the colonies for half a century or more, had burst into flame repeatedly, but never so violently as in 1763, in the Mayhew-Apthorp controversy which climaxed years of growing anxiety that plans were being made secretly to establish an American episcopate. To Mayhew, as to Presbyterian and Congregational leaders throughout the colonies, there could be little doubt that the threat was real. Many of the facts were known, facts concerning maneuvers in London and in America. Anglican leaders in New York and New Jersey had met almost publicly to petition England for an American episcopate, and there could be little doubt also of the role of the Society for the Propagation of the Gospel in this undercover operation. For if the ostensible goal of the Society was the gospelizing of the pagan Indians and Negroes, its true goal was manifestly revealed when it established missions in places like Cambridge, Massachusetts, which had not had a resident Indian since the seventeenth century and was well equipped with "orthodox" preachers. Such missions, Mayhew wrote, have "all the appearance of entering wedges . . . carrying on the crusade, or spiritual siege of our churches, with the hope that they will one day submit to an episcopal sovereign." Bishops, he wrote unblinkingly in reply to the Archbishop of Canterbury, have commonly been instruments in arbitrary reigns of "establishing a tyranny over the bodies and souls of men," and their establishment in America would mark the end of liberty in Massachusetts and elsewhere. By 1765, when the final exchanges in this pamphlet war were published, it was commonly understood in New England and elsewhere that "the stamping and episcopizing [of] our colonies were . . . *only different branches of the same plan of power.*" [16]

Fear of an ecclesiastical conspiracy against American liberties, latent among nonconformists through all of colonial history, thus erupted into public controversy at the very same time that the first impact of new British policies in civil affairs was being felt. And though it was, in an obvious sense, a limited fear (for large parts of the population identified themselves with the Anglican church and were not easily convinced that liberty was being threatened by a plot of Churchmen) it nevertheless had a profound indirect effect everywhere, for it stimulated among highly articulate leaders of public opinion, who would soon be called upon to interpret the tendency of civil affairs, a general sense that they lived in a conspiratorial world in which what the highest officials professed was not what they in fact intended, and that their words masked a malevolent design.[17]

Reinforcement for this belief came quickly. Even for those who had in no way been concerned with the threat of an episcopal establishment, the passage of the Stamp Act was not merely an impolitic and unjust law that threatened the priceless right of the individual to retain possession of his property until he or his chosen representative voluntarily gave it up to another; it was to many, also, a danger signal indicating that a more general threat existed. For though it could be argued, and in a sense proved by the swift repeal of the act, that nothing more was involved than ignorance or confusion on the part of people in power who really knew better and who, once warned by the reaction of the colonists, would not repeat the mistake — though this could be, and by many was, concluded, there nevertheless appeared to be good reason to suspect that more was involved. For from whom had the false information and evil advice come that had so misled the English government? From officials in the colonies, said John Adams, said Oxenbridge Thacher, James Otis, and Stephen Hopkins — from officials bent on overthrowing the constituted forms of government in order to satisfy their own lust for power, and not likely to relent in their passion. Some of these local plotters were easily identified. To John Adams, Josiah Quincy, and others the key figure in Massachusetts from the beginning to the end was Thomas Hutchinson who by "serpentine wiles" was befuddling and victimizing the weak, the avaricious, and the incautious in order to increase his notorious engrossment of public office. In Rhode Island it was, to James Otis, that "little, dirty, drinking, drabbing, contaminated knot of thieves, beggars, and transports . . . made up of Turks, Jews, and other infidels, with a few renegado Christians and Catholics" — the Newport junto, led by Martin Howard, Jr., which had already been accused by

Stephen Hopkins and others in Providence of "conspiring against the liberties of the colony." [18]

But even if local leaders associated with power elements in England had not been so suspect, there were grounds for seeing more behind the Stamp Act than its ostensible purpose. The official aim of the act was, of course, to bring in revenue to the English treasury. But the sums involved were in fact quite small, and "some persons . . . may be inclined to acquiesce under it." But that would be to fall directly into the trap, for the smaller the taxes, John Dickinson wrote in the most influential pamphlet published in America before 1776, the more dangerous they were, since they would the more easily be found acceptable by the incautious, with the result that a precedent would be established for making still greater inroads on liberty and property.

> Nothing is wanted at home but a PRECEDENT, the force of which shall be established by the tacit submission of the colonies . . . If the Parliament succeeds in this attempt, other statutes will impose other duties . . . and thus the Parliament will levy upon us such sums of money as they choose to take, *without any other* LIMITATION *than their* PLEASURE.[19]

But by then, in 1768, when Dickinson's *Farmer's Letters* were published as a pamphlet, more explicit evidence of a wide-ranging plot was accumulating rapidly. Not only had another revenue act, the Townshend Duties, been passed by Parliament despite all the violence of the colonists' reaction to the Stamp Act, but it was a measure that enhanced the influence of the customs administration, which for other reasons had already come under suspicion. There had been, it was realized by the late 1760's, a sudden expansion in the number of "posts in the [colonial] 'government' . . . worth the attention of persons of influence in Great Britain" — posts, Franklin explained, like the governorships, filled by persons who were

> generally strangers to the provinces they are sent to govern, have no estate, natural connection, or relation there to give them an affection for the country . . . they come only to make money as fast as they can; are sometimes men of vicious characters and broken fortunes, sent by a minister merely to get them out of the way.[20]

By the late 1760's, in the perspective of recent events, one could see that the invasion of customs officers "born with long claws like eagles," had begun as far back as the last years of the Seven Years' War and was now being reinforced by the new tax measures. The wartime Orders in Council demanding stricter enforcement of the Navigation Laws; the Sugar Act of 1764, which had multiplied the customs personnel; and the American Board of Customs Commissioners created in 1767 with "power," Americans

said, "to constitute as many under officers as they please" — all of these
developments could be seen to have provided for an "almost incredible number of inferior officers," most of whom the colonists believed to be "wretches
. . . of such infamous characters that the merchants cannot possibly think
their interest safe under their care." More important by far, however, was
their influence on government.

For there was an obvious political and constitutional danger in having such "a set of *idle drones*," such "lazy, proud, worthless *pensioners* and
placemen," in one's midst. It was nothing less than "a general maxim,"
James Wilson wrote,

> that the crown will take advantage of every opportunity of extending its
> prerogative in opposition to the privileges of the people, [and] that it is
> the interest of those who have *pensions* or *offices at will* from the crown
> to concur in all its measures.

These "baneful harpies" were instruments of power, of prerogative. They
would upset the balance of the constitution by extending "*ministerial influence* as much beyond its former bounds as the late war did the British
dominions." Parasitic officeholders, thoroughly corrupted by their obligations to those who had appointed them, would strive to "*distinguish themselves* by their sordid zeal in defending and promoting measures which *they
know beyond all question* to be *destructive* to the *just rights* and *true interests* of their country." Seeking to "*serve the ambitious purposes of great men
at home*," these "*base-spirited wretches*" would urge — were already urging
— as they logically had to, the specious attractions of "SUBMISSIVE behavior."
They were arguing

> with a plausible affectation of *wisdom* and *concern* how *prudent* it is to
> please the *powerful* — how *dangerous* to provoke them — and then comes
> in the perpetual incantation that freezes up every generous purpose of
> the soul in cold, inactive expectation — "that if there is any request to be
> made, compliance will obtain a favorable attention."

In the end, this extension of executive patronage, based on a limitless support of government through colonial taxation, would make the whole of
government "merely a ministerial engine"; by throwing off the balance of
its parts, it would destroy the protective machinery of the constitution.[21]

But even this did not exhaust the evidence that a design against
liberty was unfolding. During the same years the independence of the
judiciary, so crucial a part of the constitution, was suddenly seen to be
under heavy attack, and by the mid-1760's to have succumbed in many
places.[22]

This too was not a new problem. The status of the colonial judiciary had been a controversial question throughout the century. The Parliamentary statute of 1701 which guaranteed judges in England life tenure in their posts had been denied to the colonies, in part because properly trained lawyers were scarce in the colonies, especially in the early years, and appointments for life would prevent the replacement of ill-qualified judges by their betters, when they appeared; and in part because, judicial salaries being provided for by temporary legislative appropriations, the removal of all executive control from the judiciary, it was feared, would result in the hopeless subordination of the courts to popular influences. The status of the judiciary in the eighteenth century was therefore left open to political maneuvering in which, more often than not, the home government managed to carry its point and to make the tenure of judges as temporary as their salaries. Then suddenly, in the early 1760's, the whole issue exploded. In 1759 the Pennsylvania Assembly declared that the judges of that province would thereafter hold their offices by the same permanence of tenure that had been guaranteed English judges after the Glorious Revolution. But the law was disallowed forthwith by the crown. Opposition newspapers boiled with resentment; angry speeches were made in the Assembly; and a pamphlet appeared explaining in the fullest detail the bearing of judicial independence on constitutional freedom.

In New York the issue was even more inflamed and had wider repercussions. There, the judges of the Supreme Court, by a political maneuver of 1750, had managed to secure their appointments for life. But this tenure was interrupted by the death of George II in 1760 which required the reissuance of all crown commissions. An unpopular and politically weak lieutenant governor, determined to prevent his enemies from controlling the courts, refused to recommission the judges on life tenure. The result was a ferocious battle in which the opposition asserted New York's *"undoubted right* of having the judges of our courts on a constitutional basis," and demanded the "liberties and privileges" of Englishmen in this connection as in all others. But they were defeated, though not by the governor. In December 1761 orders were sent out from the King in Council to all the colonies, permanently forbidding the issuance of judges' commissions anywhere on any tenure but that of "the pleasure of the crown." [23]

All the colonies were affected. In some, like New Jersey, where the governor's incautious violation of the new royal order led to his removal from office, or like North Carolina, where opposition forces refused to concede and managed to keep up the fight for permanent judicial tenure throughout the entire period from 1760 to 1776, the issue was directly joined. In others, as in Massachusetts, where specific supreme court appointments were vehemently opposed by anti-administration interests, the force of the policy was indirect. But everywhere there was bitterness at the decree and fear of its implications, for everywhere it was known that judicial tenure "at the will of the crown" was "dangerous to the liberty and property of the subject," and that if the bench were occupied by "men who depended upon the smiles of the crown for their daily bread," the possibility of having an independent judiciary as an effective check upon executive power would be wholly lost.[24]

This fear was magnified by the rumor, which was circulating vigorously as early as 1768, that it was part of the administration's policy to have the salaries of the colonial judges "appointed for them by the crown, independent of the people." If this ever happened, the Boston Town Meeting asserted when the rumor was becoming actuality, it would "complete our slavery." The reasoning was simple and straightforward:

> if taxes are to be raised from us by the Parliament of Great Britain without our consent, and the men on whose opinions and decisions our properties, liberties, and lives in a great measure depend receive their support from the revenues arising from these taxes, we cannot, when we think of the depravity of mankind, avoid looking with horror on the danger to which we are exposed!

"More and more," as the people contemplated the significance of crown salaries for a judiciary that served "at pleasure," was it clear that "the designs of administration [were] totally to subvert the constitution." Any judge, the House in Massachusetts ultimately stated, who accepted such salaries would thereby declare "that he has not a due sense of the importance of an impartial administration of justice, that he is an enemy to the constitution, and has it in his heart to promote the establishment of an arbitrary government in the province." [25]

Long before this, however, another aspect of the judicial system was believed also to have come under deliberate attack. The jury system, it was said, in New York particularly but elsewhere as well, was being systematically undermined. In New York the same executive who had fought the permanent tenure of judges insisted on the legality of allowing jury decisions, on matters of fact as well as of law, to be appealed to the governor and Council. This effort, though defeated within a year by action of the Board of Trade in England, had a lasting impact on the political consciousness of New Yorkers. It was publicly assailed, in the year of the Stamp Act, as "arbitrary" and "scandalous" in its deliberate subversion of the British constitution.[26]

Associated with this but more important because more widespread in its effect was the extension and enforcement of the jurisdiction of the vice-admiralty courts — "prerogative" courts composed not of juries but of single judges whose posts were "political offices in the hands of the royal governors, to be bestowed upon deserving friends and supporters." Since these courts had jurisdiction over the enforcement of all laws of trade and navigation as well as over ordinary marine matters, they had always been potentially threatening to the interests of the colonists. But in the past, by one means or another, they had been curtailed in their effect, and much of their business had been shunted off to common law courts dominated by juries. Suddenly in the 1760's they acquired a great new importance, for it was into their hands that the burden of judicial enforcement of the new Parliamentary legislation fell. It was upon them, consequently, and upon the whole principle of "prerogative" courts that abuse was hurled as the effect of their enhanced power was felt. "What has America done," victims of the decisions of these courts asked, "to be thus particularized, to be disfranchised and stripped of so invaluable a privilege as the trial by jury?" The operations of the vice-admiralty courts, it was felt, especially after their administrative reorganization in 1767, denied Americans a crucial measure of the protection of the British constitution. "However respectable the judge may be, it is however an hardship and severity which distinguishes [defendants before this court] from the rest of Englishmen." The evils of such prerogative invasion of the judiciary could hardly be exaggerated: their "enormous created powers . . . threatens future generations in America with a curse tenfold worse than the Stamp Act." [27]

The more one looked the more one found evidences of deliberate malevolence. In Massachusetts, Thomas Hutchinson's elaborate patronage machine, long in existence but fully organized only after the arrival of Governor Francis Bernard in 1760, appeared to suspicious tribunes like Oxenbridge Thacher and John Adams to constitute a serious threat to liberty. The Hutchinsons and the Olivers and their ambitious allies, it was said (and the view was widely circulated through the colonies), had managed, by accumulating a massive plurality of offices, to engross the power of all branches of the Massachusetts government thereby building a "foundation sufficient on which to erect a tyranny."

> Bernard had all the executive, and a negative of the legislative; Hutchinson and Oliver, by their popular arts and secret intrigues, had elevated to the [Council] such a collection of crown officers, and their own relations, as to have too much influence there; and they had three of a family on the superior bench . . . This junto therefore had the legislative and executive in their control, and more natural influence over the judicial than is ever to be trusted to any set of men in the world.

With encouragement, no doubt, from England, they were stretching their power beyond all proper bounds, becoming "conspirators against the public liberty." [28]

The same evil of plural officeholding, tending to destroy the protective mechanisms of the separation of powers, was observed to be at work in South Carolina. In both cases the filiation between the engrossing of offices in England and in America could be said to be direct. The self-seeking monopolists of office in the colonies, advancing themselves and their faithful adherents "to the exclusion of much better men," Adams wrote somewhat plaintively, were as cravenly obedient to their masters in power in England as their own despicable "creatures" were to them.[29] How deep this issue ran, how powerful its threat, could be seen best when one noted the degree to which it paralleled cognate developments in England.

John Wilkes's career was crucial to the colonists' understanding of what was happening to them; his fate, the colonists came to believe, was intimately involved with their own.[30] Not only was he associated in their minds with general opposition to the government that passed the Stamp Act and the Townshend Duties, that was flooding the colonies with parasitic placemen, and that appeared to be making inroads into the constitution by weakening the judiciary and bestowing monopolies of public offices on pliant puppets — not only was he believed to be a national leader of opposition to such a government, but he had entered the public arena first as a victim and then as the successful antagonist of general warrants, which, in the form of writs of assistance, the colonists too had fought in heroic episodes known throughout the land. He had, moreover, defended the sanctity of private property against confiscation by the government. His cause was their cause. His *Number 45 North Briton* was as celebrated in the colonies as it was in England, and more generally approved of; its symbolism became part of the iconography of liberty in the colonies. His return from exile in 1768 and subsequent election to Parliament were major events to Americans. Toasts were offered to him throughout the colonies, and substantial contributions to his cause as well as adulatory letters were sent by Sons of Liberty in Virginia, Maryland, and South Carolina. A stalwart, independent opponent of encroaching government power and a believer in the true principles of the constitution, he was expected to do much in Parliament for the good of all: so the Bostonians wrote him in June 1768 "your perseverance in the *good old cause* may still prevent the great system from dashing to pieces. 'Tis from your endeavors we hope for a royal 'Pascite, ut ante, boves,' and from our attachment to 'peace and good order' we wait for a constitutional redress: being determined that the King of Great Britain shall have subjects but not slaves in these remote parts of his dominions." [31]

By February 1769 it was well known that "*the fate of Wilkes and America must stand or fall together.*" [32] The news, therefore, that by the maneuvers of the court party Wilkes had been denied the seat in Parliament to which he had been duly elected came as a profound shock to Americans. It shattered the hopes of many that the evils they saw around them had been the result not of design but of inadvertence, and it portended darker days ahead. When again, and then for a second, a third, and a fourth time Wilkes was re-elected to Parliament and still denied his seat, Americans could only watch with horror and agree with him that the rights of the Commons, like those of the colonial Houses, were being denied by a power-hungry government that assumed to itself the privilege of deciding who should speak for the people in their own branch of the legislature. Power had reached directly and brutally into the main agency of liberty. Surely Wilkes was right: the constitution was being deliberately, not inadvertently, torn up by its roots.

Meanwhile an event even more sinister in its implications had taken place in the colonies themselves. On October 1, 1768, two regiments of regular infantry, with artillery, disembarked in Boston. For many months the harassed Governor Bernard had sought some legal means or excuse for summoning military help in his vain efforts to maintain if not an effective administration then at least order in the face of Stamp Act riots, circular letters, tumultuous town meetings, and assaults on customs officials. But the arrival of troops in Boston increased rather than decreased his troubles. For to a populace steeped in the literature of English radicalism the presence of troops in a peaceful town had such portentous meaning that resistance instantly stiffened. It was not the physical threat of the troops that affected the attitudes of the Bostonians; it was the bearing their arrival had on the likely tendency of events. Viewed in the perspective of Trenchard's writings, these were not simply soldiers assembled for police duties; they were precisely what history had proved over and over again to be prime movers of the process by which unwary nations lose "that precious jewel *liberty*." Here, in bold, stark actuality, was a standing army — just such a standing army as had snuffed out freedom in Denmark. True, British regulars had been introduced into the colonies on a permanent basis at the end of the Seven Years' War; that in itself had been disquieting. But it could then be argued that troops were needed to police the newly acquired territories, and that they were not in any case to be regularly garrisoned in peaceful, populous towns.[33] No such defense could be made of the troops sent to Boston in 1768. No simple, ingenuous explanation would suffice. The true motive was only too apparent for those with eyes to see. One of the classic stages in the process of destroying free constitutions of government had been reached.

And again significant corroboration could be found in developments in England, and support furnished for the belief that events in America were only part of a larger whole. On May 10, 1768, a mob assembled in

St. George's Fields, London, in support of the imprisoned Wilkes was fired upon by the regiment of Foot Guards that had been summoned by the nervous magistrates. Several deaths resulted, the most dramatic being that of a boy, wrongly identified as a leader of the mob, who was tracked down and shot to death on orders of the commander. The political capital made of this misfortune by the Wilkesites and other anti-government groups in London was echoed loudly in the colonies, the more so when it appeared that convictions of the guilty soldiers by normal processes of the law courts were being quashed by the government. Could it be believed to be a coincidence that in February 1770 a young Bostonian was also shot to death by officers of the state? This was more than a parallel to what had happened in London: the two events were two effects of the same cause.[34]

And then, a few weeks later, came the Boston Massacre. Doubts that the troops in Boston constituted a standing army and that it was the purpose of standing armies to terrify a populace into compliance with tyrannical wills were silenced by that event. The narrative of the Massacre written by James Bowdoin and others, which was distributed everywhere in the English-speaking world, stressed the deliberateness of the shooting and the clarity of the design that lay behind the lurid event; nor was the parallel to the St. George's Fields murders neglected. The acquittal of the indicted soldiers did not alter the conviction that the Massacre was the logical work of a standing army, for it accentuated the parallel with the English case which also had concluded with acquittal; and in Boston too there was suspicion of judicial irregularities. How the murderers managed to escape was known to some, it was said, but was "too dark to explain." [35]

Unconstitutional taxing, the invasion of placemen, the weakening of the judiciary, plural officeholding, Wilkes, standing armies — these were major evidences of a deliberate assault of power upon liberty. Lesser testimonies were also accumulating at the same time: small episodes in themselves, they took on a large significance in the context in which they were received. Writs of assistance in support of customs officials were working their expected evil: "our houses, and even our bedchambers, are exposed to be ransacked, our boxes, trunks, and chests broke open, ravaged and plundered by wretches whom no prudent man would venture to employ even as menial servants." Legally convened legislatures had been "adjourned . . . to a place highly inconvenient to the members and greatly disadvantageous to the interest of the province"; they had been prorogued and dissolved at executive whim. Even the boundaries of colonies had been tampered with, whereby *"rights of soil"* had been eliminated at a stroke. When in 1772 the Boston Town Meeting met to draw up a full catalogue of the "infringements and violations" of the "rights of the colonists, and of this province in particular, as men, as Christians, and as subjects," it approved a list of twelve items, which took seventeen pamphlet pages to describe.[36]

But then, for a two-year period, there was a *détente* of sorts created by the repeal of the Townshend Duties, the withdrawal of troops from Boston, and the failure of other provocative measures to be taken. It ended abruptly, however, in the fall and winter of 1773, when, with a terrifying rush, the tendencies earlier noted were brought to fulfillment. In the space of a few weeks, all the dark, twisted roots of malevolence were finally revealed, plainly, for all to see.

The turning point was the Boston Tea Party in December 1773. Faced by this defiant resistance to intimidation, the powers at work in England, it was believed, gave up all pretense of legality — "threw off the mask," John Adams said — and moved swiftly to complete their design. In a period of two months in the spring of 1774 Parliament took its revenge in a series of coercive actions no liberty-loving people could tolerate: the Boston Port Act, intended, it was believed, to snuff out the economic life of the Massachusetts metropolis; the Administration of Justice Act, aimed at crippling judicial processes once and for all by permitting trials to be held in England for offenses committed in Massachusetts; the Massachusetts Government Act, which stripped from the people of Massachusetts the protection of the British constitution by giving over all the "democratic" elements of the province's government — even popularly elected juries and town meetings — into the hands of the executive power; the Quebec Act, which, while not devised as a part of the coercive program, fitted it nicely, in the eyes of the colonists, by extending the boundaries of a "papist" province, and one governed wholly by prerogative, south into territory claimed by Virginia, Connecticut, and Massachusetts; finally, the Quartering Act, to take effect in all colonies, which permitted the seizure for the use of troops of all buildings, public and private, deserted and occupied.

Once these coercive acts were passed there could be little doubt that "the system of slavery fabricated against America . . . is the offspring of mature deliberation." To the leaders of the Revolutionary movement there was, beyond question, "a settled, fixed plan for *enslaving* the colonies, or bringing them under arbitrary government, and indeed the nation too." By 1774 the idea "that the British government — the *King, Lords,* and *Commons* — have laid a regular plan to enslave America, and that they are now deliberately putting it in execution" had been asserted, Samuel Seabury wrote wearily but accurately, "over, and over, and over again." The less inhibited of the colonial orators were quick to point out that "the MONSTER of a standing ARMY" had sprung directly from "a PLAN . . . *systematically* laid, and pursued by the British *ministry,* near twelve years, for enslaving America"; the Boston Massacre, it was claimed, had been

"planned by Hillsborough and a knot of treacherous knaves in Boston."
Careful analysts like Jefferson agreed on the major point; in one of the most
closely reasoned of the pamphlets of 1774 the Virginian stated unambigu-
ously that though "single acts of tyranny may be ascribed to the accidental
opinion of a day . . . a series of oppressions begun at a distinguished
period and pursued unalterably through every change of ministers too
plainly prove a deliberate and systematical plan of reducing us to slavery."
And the fastidious and scholarly John Dickinson, though in 1774 he still
clung to the hope that inadvertence, at least on the part of the King, was
involved, believed that "a plan had been deliberately framed and perti-
naciously adhered to, unchanged even by frequent changes of ministers,
unchecked by any intervening gleam of humanity, to sacrifice to a passion
for arbitrary dominion the universal property, liberty, safety, honor, happiness, and prosperity of us unoffending yet devoted Americans." Some sought
to date the origins of the plot. Josiah Quincy found it in the Restoration of
Charles II; and though John Adams, with one eye on Thomas Hutchinson,
wrote in 1774 that "the conspiracy was first regularly formed and begun to
be executed in 1763 or 4," later he traced it back to the 1750's and forties
and the administration of Governor Shirley of Massachusetts. Nor were the
stages of its development neglected. They could be traced, if in no other
place then in the notorious Hutchinson letters of 1768–69, those "profoundly
secret, dark, and deep" letters which, published in 1773, totally exposed
Hutchinson's "machiavellian dissimulation," John Adams wrote, and convicted him of "junto conspiracy"; they gave proof, the Boston Committee of
Correspondence wrote, that God had "wonderfully interposed to bring to
light the plot that has been laid for us by our malicious and invidious
enemies." [37]

    But who, specifically, were these enemies, and what were their goals?
Local plotters like Hutchinson were clearly only "creatures" of greater
figures in England coordinating and impelling forward the whole effort.
There were a number of specific identifications of these master influences.
One, which appeared in 1773, claimed that at the root of the evil stood the
venerable John Stuart, Lord Bute, whose apparent absence from politics
during the previous decade could be seen as one of his more successful
dissimulations: "he has been aiming for years . . . to destroy the ancient
right of the subjects," and now was finally taking steps to "overthrow both
. . . King and state; to bring on a revolution, and to place another whom
he [is] more nearly allied to upon the throne." Believing the people to
"have too much liberty," he intended to reduce them to the "spiritless
SLAVES" they had been "in the reign of the *Stuarts*." [38] A more general
version of this view was that a Stuart-Tory party, the "corrupt, Frenchified
party in the nation," as it was described in 1766, was at work seeking to re-

verse the consequences of the Glorious Revolution. It was this notion that
led to the republication of Rapin's *Dissertation on . . . the Whigs and
Tories* in Boston in 1773; and it was this notion that furnished Jefferson
with his ultimate understanding of the "system" that sought to destroy
liberty in America.[39] Still another explanation emphasized the greed of a
"monied interest" created by the crown's financial necessities during the
Seven Years' War. The creation of this group was accompanied "by levying
of taxes, by a host of tax gatherers, and a long train of dependents of the
crown. The practice grew into system, till at length the crown found means
to break down those barriers which the constitution had assigned to each
branch of the legislature, and effectually destroyed the independence of both
Lords and Commons." [40]

The most common explanation, however — an explanation almost
universally accepted even after the Declaration of Independence placed responsibility officially on the King himself — located "the spring and cause
of all the distresses and complaints of the people in England or in America"
in "a kind of fourth power that the constitution knows nothing of, or has
not provided against." This "overruling arbitrary power, which absolutely
controls the King, Lords, and Commons," was composed, it was said, of the
"ministers and favorites" of the King, who, in defiance of God and man
alike, "extend their usurped authority infinitely too far," and, throwing off
the balance of the constitution, make their "despotic will" the authority of
the nation.

> For their power and interest is so great that they can and do procure what-
> ever laws they please, having (by power, interest, and the application of
> the people's money to *placemen* and *pensioners*) the whole legislative
> authority at their command. So that it is plain (not to say a word of a
> particular reigning arbitrary *Stuarchal* power among them) that the rights
> of the people are ruined and destroyed by ministerial *tyrannical* authority,
> and thereby . . . become a kind of slaves to the ministers of state.

This "junto of courtiers and state-jobbers," these "court-locusts," whisper-
ing in the royal ear, "instill in the King's mind a divine right of authority
to command his subjects" at the same time as they advance their "detestable
scheme" by misinforming and misleading the people.[41]

It was a familiar notion that had served in England for generations
to justify opposition to a crown that could do no wrong, and it had recently
been revived by both Pitt and Burke echoing the earlier eloquence of
Bolingbroke. It had, moreover, a particular familiarity in New England, and
elsewhere in the colonies, where people generally were acquainted with the
Book of Esther and hence had a model for a ministerial conspiracy in the
story of that "tyrannic *bloodthirsty* MINISTER OF STATE," Haman, at the

court of Ahasuerus. There he was, wrote the Newbury, Massachusetts, minister Oliver Noble in 1775, *"Haman* the *Premier,* and his junto of court *favorites, flatterers,* and *dependents* in the royal city, together with *governors* of provinces, *councilors, boards of trade, commissioners* and their *creatures, officers* and *collectors* of REVENUE, *solicitors, assistants, searchers,* and *inspectors,* down to *tide-waiters* and their *scribes,* and the good Lord knows whom and how many of them, together with the coachmen and servants of the whole . . ." — [*footnote:*] "Not that I am certain the *Persian* state had all these *officers* . . . or that the underofficers of state rode in *coaches* or chariots . . . But as the *Persian* monarchy was despotic . . . it is highly probable . . ." The story was so well known: ". . . now behold the DECREE obtained! The *bloody* PLAN ripened!" The *"cruel perpetrators of the horrid PLOT* and a *banditti* of ministerial tools through the provinces" had everything in readiness. "But behold! . . . A merciful GOD heard the cries of this oppressed people . . ." The parallels were closely drawn; Haman: Lord North; Esther and the Jews: the colonists; and Mordecai: Franklin.[42]

But why were not these manipulators of prerogative satisfied with amassing power at home? Why the attention to faraway provinces in America? Several answers were offered, besides the general one that power naturally seeks to drive itself everywhere, into every pocket of freedom. One explanation was that the court, having reached a limit in the possibilities of patronage and spoils in the British Isles, sought a quarrel with the colonies as an excuse for confiscating their wealth. "The long and scandalous list of placemen and pensioners and the general profligacy and prodigality of the present reign exceed the annual supplies. England is drained by taxes, and Ireland impoverished to almost the last farthing . . . America was the only remaining spot to which their oppression and extortion had not fully reached, and they considered her as a fallow field from which a large income might be drawn . . ." When the colonists' reaction to the Stamp Act proved that "raising a revenue in America quietly" was out of the question, it was decided to destroy their power to resist: the colonies were to be "politically broken up." And so the Tea Act was passed, not to gain a revenue but to provoke a quarrel. The ministry wished "to see America in arms . . . because it furnished them with a pretense for declaring us rebels; and persons conquered under that character forfeit their all, be it where it will or what it will, to the crown." England did not desire an accommodation of any sort, Lord North's conciliatory plan notwithstanding. "From motives of political avarice," she sought an excuse for conquest: "it is on this ground only that the continued obstinacy of her conduct can be accounted for." [43]

But perhaps the most explicit and detailed explanation of the assault upon America by a conspiratorial ministry came from the pen of a country parson in Connecticut writing "to enlighten the people of a country town not under the best advantages for information from the newspapers and other pieces wrote upon the controversy." Seeking to rouse the villagers "to a sense of the danger to which their liberties are now involved," the Rev. Ebenezer Baldwin of Danbury explained that during the last war "the state of the colonies was much more attended to than it had been in times past," and "a very exalted idea of the riches of this country" had been conveyed back to England by the returning officers and soldiers. This exciting information fitted the plans of the ministry neatly, for

> notwithstanding the excellency of the British constitution, if the ministry can secure a majority in Parliament who will come into all their measures [and] will vote as they bid them, they may rule as absolutely as they do in *France* or *Spain,* yea as in *Turkey* or *India.* And this seems to be the present plan: to secure a majority of Parliament, and thus enslave the nation with their own consent. The more places or pensions the ministry have in their gift the more easily they can *bribe* a majority of Parliament by bestowing those places on them or their friends. This makes them erect so many new and unnecessary offices in America, even so as to swallow up the whole of the revenue . . . by bestowing these places — places of considerable profit and no labor — upon the children or friends or dependents of the members of Parliament, the ministry can secure them in their interest. This doubtless is the great thing the ministry are driving at, to establish arbitrary government with the consent of Parliament. And to keep the people of England still, the first exertions of this power are upon the colonies.[44]

Thus the balance of the constitution had been thrown off by a gluttonous ministry usurping the prerogatives of the crown and systematically corrupting the independence of the Commons. Corruption was at the heart of it — the political corruption built on the general dissoluteness of the populace, so familiar in the history of tyranny and so shocking to observers of mid-eighteenth-century England. The evil, public and private, that had appalled Dickinson in 1754 had ripened, it seemed clear, in the subsequent decade. As early as 1766 there had been nervous speculation in the colonies about what would happen

> if the British empire should have filled up the measure of its iniquity and become ripe for ruin; if a proud, arbitrary, selfish, and venal spirit of corruption should ever reign in the British court and diffuse itself through all ranks in the nation; if lucrative posts be multiplied without necessity, and pensioners multiplied without bounds; if the policy of governing be by bribery and corruption, and the trade and manufactures of the nation be disregarded and trampled under foot; if all offices be bought

and sold at a high and extravagant price . . . ; and if, to support these shocking enormities and corruptions, the subjects in all quarters must be hard squeezed with the iron arms of oppression.

Two years later it was stated that

> The present involved state of the British nation, the rapacity and profuseness of many of her great men, the prodigious number of their dependents who want to be gratified with some office which may enable them to live lazily upon the labor of others, must convince us that we shall be taxed so long as we have a penny to pay, and that new offices will be constituted and new officers palmed upon us until the number is so great that we cannot by our constant labor and toil maintain any more.

By 1769 a Boston correspondent of Wilkes commented on "that torrent of corruption which 'like a general flood, has deluged all' to the eternal disgrace of the British nation," and suggested that the reason the "arbitrary and despotic" English government had "extended their ravages to America" was because they had found the British Isles too restricted an area for the full gratification of their "incessant cravings of luxury, extravagance and dissipation." [45]

That by 1774 the final crisis of the constitution, brought on by political and social corruption, had been reached was, to most informed colonists, evident; but if they had not realized it themselves they would soon have discovered it from the flood of newspapers, pamphlets, and letters that poured in on them from opposition sources in England. Again and again reports from the home country proclaimed that the English nation had departed, once and for all and completely, from the true principles of liberty: the principles not of "certain modern Whigs," as one English pamphlet of 1774, reprinted in the colonies seven times within the year of its first appearance, explained, but of "Whigs before the [Glorious] Revolution and at the time of it; I mean the principles which such men as Mr. Locke, Lord Molesworth, and Mr. Trenchard maintained with their pens, Mr. Hampden and Lord [William] Russell with their blood, and Mr. Algernon Sidney with both." To those Englishmen who in the 1770's most directly inherited and most forcefully propagated these radical principles — Richard Price, Joseph Priestley, James Burgh — the situation at home if not abroad justified, even exaggerated, the worst fears for the future of liberty that their predecessors had expressed. For these latter-day radicals had witnessed personally the threatening rise of prerogative influence in the English government and its dramatic manifestation in the Wilkes affair; and they had seen revealed the rapacity and bankruptcy of the swollen East India Company, a revelation which illuminated to them the corruption of their era as dramatically as the collapse of the South Sea Company had revealed the rottenness of the era of George I to Trenchard and Gordon. Everywhere there was cynicism and gluttonous self-seeking. What more was needed to convince one that affairs in Britain were plummeting toward complete and irrecoverable collapse? The long-awaited signs of the total degeneration of the moral qualities necessary to preserve liberty were unmistakable, and these English radicals said so, vigorously, convincingly, in a series of increasingly shrill pamphlets and letters that were read avidly, circulated, published and republished, in America.[46]

There, these ideas carried conviction to a far larger part of the population, and bore more dramatic implications than they did in England. "Liberty," John Adams wrote, "can no more exist without virtue and independence than the body can live and move without a soul," and what liberty can be expected to flow from England where "luxury, effeminacy, and venality are arrived at such a shocking pitch" and where "both electors and elected are become one mass of corruption"? It was not hard to see where England stood: it was, Adams declared, precisely at the point "where the Roman republic was when Jugurtha left it, and pronounced it 'a venal city, ripe for destruction, if it can only find a purchaser.'" The analogy to the decline and fall of Rome and its empire was intriguing and informative; others carried it further and became more specific. Like Rome in its decline, England, "from being the nursery of heroes, became the residence of musicians, pimps, panders, and catamites." The swift decline of her empire, which, it was observed, had reached its peak only between 1758 and the Stamp Act, resulted from the same poison that had proved so fatal to free states in classical antiquity: the corruption, effeminacy, and languor that came from "the riches and luxuries of the East" and led to a calamitous "decay of virtue" and the collapse of the constitution. So often, so stridently, and so convincingly was it said in the colonies that in England "luxury has arrived to a great pitch; and it is a universal maxim that luxury indicates the declension of a state" — so often was it argued that vigor was gone, exhaustion and poverty approaching, that those who would defend British policy were obliged to debate the point: to assert the health and strength of English society, arguing, as Samuel Seabury did, that England was a "vigorous matron, just approaching a green old age; and with spirit and strength sufficient to chastise her undutiful and rebellious children" and not at all, as his adversary Alexander Hamilton had pictured her, "an old, wrinkled, withered, worn-out hag." [47]

The fact that the ministerial conspiracy against liberty had risen from corruption was of the utmost importance to the colonists. It gave a radical new meaning to their claims: it transformed them from constitutional arguments to expressions of a world regenerative creed. For they knew that England was one of the last refuges of the ancient gothic constitution that had once flourished everywhere in the civilized world. By far "the greatest part of the human race," it was known, already lies in "total subjection to their rulers." Throughout the whole continent of Asia people are reduced "to such a degree of abusement and degradation"

> that the very idea of liberty is unknown among them. In *Africa,* scarce any human beings are to be found but barbarians, tyrants, and slaves: all equally remote from the true dignity of human nature and from a well-regulated state of society. Nor is *Europe* free from the curse. Most of her nations are forced to drink deep of the bitter cup. And in those in which freedom seem to have been established, the vital flame is going out. Two kingdoms, those of *Sweden* and *Poland,* have been betrayed and enslaved in the course of one year. The free towns of *Germany* can remain free no longer than their potent neighbors shall please to let them. *Holland* has got the forms if she has lost the spirit of a free country. *Switzerland* alone is in the full and safe possession of her freedom.

And if now, in this deepening gloom, the light of liberty went out in Britain too — in Britain, where next to "self-preservation, political liberty is the main aim and end of her constitution" — if, as events clearly portended and as "senators and historians are repeatedly predicting . . . continued corruption and standing armies will prove mortal distempers in her constitution" — what then? What refuge will liberty find?

"To our own country," it was answered, "must we look for the biggest part of that liberty and freedom that yet remains, or is to be expected, among mankind . . . For while the greatest part of the nations of the earth are held together under the yoke of universal slavery, the North American provinces yet remain *the country of free men:* the *asylum,* and the last, to which such may yet flee from the common deluge." More than that: "our native country . . . bids the fairest of any to promote *the perfection and happiness of mankind.*" No one, of course, can predict "the state of mankind in future ages." But insofar as one can judge the ultimate "designs of providence by the number and power of the causes that are already at work, we shall be led to think that the perfection and happiness of mankind is to be carried further in America than it has ever yet been in any place." Consider the growth the colonies had enjoyed in so short a time — growth in all ways, but especially in population: a great natural increase it had been, supplemented by multitudes from Europe, "tired out with the miseries they are doomed to at home," migrating to America "as the only country in which they can find food, raiment, and rest." Consider also the physical vigor of the people. But above all consider the moral health of the people and of the body politic.

The fatal arts of luxury and corruption are but comparatively beginning among us . . . Nor is corruption yet established as the common principle in public affairs. Our representatives are not chosen by bribing, corrupting, or buying the votes of the electors. Nor does it take one half of the revenue of a province to manage her house of commons . . . We have been free also from the burden and danger of standing armies . . . Our defenses has been our *militia* . . . the general operation of things among ourselves indicate strong tendencies towards a state of greater perfection and happiness than mankind has yet seen.

No one, therefore, can conceive of the cause of America as "the cause of a mob, of a party, or a faction." The cause of America "is the cause of *self-defense*, of *public faith*, and of the *liberties of mankind* . . . 'In our destruction, liberty itself expires, and human nature will despair of evermore regaining its first and original dignity.' " [48]

This theme, elaborately orchestrated by the colonial writers, marked the fulfillment of the ancient idea, deeply embedded in the colonists' awareness, that America had from the start been destined to play a special role in history. The controversy with England, from its beginning in the early 1760's, had lent support to that belief, so long nourished by so many different sources: the covenant theories of the Puritans, certain strands of Enlightenment thought, the arguments of the English radicals, the condition of life in the colonies, even the conquest of Canada. It had been the Stamp Act that had led John Adams to see in the original settlement of the colonies "the opening of a grand scene and design in providence for the illumination of the ignorant and the emancipation of the slavish part of mankind all over the earth." And Jonathan Mayhew, celebrating the conclusion of the same episode, had envisioned future streams of refugees escaping from a Europe sunk in "luxury, debauchery, venality, intestine quarrels, or other vices." It was even possible, Mayhew had added, "who knows?" that "our liberties being thus established, . . . on some future occasion . . . we or our posterity may even have the great felicity and honor to . . . keep Britain herself from ruin." [49]

Now, in 1774, that "future occasion" was believed to be at hand. After the passage of the Coercive Acts it could be said that "all the spirit of patriotism or of liberty now left in England" was no more than "the last snuff of an expiring lamp," while "the same sacred flame . . . which once showed forth such wonders in Greece and in Rome . . . burns brightly and strongly in America." Who ought then to suppress as "whimsical and enthusiastical" the belief that the colonies were to become "the foundation of a great and mighty empire, the largest the world ever saw to be founded on such principles of liberty and freedom, both civil and religious . . . [and] which shall be the principal seat of that glorious kingdom which Christ snall erect upon earth in the latter days"? It was the hand of God that was "in America now giving a new epocha to the history of the world." [50]

In the invigorating atmosphere of such thoughts, the final conclusion of the colonists' logic could be drawn not with regret but with joy. For while everyone knew that when tyranny is abroad "submission is a crime"; while they readily acknowledged that "no obedience is due to arbitrary, unconstitutional edicts calculated to enslave a free people"; and while they knew that the invasion of the liberties of the people "constitutes a state of war with the people" who may properly use "all the power which God has given them" to protect themselves — nevertheless they hesitated to come to a final separation even after Lexington and Bunker Hill. They hesitated, moving slowly and reluctantly, protesting "before God and the world that the utmost of [our] wish is that things may return to their old channel." They hesitated because their *"sentiments of duty and affection"* were sincere; they hesitated because their respect for constituted authority was great; and they hesitated too because their future as an independent people was a matter of doubt, full of the fear of the unknown.[51]

What would an independent American nation be? A republic, necessarily — and properly, considering the character and circumstances of the people. But history clearly taught that republics were delicate polities, quickly degenerating into anarchy and tyranny; it was impossible, some said, to "recollect a single instance of a nation who supported this form of government for any length of time or with any degree of greatness." Others felt that independence might "split and divide the empire into a number of petty, insignificant states" that would easily fall subject to the will of "some foreign tyrant, or the more intolerable despotism of a few American demogogues"; the colonies might end by being "parceled out, Poland-like."

But if what the faint-hearted called "the ill-shapen, diminutive brat, INDEPENDENCY" contained within it all that remained of freedom; if it gave promise of growing great and strong and becoming the protector and propagator of liberty everywhere; if it were indeed true that "the cause of America is in a great measure the cause of all mankind"; if " 'Tis not the concern of a day, a year, or an age; posterity are virtually involved in the contest, and will be more or less affected even to the end of time by our proceedings now" — if all of this were true, ways would be found by men inspired by such prospects to solve the problems of a new society and government. And so let every lover of mankind, every hater of tyranny,

> stand forth! Every spot of the old world is overrun with oppression. Freedom hath been hunted round the globe. Asia and Africa have long expelled her. Europe regards her like a stranger, and England hath given her warning to depart. O! receive the fugitive, and prepare in time an asylum for mankind.[52]

Rhetoric and Reality in the American Revolution

GORDON S. WOOD

Bailyn's student, Gordon S. Wood (1933–   ), former fellow at the Institute of Early American History and Culture at Colonial Williamsburg and now associate professor of history at Brown University, wonders in the following article whether Bailyn's stress on ideas overlooks the real causes of why the colonists thought as they did and, therefore, why they revolted. He provides a valuable summary of Bailyn's aims and achievements in redirecting the post-World War II emphasis upon the revolutionists' principles and conscious espousal of ideals to a consideration of dynamic growth and transformation. Essentially, Wood sees Bailyn's work as a bridge between the newer idealist or neo-whig interpretation and the older economic or progressive interpretation, which he calls behaviorist. The elucidation of his argument summarizes the dilemma of current historical analysis of the Revolution and also exemplifies it in many ways.

Wood's description of this dilemma illustrates the very problem he discusses. To what extent does he both posit and deny a dichotomy between ideals and interests, between the conceptual world of people and their real motives? Is he consistent in his description of the relation between motivation and causation? Does he at times see the whole question of explanation in terms of motivation? Does he at other times maintain that no matter how complete the knowledge of motives and regardless of whether they are conscious or unconscious, complete analysis of causation involves still more than knowledge of motivation? Does he tell us what that "more" is? In his own example drawn from Virginia politics, he maintains that the rhetoric resulted from the colonists' anxiety produced by the grave social crisis they did not fully understand. Yet, does his example really move beyond an analysis of motivation, even though he has shifted the motives beyond either conscious ideals or crass interests? His long book, The Creation of the American Republic, 1776–1787 *(Chapel Hill: University of North Carolina Press, 1969), again asserts that the colonists went to war because of a fundamental social disequilibrium, but again he neither proves his contention nor devotes much space to it.*

In summary, the dilemma Wood sees so well and exemplifies equally well revolves about the whole problem of the model of

*explanation used in contemporary thinking about the behavior
of men. He, like others on the frontiers of historical knowledge,
is seeking new ways of reconciling traditional views of men's
ideas and actions by combining cultural beliefs and values with
the independent reconstruction of actual practices in the social
structure. In Wood's case, this synthesis links personal principles
and interests to societal disequilibrium as the source of the
anxiety that motivates men to immediate action.*

If any catch phrase is to characterize the work being done on the
American Revolution by this generation of historians, it will probably be
"the American Revolution considered as an intellectual movement." [1]* For
we now seem to be fully involved in a phase of writing about the Revolution in which the thought of the Revolutionaries, rather than their social
and economic interests, has become the major focus of research and analysis.
This recent emphasis on ideas is not of course new, and indeed right from
the beginning it has characterized almost all our attempts to understand the
Revolution. The ideas of a period which Samuel Eliot Morison and Harold
Laski once described as, next to the English revolutionary decades of the
seventeenth century, the most fruitful era in the history of Western political
thought could never be completely ignored in any phase of our history
writing.[2]

It has not been simply the inherent importance of the Revolutionary ideas, those "great principles of freedom," [3] that has continually attracted the attention of historians. It has been rather the unusual nature
of the Revolution and the constant need to explain what on the face of it
seems inexplicable that has compelled almost all interpreters of the Revolution, including the participants themselves, to stress its predominantly intellectual character and hence its uniqueness among Western revolutions.
Within the context of Revolutionary historiography the one great effort to
disparage the significance of ideas in the Revolution — an effort which dominated our history writing in the first half of the twentieth century — becomes something of an anomaly, a temporary aberration into a deterministic
social and economic explanation from which we have been retreating for
the past two decades. Since roughly the end of World War II we have witnessed a resumed and increasingly heightened insistence on the primary

Reprinted by permission from Gordon S. Wood, "Rhetoric and Reality
in the American Revolution," *William and Mary Quarterly*, XXIII,
3d Ser. (January, 1966), pp. 3–32.
* [See pp. 167–171 for notes to this article. — Ed.]

significance of conscious beliefs, and particularly of constitutional principles, in explaining what once again has become the unique character of the American Revolution. In the hands of idealist-minded historians the thought and principles of the Americans have consequently come to re-possess that explanative force which the previous generation of materialist-minded historians had tried to locate in the social structure.

Indeed, our renewed insistence on the importance of ideas in ex-plaining the Revolution has now attained a level of fullness and sophistica-tion never before achieved, with the consequence that the economic and social approach of the previous generation of behaviorist historians has never seemed more anomalous and irrelevant than it does at present. Yet paradoxically it may be that this preoccupation with the explanatory power of the Revolutionary ideas has become so intensive and so refined, assumed such a character, that the apparently discredited social and economic ap-proach of an earlier generation has at the same time never seemed more attractive and relevant. In other words, we may be approaching a crucial juncture in our writing about the Revolution where idealism and behavior-ism meet.

I

It was the Revolutionaries themselves who first described the pecu-liar character of what they had been involved in. The Revolution, as those who took stock at the end of three decades of revolutionary activity noted, was not "one of those events which strikes the public eye in the subversions of laws which have usually attended the revolutions of governments." Be-cause it did not seem to have been a typical revolution, the sources of its force and its momentum appeared strangely unaccountable. "In other revo-lutions, the sword has been drawn by the arm of offended freedom, under an oppression that threatened the vital powers of society." [4] But this seemed hardly true of the American Revolution. There was none of the legendary tyranny that had so often driven desperate peoples into revolution. The Americans were not an oppressed people; they had no crushing imperial shackles to throw off. In fact, the Americans knew they were probably freer and less burdened with cumbersome feudal and monarchical restraints than any part of mankind in the eighteenth century. To its victims, the Tories, the Revolution was truly incomprehensible. Never in history, said Daniel Leonard, had there been so much rebellion with so "little real cause." It was, wrote Peter Oliver, "the most wanton and unnatural rebellion that ever existed." [5] The Americans' response was out of all proportion to the stimuli. The objective social reality scarcely seemed capable of explaining a revolution.

Yet no American doubted that there had been a revolution. How then was it to be justified and explained? If the American Revolution, lacking "those mad, tumultuous actions which disgraced many of the great revolutions of antiquity," was not a typical revolution, what kind of revolution was it? If the origin of the American Revolution lay not in the usual passions and interests of men, wherein did it lay? Those Americans who looked back at what they had been through could only marvel at the rationality and moderation, "supported by the energies of well weighed choice," involved in their separation from Britain, a revolution remarkably "without violence or convulsion." [6] It seemed to be peculiarly an affair of the mind. Even two such dissimilar sorts of Whigs as Thomas Paine and John Adams both came to see the Revolution they had done so much to bring about as especially involved with ideas, resulting from "a mental examination," a change in "the minds and hearts of the people." [7] The Americans were fortunate in being born at a time when the principles of government and freedom were better known than at any time in history. The Americans had learned "how to define the rights of nature, — how to search into, to distinguish, and to comprehend, the principles of physical, moral, religious, and civil liberty," how, in short, to discover and resist the forces of tyranny before they could be applied. Never before in history had a people achieved "a revolution by reasoning" alone.[8]

The Americans, "born the heirs of freedom," [9] revolted not to create but to maintain their freedom. American society had developed differently from that of the Old World. From the time of the first settlements in the seventeenth century, wrote Samuel Williams in 1794, "every thing tended to produce, and to establish the spirit of freedom." While the speculative philosophers of Europe were laboriously searching their minds in an effort to decide the first principles of liberty, the Americans had come to experience vividly that liberty in their everyday lives. The American Revolution, said Williams, joined together these enlightened ideas with America's experience. The Revolution was thus essentially intellectual and declaratory: it "explained the business to the world, and served to confirm what nature and society had before produced." "All was the result of reason. . . ." [10] The Revolution had taken place not in a succession of eruptions that had crumbled the existing social structure, but in a succession of new thoughts and new ideas that had vindicated that social structure.

The same logic that drove the participants to view the Revolution as peculiarly intellectual also compelled Moses Coit Tyler, writing at the end of the nineteenth century, to describe the American Revolution as "preeminently a revolution caused by ideas, and pivoted on ideas." That ideas played a part in all revolutions Tyler readily admitted. But in most revolutions, like that of the French, ideas had been perceived and acted upon only when the social reality had caught up with them, only when the ideas had been given meaning and force by long-experienced "real evils." The American Revolution, said Tyler, had been different: it was directed "not against tyranny inflicted, but only against tyranny anticipated." The Americans revolted not out of actual suffering but out of reasoned principle. "Hence, more than with most other epochs of revolutionary strife, our epoch of revolutionary strife was a strife of ideas: a long warfare of political logic; a succession of annual campaigns in which the marshalling of arguments not only preceded the marshalling of armies, but often exceeded them in impression upon the final result." [11]

II

It is in this historiographical context developed by the end of the nineteenth century, this constant and at times extravagant emphasis on the idealism of the Revolution, that the true radical quality of the Progressive generation's interpretation of the Revolution becomes so vividly apparent. For the work of these Progressive historians was grounded in a social and economic explanation of the Revolutionary era that explicitly rejected the causal importance of ideas. These historians could scarcely have avoided the general intellectual climate of the first part of the twentieth century which regarded ideas as suspect. By absorbing the diffused thinking of Marx and Freud and the assumptions of behaviorist psychology, men had come to conceive of ideas as ideologies or rationalizations, as masks obscuring the underlying interests and drives that actually determined social behavior. For too long, it seemed, philosophers had reified thought, detaching ideas from the material conditions that produced them and investing them with an independent will that was somehow alone responsible for the determination of events.[12] As Charles Beard pointed out in his introduction to the 1935 edition of *An Economic Interpretation of the Constitution*, previous historians of the Constitution had assumed that ideas were "entities, particularities, or forces, apparently independent of all earthly considerations coming under the head of 'economic.' " It was Beard's aim, as it was the aim of many of his contemporaries, to bring into historical consideration "those realistic features of economic conflict, stress, and strain" which previous interpreters of the Revolution had largely ignored.[13] The product of this aim was a generation or more of historical writing about the Revolutionary period (of which Beard's was but the most famous expression) that sought to explain the Revolution and the formation of the Constitution in terms of socio-economic relationships and interests rather than in terms of ideas.[14]

Curiously, the consequence of this reversal of historical approaches was not the destruction of the old-fashioned conception of the nature of ideas. As Marx had said, he intended only to put Hegel's head in its rightful place; he had no desire to cut it off. Ideas as rationalization, as ideology, remained — still distinct entities set in opposition to interests, now however lacking any deep causal significance, becoming merely a covering superstructure for the underlying and determinative social reality. Ideas therefore could still be the subject of historical investigation, as long as one kept them in their proper place, interesting no doubt in their own right but not actually counting for much in the movement of events.

Even someone as interested in ideas as Carl Becker never seriously considered them to be in any way determinants of what happened. Ideas fascinated Becker, but it was as superstructure that he enjoyed examining them, their consistency, their logic, their clarity, the way men formed and played with them. In his *Declaration of Independence: A Study in the History of Political Ideas* the political theory of the Americans takes on an unreal and even fatuous quality. It was as if ideas were merely refined tools to be used by the colonists in the most adroit manner possible. The entire Declaration of Independence, said Becker, was calculated for effect, designed primarily "to convince a candid world that the colonies had a moral and legal right to separate from Great Britain." The severe indictment of the King did not spring from unfathomable passions but was contrived, conjured up, to justify a rebellion whose sources lay elsewhere. Men to Becker were never the victims of their thought, always the masters of it. Ideas were a kind of legal brief. "Thus step by step, from 1764 to 1776, the colonists modified their theory to suit their needs." [15] The assumptions behind Becker's 1909 behaviorist work on New York politics in the Revolution and his 1922 study of the political ideas in the Declaration of Independence were more alike than they at first might appear.

Bringing to their studies of the Revolution similar assumptions about the nature of ideas, some of Becker's contemporaries went on to expose starkly the implications of those assumptions. When the entire body of Revolutionary thinking was examined, these historians could not avoid being struck by its generally bombastic and overwrought quality. The ideas expressed seemed so inflated, such obvious exaggerations of reality, that they could scarcely be taken seriously. The Tories were all "wretched hirelings, and execrable parricides"; George III, the "tyrant of the earth," a "monster in human form"; the British soldiers, "a mercenary, licentious rabble of banditti," intending to "tear the bowels and vitals of their brave but peaceable fellow subjects, and *to wash the ground with a profusion of innocent blood.*" [16] Such extravagant language, it seemed, could be nothing but calculated deception, at best an obvious distortion of fact, designed to incite and mold a revolutionary fervor. "The stigmatizing of British policy as 'tyranny,' 'oppression' and 'slavery,' " wrote Arthur M. Schlesinger, the dean of the Progressive historians, "had little or no objective reality, at least prior to the Intolerable Acts, but ceaseless repetition of the charge kept emotions at fever pitch." [17]

Indeed, so grandiose, so overdrawn, it seemed, were the ideas that the historians were necessarily led to ask not whether such ideas were valid but why men should have expressed them. It was not the content of such ideas but the function that was really interesting. The Revolutionary rhetoric, the profusion of sermons, pamphlets, and articles in the patriotic cause, could best be examined as propaganda, that is, as a concerted and self-conscious effort by agitators to manipulate and shape public opinion. Because of the Progressive historians' view of the Revolution as the movement of class minorities bent on promoting particular social and economic interests, the conception of propaganda was crucial to their explanation of what seemed to be a revolutionary consensus. Through the use of ideas in provoking hatred and influencing opinion and creating at least "an appearance of unity," the influence of a minority of agitators was out of all proportion to their number. The Revolution thus became a display of extraordinary skillfulness in the manipulation of public opinion. In fact, wrote Schlesinger, "no disaffected element in history has ever risen more splendidly to the occasion." [18]

Ideas thus became, as it were, parcels of thought to be distributed and used where they would do the most good. This propaganda was not of course necessarily false, but it was always capable of manipulation. "Whether the suggestions are to be true or false, whether the activities are to be open or concealed," wrote Philip Davidson, "are matters for the propagandist to decide." Apparently ideas could be turned on or off at will, and men controlled their rhetoric in a way they could not control their interests. Whatever the importance of propaganda, its connection with social reality was tenuous. Since ideas were so self-consciously manageable, the Whigs were not actually expressing anything meaningful about themselves but were rather feigning and exaggerating for effect. What the Americans said could not be taken at face value but must be considered as a rhetorical disguise for some hidden interest. The expression of even the classic and well-defined natural rights philosophy became, in Davidson's view, but "the propagandist's rationalization of his desire to protect his vested interests." [19]

With this conception of ideas as weapons shrewdly used by designing propagandists, it was inevitable that the thought of the Revolutionaries should have been denigrated. The Revolutionaries became by implication hypocritical demagogues, "adroitly tailoring their arguments to changing conditions." Their political thinking appeared to possess neither consistency nor significance. "At best," said Schlesinger in an early summary of his interpretation, "an exposition of the political theories of the anti-parliamentary party is an account of their retreat from one strategic position to another." So the Whigs moved, it was strongly suggested, easily if not frivolously from a defense of charter rights, to the rights of Englishmen, and finally to the rights of man, as each position was exposed and became untenable. In short, concluded Schlesinger, the Revolution could never be understood if it were regarded "as a great forensic controversy over abstract governmental rights." [20]

III

It is essentially on this point of intellectual consistency that Edmund S. Morgan has fastened for the past decade and a half in an attempt to bring down the entire interpretive framework of the socio-economic argument. If it could be shown that the thinking of the Revolutionaries was not inconsistent after all, that the Whigs did not actually skip from one constitutional notion to the next, then the imputation of Whig frivolity and hypocrisy would lose its force. This was a central intention of Morgan's study of the political thought surrounding the Stamp Act. As Morgan himself has noted and others have repeated, "In the last analysis the significance of the Stamp Act crisis lies in the emergence, not of leaders and methods and organizations, but of well-defined constitutional principles." As early as 1765 the Whigs "laid down the line on which Americans stood until they cut their connections with England. Consistently from 1765 to 1776 they denied the authority of Parliament to tax them externally or internally; consistently they affirmed their willingness to submit to whatever legislation Parliament should enact for the supervision of the empire as a whole." [21] This consistency thus becomes, as one scholar's survey of the current interpretation puts it, "an indication of American devotion to principle." [22]

It seemed clear once again after Morgan's study that the Americans were more sincerely attached to constitutional principles than the behaviorist historians had supposed, and that their ideas could not be viewed as simply manipulated propaganda. Consequently the cogency of the Progressive historians' interpretation was weakened if not unhinged. And as the evidence against viewing the Revolution as rooted in internal class-conflict continued to mount from various directions, it appeared more and more comprehensible to accept the old-fashioned notion that the Revolution was after all the consequence of "a great forensic controversy over abstract governmental rights." There were, it seemed, no deprived and depressed populace yearning for a participation in politics that had long been denied; no coherent merchant class victimizing a mass of insolvent debtors; no seething discontent with the British mercantile system; no privileged aristocracy, protected by law, anxiously and insecurely holding power against a clamoring democracy. There was, in short, no internal class upheaval in the Revolution.[23]

If the Revolution was not to become virtually incomprehensible, it must have been the result of what the American Whigs always contended it was — a dispute between Mother Country and colonies over constitutional liberties. By concentrating on the immediate events of the decade leading up to independence, the historians of the 1950's have necessarily fled from the economic and social determinism of the Progressive historians. And by emphasizing the consistency and devotion with which Americans held their constitutional beliefs they have once again focused on what seems to be the extraordinary intellectuality of the American Revolution and hence its uniqueness among Western revolutions. This interpretation, which, as Jack R. Greene notes, "may appropriately be styled neo-whig," has turned the Revolution into a rationally conservative movement, involving mainly a constitutional defense of existing political liberties against the abrupt and unexpected provocations of the British government after 1760. "The issue then, according to the neo-whigs, was no more and no less than separation from Britain and the preservation of American liberty." The Revolution has therefore become "more political, legalistic, and constitutional than social or economic." Indeed, some of the neo-Whig historians have implied not just that social and economic conditions were less important in bringing on the Revolution as we once thought, but rather that the social situation in the colonies had little or nothing to do with causing the Revolution. The Whig statements of principle iterated in numerous declarations appear to be the only causal residue after all the supposedly deeper social and economic causes have been washed away. As one scholar who has recently investigated and carefully dismissed the potential social and economic issues in pre-Revolutionary Virginia has concluded, "What remains as the fundamental issue in the coming of the Revolution, then, is nothing more than the contest over constitutional rights." [24]

In a different way Bernard Bailyn in a recent article has clarified and reinforced this revived idealistic interpretation of the Revolution. The accumulative influence of much of the latest historical writing on the character of eighteenth-century American society has led Bailyn to the same insight expressed by Samuel Williams in 1794. What made the Revolution truly revolutionary was not the wholesale disruption of social groups and political institutions, for compared to other revolutions such disruption was slight; rather it was the fundamental alteration in the Americans' structure of values, the way they looked at themselves and their institutions. Bailyn has seized on this basic intellectual shift as a means of explaining the apparent contradiction between the seriousness with which the Americans took their Revolutionary ideas and the absence of radical social and institutional change. The Revolution, argues Bailyn, was not so much the transformation as the realization of American society.

The Americans had been gradually and unwittingly preparing themselves for such a mental revolution since they first came to the New World in the seventeenth century. The substantive changes in American society had taken place in the course of the previous century, slowly, often imperceptibly, as a series of small piecemeal deviations from what was regarded by most Englishmen as the accepted orthodoxy in society, state, and religion. What the Revolution marked, so to speak, was the point when the Americans suddenly blinked and saw their society, its changes, its differences, in a new perspective. Their deviation from European standards, their lack of an established church and a titled aristocracy, their apparent rusticity and general equality, now became desirable, even necessary, elements in the maintenance of their society and politics. The comprehending and justifying, the endowing with high moral purpose, of these confusing and disturbing social and political divergences, Bailyn concludes, was the American Revolution.[25]

Bailyn's more recent investigation of the rich pamphlet literature of the decades before Independence has filled out and refined his idealist interpretation, confirming him in his "rather old-fashioned view that the American Revolution was above all else an ideological-constitutional struggle and not primarily a controversy between social groups undertaken to force changes in the organization of society." While Bailyn's book-length introduction to the first of a multivolumed edition of Revolutionary pamphlets makes no effort to stress the conservative character of the Revolution and indeed emphasizes (in contrast to the earlier article) its radicalism and the dynamic and transforming rather than the rationalizing and declarative quality of Whig thought, it nevertheless represents the culmination of the idealist approach to the history of the Revolution. For "above all else," argues Bailyn, it was the Americans' world-view, the peculiar bundle of notions and beliefs they put together during the imperial debate, "that in the end propelled them into Revolution." Through his study of the Whig pamphlets Bailyn became convinced "that the fear of a comprehensive conspiracy against liberty throughout the English-speaking world — a conspiracy believed to have been nourished in corruption, and of which, it was felt, oppression in America was only the most immediately visible part — lay at the heart of the Revolutionary movement." No one of the various acts and measures of the British government after 1763 could by itself have provoked the extreme and violent response of the American Whigs. But when linked together they formed in the minds of the Americans, imbued with a particular historical understanding of what constituted tyranny, an extensive and frightening program designed to enslave the New World. The Revolution becomes comprehensible only when the mental framework, the Whig worldview into which the Americans fitted the events of the 1760's and 1770's, is known. "It is the development of this view to the point of overwhelming persuasiveness to the majority of American leaders and the meaning this view gave to the events of the time, and not simply an accumulation of grievances," writes Bailyn, "that explains the origins of the American Revolution." [26]

It now seems evident from Bailyn's analysis that it was the Americans' peculiar conception of reality more than anything else that convinced them that tyranny was afoot and that they must fight if their liberty was to survive. By an emphatic understanding of a wide range of American thinking Bailyn has been able to offer us a most persuasive argument for the importance of ideas in bringing on the Revolution. Not since Tyler has the intellectual character of the Revolution received such emphasis and never before has it been set out so cogently and completely. It would seem that the idealist explanation of the Revolution has nowhere else to go.[27]

IV

Labeling the recent historical interpretations of the Revolution as "neo-whig" is indeed appropriate, for, as Page Smith has pointed out, "After a century and a half of progress in historical scholarship, in research techniques, in tools and methods, we have found our way to the interpretation held, substantially, by those historians who themselves participated in or lived through the era of, the Revolution." By describing the Revolution as a conservative, principled defense of American freedom against the provocations of the English government, the neo-Whig historians have come full circle to the position of the Revolutionaries themselves and to the interpretation of the first generation of historians.[28] Indeed, as a consequence of this historical atavism, praise for the contemporary or early historians has become increasingly common.

But to say "that the Whig interpretation of the American Revolution may not be as dead as some historians would have us believe" is perhaps less to commend the work of David Ramsay and George Bancroft than to indict the approach of recent historians.[29] However necessary and rewarding the neo-Whig histories have been, they present us with only a partial perspective on the Revolution. The neo-Whig interpretation is intrinsically polemical; however subtly presented, it aims to justify the Revolution. It therefore cannot accommodate a totally different, an opposing, perspective, a Tory view of the Revolution. It is for this reason that the recent publication of Peter Oliver's "Origin and Progress of the American Rebellion" is of major significance, for it offers us — "by attacking the hallowed traditions

of the revolution, challenging the motives of the founding fathers, and de-
picting revolution as passion, plotting, and violence" — an explanation of
what happened quite different from what we have been recently accustomed
to.[30] Oliver's vivid portrait of the Revolutionaries with his accent on their
vicious emotions and interests seriously disturbs the present Whiggish interpretation of the Revolution. It is not that Oliver's description of, say,
John Adams as madly ambitious and consumingly resentful is any more correct than Adams's own description of himself as a virtuous and patriotic
defender of liberty against tyranny. Both interpretations of Adams are in a
sense right, but neither can comprehend the other because each is preoccu-
pied with seemingly contradictory sets of motives. Indeed, it is really these
two interpretations that have divided historians of the Revolution ever
since.

    Any intellectually satisfying explanation of the Revolution must en-
compass the Tory perspective as well as the Whig, for if we are compelled
to take sides and choose between opposing motives — unconscious or avowed,
passion or principle, greed or liberty — we will be endlessly caught up in the
polemics of the participants themselves. We must, in other words, eventually dissolve the distinction between conscious and unconscious motives, between the Revolutionaries' stated intentions and their supposedly hidden
needs and desires, a dissolution that involves somehow relating beliefs and
ideas to the social world in which they operate. If we are to understand the
causes of the Revolution we must therefore ultimately transcend this problem of motivation. But this we can never do as long as we attempt to explain
the Revolution mainly in terms of the intentions of the participants. It is
not that men's motives are unimportant; they indeed make events, including
revolutions. But the purposes of men, especially in a revolution, are so
numerous, so varied, and so contradictory that their complex interaction
produces results that no one intended or could even foresee. It is this interaction and these results that recent historians are referring to when they
speak so disparagingly of those "underlying determinants" and "impersonal
and inexorable forces" bringing on the Revolution. Historical explanation
which does not account for these "forces," which, in other words, relies
simply on understanding the conscious intentions of the actors, will thus
be limited. This preoccupation with men's purposes was what restricted
the perspectives of the contemporaneous Whig and Tory interpretations;
and it is still the weakness of the neo-Whig histories, and indeed of any
interpretation which attempts to explain the events of the Revolution by
discovering the calculations from which individuals supposed themselves
to have acted.

    No explanation of the American Revolution in terms of the inten-
tions and designs of particular individuals could have been more crudely

put than that offered by the Revolutionaries themselves. American Whigs, like men of the eighteenth century generally, were fascinated with what seemed to the age to be the newly appreciated problem of human motivation and causation in the affairs of the world. In the decade before independence the Americans sought endlessly to discover the supposed calculations and purposes of individuals or groups that lay behind the otherwise incomprehensible rush of events. More than anything else perhaps, it was this obsession with motives that led to the prevalence in the eighteenth century of beliefs in conspiracies to account for the confusing happenings in which men found themselves caught up. Bailyn has suggested that this common fear of conspiracy was "deeply rooted in the political awareness of eighteenth-century Britons, involved in the very structure of their political life"; it "reflected so clearly the realities of life in an age in which monarchical autocracy flourished, [and] in which the stability and freedom of England's 'mixed' constitution was a recent and remarkable achievement." [31] Yet it might also be argued that the tendency to see conspiracy behind what happened reflected as well the very enlightenment of the age. To attribute events to the designs and purposes of human agents seemed after all to be an enlightened advance over older beliefs in blind chance, providence, or God's interventions. It was rational and scientific, a product of both the popularization of politics and the secularization of knowledge. It was obvious to Americans that the series of events in the years after 1763, those "unheard of intolerable calamities, spring not of the dust, come not causeless." "Ought not the PEOPLE therefore," asked John Dickinson, "to watch? to observe facts? to search into causes? to investigate designs?" [32] And these causes and designs could be traced to individuals in high places, to ministers, to royal governors, and their lackeys. The belief in conspiracy grew naturally out of the enlightened need to find the human purposes behind the multitude of phenomena, to find the causes for what happened in the social world just as the natural scientist was discovering the causes for what happened in the physical world.[33] It was a necessary consequence of the search for connections and patterns in events. The various acts of the British government, the Americans knew, should not be "regarded according to the simple force of each, but as parts of a system of oppression." [34] The Whigs' intense search for the human purposes behind events was in fact an example of the beginnings of modern history.

In attempting to rebut those interpretations disparaging the colonists' cause, the present neo-Whig historians have been drawn into writing as partisans of the Revolutionaries. And they have thus found themselves entangled in the same kind of explanation used by the original antagonists, an explanation, despite obvious refinements, still involved with the discovery of motives and its corollary, the assessing of a personal sort of responsibility for what happened. While most of the neo-Whig historians have not gone so far as to see conspiracy in British actions (although some have come close),[35] they have tended to point up the blundering and stupidity of British officials in contrast to "the breadth of vision" that moved the Americans. If George III was in a position of central responsibility in the British government, as English historians have recently said, then, according to Edmund S. Morgan, "he must bear most of the praise or blame for the series of measures that alienated and lost the colonies, and it is hard to see how there can be much praise." By seeking "to define issues, fix responsibilities," and thereby to shift the "burden of proof" onto those who say the Americans were narrow and selfish and the empire was basically just and beneficent, the neo-Whigs have attempted to redress what they felt was an unfair neo-Tory bias of previous explanations of the Revolution; [36] they have not, however, challenged the terms of the argument. They are still obsessed with why men said they acted and with who was right and who was wrong. Viewing the history of the Revolution in this judicatory manner has therefore restricted the issues over which historians have disagreed to those of motivation and responsibility, the very issues with which the participants themselves were concerned.

The neo-Whig "conviction that the colonists' attachment to principle was genuine" [37] has undoubtedly been refreshing, and indeed necessary, given the Tory slant of earlier twentieth-century interpretations. It now seems clearer that the Progressive historians, with their naive and crude reflex conception of human behavior, had too long treated the ideas of the Revolution superficially if not superciliously. Psychologists and sociologists' are now willing to grant a more determining role to beliefs, particularly in revolutionary situations. It is now accepted that men act not simply in response to some kind of objective reality but to the meaning they give to that reality. Since men's beliefs are as much a part of the given stimuli as the objective environment, the beliefs must be understood and taken seriously if men's behavior is to be fully explained. The American Revolutionary ideas were more than cooked up pieces of thought served by an aggressive and interested minority to a gullible and unsuspecting populace. The concept of propaganda permitted the Progressive historians to account for the presence of ideas but it prevented them from recognizing ideas as an important determinant of the Americans' behavior. The weight attributed to ideas and constitutional principles by the neo-Whig historians was thus an essential corrective to the propagandist studies.

Yet in its laudable effort to resurrect the importance of ideas in historical explanation much of the writing of the neo-Whigs has tended to return to the simple nineteenth-century intellectualist assumption that history is the consequence of a rational calculation of ends and means, that what happened was what was consciously desired and planned. By supposing "that individual actions and immediate issues are more important than underlying determinants in explaining particular events," by emphasizing conscious and articulated motives, the neo-Whig historians have selected and presented that evidence which is most directly and clearly expressive of the intentions of the Whigs, that is, the most well-defined, the most constitutional, the most reasonable of the Whig beliefs, those found in their public documents, their several declarations of grievances and causes. It is not surprising that for the neo-Whigs the history of the American Revolution should be more than anything else "the history of the Americans' search for principles." [38] Not only, then, did nothing in the Americans' economic and social structure really determine their behavior, but the colonists in fact acted from the most rational and calculated of motives: they fought, as they said they would, simply to defend their ancient liberties against British provocation.

By implying that certain declared rational purposes are by themselves an adequate explanation for the Americans' revolt, in other words that the Revolution was really nothing more than a contest over constitutional principles, the neo-Whig historians have not only threatened to deny what we have learned of human psychology in the twentieth century, but they have also in fact failed to exploit fully the terms of their own idealist approach by not taking into account all of what the Americans believed and said. Whatever the deficiencies and misunderstandings of the role of ideas in human behavior present in the propagandist studies of the 1930's, these studies did for the first time attempt to deal with the entirety and complexity of American Revolutionary thought — to explain not only all the well-reasoned notions of law and liberty that were so familiar but, more important, all the irrational and hysterical beliefs that had been so long neglected. Indeed, it was the patent absurdity and implausibility of much of what the Americans said that lent credence and persuasiveness to their mistrustful approach to the ideas. Once this exaggerated and fanatical rhetoric was uncovered by the Progressive historians, it should not have subsequently been ignored — no matter how much it may have impugned the reasonableness of the American response. No widely expressed ideas can be dismissed out of hand by the historian.

In his recent analysis of Revolutionary thinking Bernard Bailyn has avoided the neo-Whig tendency to distort the historical reconstruction of the American mind. By comprehending "the assumptions, beliefs, and ideas that lay behind the manifest events of the time," Bailyn has attempted to get inside the Whigs' mind, and to experience vicariously all of what they thought and felt, both their rational constitutional beliefs and their hysterical and emotional ideas as well. The inflammatory phrases, "slavery," "corruption," "conspiracy," that most historians had either ignored or readily dismissed as propaganda, took on a new significance for Bailyn. He came "to suspect that they meant something very real to both the writers and their readers: that there were real fears, real anxieties, a sense of real danger behind these phrases, and not merely the desire to influence by rhetoric and propaganda the inert minds of an otherwise passive populace." [39] No part of American thinking, Bailyn suggests — not the widespread belief in a ministerial conspiracy, not the hostile and vicious indictments of individuals, not the fear of corruption and the hope for regeneration, not any of the violent seemingly absurd distortions and falsifications of what we now believe to be true, in short, none of the frenzied rhetoric — can be safely ignored by the historian seeking to understand the causes of the Revolution.

Bailyn's study, however, represents something other than a more complete and uncorrupted version of the common idealist interpretations of the Revolution. By viewing from the "interior" the Revolutionary pamphlets, which were "to an unusual degree, *explanatory*," revealing "not merely positions taken but the reasons why positions were taken," Bailyn like any idealist historian has sought to discover the motives the participants themselves gave for their actions, to re-enact their thinking at crucial moments, and thereby to recapture some of the "unpredictable reality" of the Revolution.[40] But for Bailyn the very unpredictability of the reality he has disclosed has undermined the idealist obsession with explaining why, in the participants' own estimation, they acted as they did. Ideas emerge as more than explanatory devices, as more than indicators of motives. They become as well objects for analysis in and for themselves, historical events in their own right to be treated as other historical events are treated. Although Bailyn has examined the Revolutionary ideas subjectively from the inside, he has also analyzed them objectively from the outside. Thus, in addition to a contemporary Whig perspective, he presents us with a retrospective view of the ideas — their complexity, their development, and their consequences — that the actual participants did not have. In effect his essay represents what has been called "a Namierism of the history of ideas," [41] a structural analysis of thought that suggests a conclusion about the movement of history not very different from Sir Lewis Namier's, where history becomes something "started in ridiculous beginnings, while small men did things both infinitely smaller and infinitely greater than they knew." [42]

In his *England in the Age of the American Revolution* Namier attacked the Whig tendency to overrate "the importance of the conscious will and purpose in individuals." Above all he urged us "to ascertain and recognize the deeper irrelevancies and incoherence of human actions, which are not so much directed by reason, as invested by it *ex post facto* with the appearances of logic and rationality," to discover the unpredictable reality, where men's motives and intentions were lost in the accumulation and momentum of interacting events. The whole force of Namier's approach tended to squeeze the intellectual content out of what men did. Ideas setting forth principles and purposes for action, said Namier, did not count for much in the movement of history.[43]

In his study of the Revolutionary ideas Bailyn has come to an opposite conclusion: ideas counted for a great deal, not only being responsible for the Revolution but also for transforming the character of American society. Yet in his hands ideas lose that static quality they have commonly had for the Whig historians, the simple statements of intention that so exasperated Namier. For Bailyn the ideas of the Revolutionaries take on an elusive and unmanageable quality, a dynamic self-intensifying character that transcended the intentions and desires of any of the historical participants. By emphasizing how the thought of the colonists was "strangely reshaped, turned in unfamiliar directions," by describing how the Americans "indeliberately, half-knowingly" groped toward "conclusions they could not themselves clearly perceive," by demonstrating how new beliefs and hence new actions were the responses not to desire but to the logic of developing situations, Bailyn has wrested the explanation of the Revolution out of the realm of motivation in which the neo-Whig historians had confined it.

With this kind of approach to ideas, the degree of consistency and devotion to principles become less important, and indeed the major issues of motivation and responsibility over which historians have disagreed become largely irrelevant. Action becomes not the product of rational and conscious calculation but of dimly perceived and rapidly changing thoughts and situations, "where the familiar meaning of ideas and words faded away into confusion, and leaders felt themselves peering into a haze, seeking to bring shifting conceptions somehow into focus." Men become more the victims than the manipulators of their ideas, as their thought unfolds in ways few anticipated, "rapid, irreversible, and irresistible," creating new problems, new considerations, new ideas, which have their own unforeseen implications. In this kind of atmosphere the Revolution, not at first desired by the Americans, takes on something of an inevitable character, moving through a process of escalation into levels few had intended or perceived. It no longer makes sense to assign motives or responsibility to particular individuals for the totality of what happened. Men were involved in a complicated web of phenomena, ideas, and situations, from which in retrospect escape seems impossible.[44]

By seeking to uncover the motives of the Americans expressed in the Revolutionary pamphlets, Bailyn has ended by demonstrating the autonomy of ideas as phenomena, where the ideas operate, as it were, over the heads of the participants, taking them in directions no one could have foreseen. His

discussion of Revolutionary thought thus represents a move back to a deterministic approach to the Revolution, a determinism, however, which is
different from that which the neo-Whig historians have so recently and self-
consciously abandoned. Yet while the suggested determinism is thoroughly
idealist — indeed never before has the force of ideas in bringing on the
Revolution been so emphatically put — its implications are not. By helping
to purge our writing about the Revolution of its concentration on constitutional principles and its stifling judicial-like preoccupation with motivation
and responsibility, the study serves to open the way for new questions and
new appraisals. In fact, it is out of the very completeness of his idealist
interpretation, out of his exposition of the extraordinary nature — the very
dynamism and emotionalism — of the Americans' thought that we have the
evidence for an entirely different, a behaviorist, perspective on the causes of
the American Revolution. Bailyn's book-length introduction to his edition
of Revolutionary pamphlets is therefore not only a point of fulfillment for
the idealist approach to the Revolution, it is also a point of departure for
a new look at the social sources of the Revolution.

v

It seems clear that historians of eighteenth-century America and the
Revolution cannot ignore the force of ideas in history to the extent that
Namier and his students have done in their investigations of eighteenth-
century English politics. This is not to say, however, that the Namier approach to English politics has been crucially limiting and distorting. Rather
it may suggest that the Namier denigration of ideas and principles is inap-
plicable for American politics because the American social situation in
which ideas operated was very different from that of eighteenth-century
England. It may be that ideas are less meaningful to a people in a socially
stable situation. Only when ideas have become stereotyped reflexes do evasion and hypocrisy and the Namier mistrust of what men believe become
significant. Only in a relatively settled society does ideology become a kind
of habit, a bundle of widely shared and instinctive conventions, offering
ready-made explanations for men who are not being compelled to ask any
serious questions. Conversely, it is perhaps only in a relatively unsettled, dis-
ordered society, where the questions come faster than men's answers, that
ideas become truly vital and creative.[45]

Paradoxically it may be the very vitality of the Americans' ideas,
then, that suggests the need to examine the circumstances in which they
flourished. Since ideas and beliefs are ways of perceiving and explaining the
world, the nature of the ideas expressed is determined as much by the character of the world being confronted as by the internal development of inherited and borrowed conceptions. Out of the multitude of inherited and

transmitted ideas available in the eighteenth century, Americans selected and emphasized those which seemed to make meaningful what was happening to them. In the colonists' use of classical literature, for example, "their detailed knowledge and engaged interest covered only one era and one small group of writers," Plutarch, Livy, Cicero, Sallust, and Tacitus — those who "had hated and feared the trends of their own time, and in their writing had contrasted the present with a better past, which they endowed with qualities absent from their own, corrupt era." [46] There was always, in Max Weber's term, some sort of elective affinity between the Americans' interests and their beliefs, and without that affinity their ideas would not have possessed the peculiar character and persuasiveness they did. Only the most revolutionary social needs and circumstances could have sustained such revolutionary ideas.[47]

When the ideas of the Americans are examined comprehensively, when all of the Whig rhetoric, irrational as well as rational, is taken into account, one cannot but be struck by the predominant characteristics of fear and frenzy, the exaggerations and the enthusiasm, the general sense of social corruption and disorder out of which would be born a new world of benevolence and harmony where Americans would become the "eminent examples of every divine and social virtue." [48] As Bailyn and the propaganda studies have amply shown, there is simply too much fanatical and millennial thinking even by the best minds that must be explained before we can characterize the Americans' ideas as peculiarly rational and legalistic and thus view the Revolution as merely a conservative defense of constitutional liberties. To isolate refined and nicely-reasoned arguments from the writings of John Adams and Jefferson is not only to disregard the more inflamed expressions of the rest of the Whigs but also to overlook the enthusiastic extravagance — the paranoiac obsession with a diabolical Crown conspiracy and the dream of a restored Saxon era — in the thinking of Adams and Jefferson themselves.

The ideas of the Americans seem, in fact, to form what can only be called a revolutionary syndrome. If we were to confine ourselves to examining the Revolutionary rhetoric alone, apart from what happened politically or socially, it would be virtually impossible to distinguish the American Revolution from any other revolution in modern Western history. In the kinds of ideas expressed the American Revolution is remarkably similar to the seventeenth-century Puritan Revolution and to the eighteenth-century French Revolution: the same general disgust with a chaotic and corrupt world, the same anxious and angry bombast, the same excited fears of conspiracies by depraved men, the same utopian hopes for the construction of a new and virtuous order.[49] It was not that this syndrome of ideas was simply transmitted from one generation or from one people to another. It was

rather perhaps that similar, though hardly identical, social situations called
forth within the limitations of inherited and available conceptions similar
modes of expression. Although we need to know much more about the sociology of revolutions and collective movements, it does seem possible that
particular patterns of thought, particular forms of expression, correspond to
certain basic social experiences. There may be, in other words, typical modes
of expression, typical kinds of beliefs and values, characterizing a revolutionary situation, at least within roughly similar Western societies. Indeed,
the types of ideas manifested may be the best way of identifying a collective
movement as a revolution. As one student of revolutions writes, "It is on the
basis of a knowledge of men's beliefs that we can distinguish their behaviour
from riot, rebellion or insanity." [50]

It is thus the very nature of the Americans' rhetoric — its obsession
with corruption and disorder, its hostile and conspiratorial outlook, and its
millennial vision of a regenerated society — that reveals as nothing else apparently can the American Revolution as a true revolution with its sources
lying deep in the social structure. For this kind of frenzied rhetoric could
spring only from the most severe sorts of social strain. The grandiose and
feverish language of the Americans was indeed the natural, even the inevitable, expression of a people caught up in a revolutionary situation, deeply
alienated from the existing sources of authority and vehemently involved in
a basic reconstruction of their political and social order. The hysteria of the
Americans' thinking was but a measure of the intensity of their revolutionary passions. Undoubtedly the growing American alienation from British
authority contributed greatly to this revolutionary situation. Yet the very
weakness of the British imperial system and the accumulating ferocity of
American antagonism to it suggests that other sources of social strain were
being fed into the revolutionary movement. It may be that the Progressive
historians in their preoccupation with internal social problems were more
right than we have recently been willing to grant. It would be repeating
their mistake, however, to expect this internal social strain necessarily to
take the form of coherent class conflict or overt social disruption. The
sources of revolutionary social stress may have been much more subtle but
no less severe.

Of all of the colonies in the mid-eighteenth century, Virginia seems
the most settled, the most lacking in obvious social tensions. Therefore, as it
has been recently argued, since conspicuous social issues were nonexistent,
the only plausible remaining explanation for the Virginians' energetic and
almost unanimous commitment to the Revolution must have been their devotion to constitutional principles.[51] Yet it may be that we have been looking for the wrong kind of social issues, for organized conflicts, for conscious
divisions, within the society. It seems clear that Virginia's difficulties were

not the consequence of any obvious sectional or class antagonism, Tidewater versus Piedmont, aristocratic planters versus yeomen farmers. There was apparently no discontent with the political system that went deep into the social structure. But there does seem to have been something of a social crisis within the ruling group itself, which intensely aggravated the Virginians' antagonism to the imperial system. Contrary to the impression of confidence and stability that the Virginia planters have historically acquired, they seemed to have been in very uneasy circumstances in the years before the Revolution. The signs of the eventual nineteenth-century decline of the Virginia gentry were, in other words, already felt if not readily apparent.

The planters' ability to command the acquiescence of the people seems extraordinary compared to the unstable politics of the other colonies. But in the years before independence there were signs of increasing anxiety among the gentry over their representative role. The ambiguities in the relationship between the Burgesses and their constituents erupted into open debate in the 1750's. And men began voicing more and more concern over the mounting costs of elections and growing corruption in the soliciting of votes, especially by "those who have neither natural nor acquired parts to recommend them." [52] By the late sixties and early seventies the newspapers were filled with warnings against electoral influence, bribery, and vote seeking. The freeholders were stridently urged to "strike at the Root of this growing Evil; be influenced by Merit alone," and avoid electing "obscure and inferior persons." [53] It was as if ignoble ambition and demagoguery, one bitter pamphlet remarked, were a "Daemon lately come among us to disturb the peace and harmony, which had so long subsisted in this place." [54] In this context Robert Munford's famous play, *The Candidates*, written in 1770, does not so much confirm the planters' confidence as it betrays their uneasiness with electoral developments in the colony, "when coxcombs and jockies can impose themselves upon it for men of learning." Although disinterested virtue eventually wins out, Munford's satire reveals the kinds of threats the established planters faced from ambitious knaves and blockheads who were turning representatives into slaves of the people.[55]

By the eve of the Revolution the planters were voicing a growing sense of impending ruin, whose sources seemed in the minds of many to be linked more and more with the corrupting British connection and the Scottish factors, but for others frighteningly rooted in "our Pride, our Luxury, and Idleness." [56] The public and private writings of Virginians became obsessed with "corruption," "virtue," and "luxury." The increasing defections from the Church of England, even among ministers and vestrymen, and the remarkable growth of dissent in the years before the Revolution, "so much complained of in many parts of the colony," further suggests some sort of social stress. The strange religious conversions of Robert Carter may represent only the most dramatic example of what was taking place less frenziedly elsewhere among the gentry.[57] By the middle of the eighteenth century it was evident that many of the planters were living on the edge of bankruptcy, seriously overextended and spending beyond their means in an almost frantic effort to fulfill the aristocratic image they had created of themselves.[58] Perhaps the importance of the Robinson affair in the 1760's lies not in any constitutional changes that resulted but in the shattering effect the disclosures had on that virtuous image.[59] Some of the planters expressed openly their fears for the future, seeing the products of their lives being destroyed in the reckless gambling and drinking of their heirs, who, as Landon Carter put it, "play away and play it all away." [60]

The Revolution in Virginia, "produced by the wantonness of the Gentleman," as one planter suggested,[61] undoubtedly gained much of its force from this social crisis within the gentry. Certainly more was expected from the Revolution than simply a break from British imperialism, and it was not any crude avoidance of British debts.[62] The Revolutionary reforms, like the abolition of entail and primogeniture, may have signified something other than mere symbolic legal adjustments to an existing reality. In addition to being an attempt to make the older Tidewater plantations more economically competitive with lands farther west, the reforms may have represented a real effort to redirect what was believed to be a dangerous tendency in social and family development within the ruling gentry. The Virginians were not after all aristocrats who could afford having their entailed families' estates in the hands of weak or ineffectual eldest sons. Entail, as the preamble to the 1776 act abolishing it stated, had often done "injury to the morals of youth by rendering them independent of, and disobedient to, their parents." [63] There was too much likelihood, as the Nelson family sadly demonstrated, that a single wayward generation would virtually wipe out what had been so painstakingly built.[64] George Mason bespoke the anxieties of many Virginians when he warned the Philadelphia Convention in 1787 that "our own Children will in a short time be among the general mass." [65]

Precisely how the strains within Virginia society contributed to the creation of a revolutionary situation and in what way the planters expected independence and republicanism to alleviate their problems, of course, need to be fully explored. It seems clear, however, from the very nature of the ideas expressed that the sources of the Revolution in Virginia were much more subtle and complicated than a simple antagonism to the British government. Constitutional principles alone do not explain the Virginians' almost unanimous determination to revolt. And if the Revolution in the seemingly stable colony of Virginia possessed internal social roots, it is to be expected that the other colonies were experiencing their own forms of social strain that in a like manner sought mitigation through revolution and republicanism.

It is through the Whigs' ideas, then, that we may be led back to take up where the Progressive historians left off in their investigation of the internal social sources of the Revolution. By working through the ideas — by reading them imaginatively and relating them to the objective social world they both reflected and confronted — we may be able to eliminate the unrewarding distinction between conscious and unconscious motives, and eventually thereby to combine a Whig with a Tory, an idealist with a behaviorist, interpretation. For the ideas, the rhetoric, of the Americans was never obscuring but remarkably revealing of their deepest interests and passions. What they expressed may not have been for the most part factually true, but it was always psychologically true. In this sense their rhetoric was never detached from the social and political reality; and indeed it becomes the best entry into an understanding of that reality. Their repeated overstatements of reality, their incessant talk of "tyranny" when there seems to have been no real oppression, their obsession with "virtue," "luxury," and "corruption," their devotion to "liberty" and "equality" — all these notions were neither manipulated propaganda nor borrowed empty abstractions, but ideas with real personal and social significance for those who used them. Propaganda could never move men to revolution. No popular leader, as John Adams put it, has ever been able "to persuade a large people, for any length of time together, to think themselves wronged, injured, and oppressed, unless they really were, and saw and felt it to be so." [66] The ideas had relevance; the sense of oppression and injury, although often displaced onto the imperial system, was nonetheless real. It was indeed the meaningfulness of the connection between what the Americans said and what they felt that gave the ideas their propulsive force and their overwhelming persuasiveness.

It is precisely the remarkable revolutionary character of the Americans' ideas now being revealed by historians that best indicates that something profoundly unsettling was going on in the society, that raises the question, as it did for the Progressive historians, why the Americans should have expressed such thoughts. With their crude conception of propaganda the Progressive historians at least attempted to grapple with the problem. Since we cannot regard the ideas of the Revolutionaries as simply propaganda, the question still remains to be answered. "When 'ideas' in full cry drive past," wrote Arthur F. Bentley in his classic behavioral study, *The Process of Government,* "the thing to do with them is to accept them as an indication that something is happening; and then search carefully to find out what it really is they stand for, what the factors of the social life are that are expressing themselves through the ideas." [67] Precisely because they sought to understand both the Revolutionary ideas and American society, the behaviorist historians of the Progressive generation, for all of their crude conceptualizations, their obsession with "class" and hidden economic interests, and their treatment of ideas as propaganda, have still offered us an explanation of the Revolutionary era so powerful and so comprehensive that no purely intellectual interpretation will ever replace it.

The Effects of British Imperial Policy upon Colonial Welfare

ROBERT PAUL THOMAS

As the title of this selection suggests, the argument over the benefits and costs to the colonists of the British mercantile system still continues. In this article, Robert P. Thomas (1938–), associate professor of economics at the University of Washington, initiated the most recent phase of the controversy by applying the tools and theory of the so-called new economic history to the questions involved. Proceeding from a model of the colonial economy and its counterfactual alternatives reconstructed according to modern economic theory, Thomas considers hypotheses and gives his tentative answers based upon statistical analysis. In doing this, he conveniently summarizes the opposing viewpoints of previous historical writing on the questions in addition to offering his conclusions. The application of the new economic history approach to this problem of traditional historical concern has aroused as much debate in the historical profession as Thomas's findings. While other economic historians generally agree with the approach, they question his findings because of the factors he omitted in his model or because of the unreliability of his reconstructed statistics. More traditional historians wonder about the relevance of the whole approach as well as the seemingly oversimple model he employed.

For a long time many historians believed that the effects of the mercantile system upon the colonists' welfare were a basic cause of the Revolution, for they presumed English pressure upon colonists' pocketbooks precipitated the outcry against the mother country and the defense of colonial rights. For them, economic

*interest determined political strategy, and the rhetoric of rights
conveniently concealed crasser motives. Is this the premise of
Thomas's article? If his conclusion about the small cost to the
colonists of the mercantile system is correct, does it bolster the
arguments of the idealist interpreters of the nature and causes of
the Revolution? If Thomas is wrong, does he disprove the idealist interpreters? Does he support the class conflict interpretation?
Does an objective evaluation of the costs and benefits of the mercantile system by a historian today tell us much about what the
men of the time thought were its effects? In discussing motivation, are the views of the actors or of modern observers more important? Does Thomas's article tell us much about why the
colonists went to war?*

Historians have long debated whether the American colonies on
balance benefited or were hindered by British imperial regulation. George
Bancroft thought the regulations worked a definite hardship on the colonies. George L. Beer believed these regulations nicely balanced and that
the colonies shared in the general advantages. Lawrence Harper, in a now
classic article, actually attempted to calculate the cost and found the British
policies "placed a heavy burden upon the colonies." [1]* Oliver Dickerson
wrote that "no case can be made . . . that such laws were economically
oppressive," [2] while Curtis P. Nettels, writing at the same time to the same
point, stated: "British policy as it affected the colonies after 1763 was restrictive, injurious, negative." [3] It is quite evident that a difference of opinion
exists among reputable colonial historians over this important historical
issue.

In this paper an effort is made to meet this issue head on. I shall
attempt to measure, relative to a hypothetical alternative, the extent of the
burdens and benefits stemming from imperial regulation of the foreign commerce of the thirteen colonies. The main instruments of this regulation were
the Navigation Acts, and we shall confine our attention to evaluating the
effect of these Acts upon colonial welfare. Various other imperial regulations such as the Revenue Acts, enacted after 1764, the modification of
naturalization and land regulations, the interference with colonial issues of
paper money, and the various regulations discouraging manufactures will

Reprinted by permission from Robert P. Thomas, "A Quantitative
Approach to the Study of the Effects of British Imperial Policy upon
Colonial Welfare: Some Preliminary Findings," *Journal of Economic
History*, XXV (December, 1965), pp. 615–638.
* [See pp. 171–173 for notes to this article. — Ed.]

not be dealt with in this paper. The assumption is that the direct effects of these regulations upon the economic welfare of the American colonists were insignificant compared to the effects of the Navigation Acts.[4]

The hypothesis of this paper is that membership in the British Empire, after 1763, did not impose a significant hardship upon the American colonies. To test this hypothesis I shall endeavor to bias the estimates against the hypothesis, thus not attempting to state what actually would have happened but only that it would not have amounted to as much as my estimate. The end result will, therefore, err on the side of overstating the real costs of the Navigation Acts to the thirteen colonies.

The traditional tools of economic theory will guide the preparation of these estimates. Two series of estimates will be prepared where possible: one, an annual average for the period 1763–1772, based upon official values; the other, for the single year 1770. The official trade statistics for the year 1770 have been adjusted to make them more accurate.[5]

I

> Is it legitimate for the historian to consider alternative possibilities
> to events which have happened? . . . To say that a thing happened the
> way it did is not at all illuminating. We can understand the signifi-
> cance of what did happen only if we contrast it with what might have
> happened.
>
> MORRIS RAPHAEL COHEN [6]

All attempts at measurement require a standard to which the object being measured is made relative or compared. In the case of this paper, the colonies either on balance benefited or were burdened by British imperialism, relative to how they would have fared under some alternative political situation. The problem is to pick the most probable alternative situation.

The only reasonable alternative in this case is to calculate the burdens or benefits of British regulation relative to how the colonies would have fared outside the British Empire but still within a mercantilist world. Considered within this political environment there is little doubt that prior to February 1763, when the Treaty of Paris was signed, the American colonies on balance benefited from membership in the British Empire. Before that date, the colonies were threatened on two sides by two superior colonial powers. C. M. Andrews has pointed out that, before 1763, in addition to remaining within the protection of Great Britain, the American colonies had only one other alternative: domination by another European power, probably France or Spain. Clearly, from a colonial point of view, belonging to the British Empire was superior to membership in any other.[7]

The French and Indian War ended the menace of foreign domination through the cession to Great Britain of Canada by the French and of

Florida by Spain.[8] Immediately, thereupon, several Englishmen voiced their fears that these spoils of victory, by removing the foreign threat, made inevitable the independence of the American colonies.[9] Even the French Foreign Minister, Choisoul, lent his his voice to this speculation when, soon after the Treaty of Paris, he predicted the eventual coming of the American Revolution. In 1764, Choisoul went so far as to send his agents to America to watch developments.[10] Knollenberg has pointed out that English suspicions of a desire for independence on the part of the colonies do not prove that the suspicions were well founded.[11] They do, however, suggest that an independent America was, by 1763, a distinct possibility; and thereafter the American colonists possessed another alternative to membership in a European empire. This alternative was an independent existence outside the British Empire but still within a mercantilist world.

The alternative situation that I shall employ to calculate the economic effects of the Navigation Acts after 1763 is that of a free and independent thirteen colonies outside the British Empire. This new nation would, therefore, be subject to most of the same restrictions hindering foreign nations attempting to carry on commerce with the eighteenth-century British Empire.[12]

II

> Had the wealth and economic potential of the thirteen Atlantic colonies depended solely on farming, their growth history might have paralleled that of many another slowly developing agricultural settlement. However . . . an indigenous commercial economy developed, unique in colonial history and conducive to sustained growth.
>
> GEORGE ROGERS TAYLOR [13]

This "unique" commercial economy developed within the British Empire subject to the rules and regulations of the Navigation Acts. The American colonies in a sense grew up with the empire, which after the successful conclusion of the Seven Years' War in February 1763, was the wealthiest, most populous colonial empire in the world. It included the kingdom of Great Britain and Ireland with the outlying islands of Europe; trading forts on the Gold Coast of Africa; enclaves in India, and some minor islands in Asia; Newfoundland, Hudson Bay, Nova Scotia, Quebec, the thirteen American colonies, East Florida, and West Florida on the continent of North America; the Bahamas, Bermuda, Jamaica, Antigua, Barbados, and the Leeward and Windward groups of minor islands in the West Indies, as well as the settlement of Belize in Central America.

The American colonies by 1763 formed the foundation of Great Britain's Atlantic empire and had become, as a group, England's most important commercial ally.[14] The basis of this commerce was a vigorous colonial export trade. The total exports in 1770 amounted to £3,165,225. Trade with Great Britain and Ireland accounted for 50 per cent of colonial exports. The West Indies trade constituted another 30 per cent, and commerce with southern Europe and the Wine Islands, another 17 per cent. Trade with Africa and South America accounted for most of the residual.

The colonists, of course, used their exports to purchase imports. They were Great Britain's most important customer and Great Britain their most important supplier. The British Isles shipped to the American colonies in 1768 (a year for which a detailed breakdown is available) £2,157,000 worth of goods, or nearly 75 per cent of all colonial imports, which totaled £2,890,000. Of this, £421,000 were British reexports from northern Europe.[15] The West Indies, the other important source of imports, accounted for 20.5 per cent of the colonial imports; southern Europe and the Wine Islands, 2.9 per cent; and Africa, a little less than 2.0 per cent.

The thirteen American colonies carried on this foreign commerce subject to the constraints of a series of laws designed to alter the trade of the British Empire in the interests of the mother country.[16] This commercial system can be viewed as being made up of four types of laws: (1) laws regulating the nationality, crews, and ownership of the vessels in which goods could be shipped; (2) statutes regulating the destination to which certain goods could be shipped; (3) laws designed to encourage specific primary industries via an elaborate system of rebates, drawbacks, import and export bounties, and export taxes; (4) direct prohibition of colonial industries and practices that tended to compete with English industries or to harm a prominent sector of the British economy or even, occasionally, the economy of a British colony.[17] These laws, it should be stressed, did not regulate the American colonies alone, but with occasional local modifications applied equally to the entire British Empire.

The laws regulating the nationality of vessels were designed to insure a monopoly of the carrying trade of the empire to ships of the empire. In the seventeenth and eighteenth centuries the freight factor on goods traded internationally probably averaged at least 20 per cent, and these laws were designed to insure that this revenue stayed within the empire.[18] The Navigation Acts also insured, to the extent that they were effective, that England would be the entrepôt of the empire and that the distributing trade would be centered in the British Isles.

The commodity clauses of these various regulatory Acts controlled the destination to which certain goods could be shipped. These enumerated commodities generally could be shipped only to England. The original list contained tobacco, sugar, indigo, cotton-wool, ginger, fustic and other dyewoods. Later, naval stores, hemp, rice, molasses, beaver skins, furs, and copper ore were added. The Sugar Act of 1764 added coffee, pimiento, coconuts, whale fins, raw silk, hides and skins, potash and pearl ash to the list. In 1766, the law was amended to prohibit the direct export of any colonial product north of Cape Finisterre.

There were exceptions and compensations to these commodity clauses which benefited the American colonies. Rice, after 1730, could be directly exported south of Cape Finisterre and, after 1764, to South America. Tobacco was given a monopoly in Great Britain, as its local cultivation was prohibited. While the list appears extensive, of the enumerated commodities only tobacco, indigo, copper ore, naval stores, hemp, furs and skins, whale fins, raw silk, and potash and pearl ash were products of the thirteen colonies, and only tobacco, rice, and perhaps indigo and naval stores could be considered major exports of the colonies that later became the United States.

An elaborate series of laws was enacted by the English Parliament to encourage specific industries in the interest of a self-sufficient empire. These included preferential tariffs for certain goods of colonial origin. A distinctive feature of these laws was an elaborate system of rebates and drawbacks to encourage the exports of certain commodities from England and extensive bounties to encourage the production of specific goods for export to Great Britain.

Most enumerated goods benefited from a preferential duty. These goods were thus given a substantial advantage in the markets of the mother country. Goods receiving preferential treatment included cotton-wool, ginger, sugar, molasses, coffee, tobacco, rice, naval stores, pitch, rosin, hemp, masts, whale fins, raw silk, potash and pearl ash, bar and pig iron, and various types of lumber. Certain of these goods also received draw backs of various amounts upon their reexport from Great Britain. Foreign goods competing in the English market with enumerated colonial commodities were thus subject to a disadvantage from these preferential duties.

A system of bounties was also implemented to encourage the production of specific commodities in the colonies or to allow the British manufacturers to compete with foreign exports in the colonial markets. The production of naval stores, silk, lumber, indigo, and hemp was encouraged in the colonies with bounties. In the mother country the manufacture of linen, gunpowder, silks, and many nonwoolen textiles was encouraged by a bounty to allow these products to compete with similar foreign manufactures in the colonial markets.

Certain of the colonial commodities favored by legislation were given what amounted to a monopoly of the home market of the mother country. The colonial production of tobacco, naval stores, sugar and sugar products was so favored. In the case of tobacco, the major share of total imports was reexported, so the local monopoly proved not a great boon.

In economic terms, the Navigation Acts were designed to insure that the vast bulk of the empire's carrying trade was in ships owned by Englishmen. The design of the commodity clauses was to alter the terms of trade to the disadvantage of the colonists, by making all foreign imports into the colonies, and many colonial exports whose final destination was the Continent, pass through England. The effect was to make colonial imports more expensive and colonial exports less remunerative by increasing the transportation costs of both. Finally, through tariff preferences, bounties, and outright prohibitions, resources were allocated from more efficient uses to less.

I shall approach the problem of assessing the overall effect of the various British regulations of trade by considering their effect on the following aspects of the colonial economy: (1) exports of colonial products; (2) imports into the colonies; (3) colonial foreign commerce; and (4) colonial shipping earnings. An assessment will then be undertaken of compensating benefits arising from membership in the British Empire. Finally, an attempt will be made to strike a balance on the total impact of British imperial policy upon the colonial economy.

III

The enumeration of key colonial exports in various Acts . . . hit at colonial trade both coming and going. The Acts . . . placed a heavy burden upon the colonies.

LAWRENCE HARPER [19]

In spite of the extravagant language that has been used to condemn the system, the grower of enumerated commodities was not enslaved by the legal provisions of enumeration . . . . Enumeration clearly did not hamper the expansion of the tobacco raising business in America . . . . It has been assumed by many writers that enumeration imposed a serious burden upon rice planters. The ascertainable facts do not support this assumption.

OLIVER DICKERSON [20]

The export trade between the colonies and the mother country was subjected to regulations which significantly altered its value and composition over what it would have been if the colonies had been independent. The total adjusted value of exports from the American colonies to Great Britain in 1770 was £1,458,000, of which £1,107,000, or 76 per cent, were enumerated goods. Such goods were required to be shipped directly to Great Britain. The largest part, 85.4 per cent, of the enumerated goods was subsequently reexported to northern Europe and thus when competing in these markets bore the burden of an artificial, indirect routing through England to the Continent. The costs of this indirect route took the form of an added transhipment, with the consequent port charges and fees, middlemen's commissions, and what import duties were retained upon reexport. The

enumerated goods consumed in England benefited from preferential duties
relative to goods of foreign production. A few of these enumerated commodities also were favored with import bounties.

The additional transport costs borne by enumerated goods upon
their reexport had the effect of lowering the prices received by the colonial
producer and depressing the quantity exported. In economic terms, the
world market price as shown in Graph 1 would, in the absence of regulation,
be P_2 and exports would be Q_2. The effect of the additional cost of shipment through England is to raise the price to the consumer to P_3. Colonial
exports, consequently, are reduced to Q_1. Therefore, both consumers and
producers suffer from the enumeration of colonial exports whose final
destination is not England.

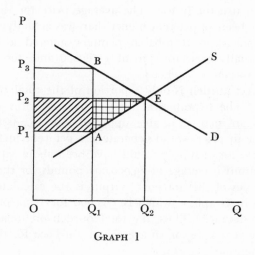

GRAPH 1

The incidence of this burden depends upon the elasticities of supply
and demand for the product. The direct cost to the producer as shown in
Graph 1 is the unit burden times the quantity produced $(P_2P_1 \cdot Q_1)$.[21] The
burden on the reduced output is equal to the return that would be earned
on the additional output over what the resources would earn in their next-
best alternative. This cost is illustrated by the shaded triangle in Graph 1
and represents the sum of the direct and indirect burdens.

In order to calculate the direct burden borne by the colonial producers of enumerated goods that were reexported from England, we need to
know three separate time series. In the case of tobacco, we need to know
the world market price in a European port, the price actually received in the
colonies, and the actual reexports of tobacco from England — all three of
which are readily available.[22]

The price that would have existed in the colonies in the absence of enumeration can be estimated, given the above information. It was estimated by dividing the observed Amsterdam price of Virginia tobacco before the Revolution by the ratio of Amsterdam to Philadelphia tobacco prices after the Revolution.[23] The postwar ratio of prices reflects the advantages received by the colonists by shipping directly to northern Europe rather than indirectly through England. This procedure provides us with an estimate of the price of tobacco in the colonies (P_2 on Graph 1) had tobacco not been subject to enumeration. The difference between the estimated price (P_2) and the actual price (P_1) is the unit burden suffered by reexported colonial tobacco.

Calculated in this manner, the price of tobacco in 1770 colonial America, had the colonies been independent, would have been over 49 per cent higher than it actually was. The average price for the decade 1763–1772 would have been 34 per cent higher than was actually recorded. These higher prices indicate that tobacco planters suffered a burden on the tobacco they actually grew in 1770 of £262,000 and, for the decade, an average annual burden of £177,000.

The direct burden is only a portion of the total colonial loss due to enumeration. The hypothetical higher tobacco prices would certainly have stimulated an increase in the supply of tobacco. Assuming that a 1 per cent increase in price would generate a 1 per cent increase in supply, the resulting increase in supply would have been about 39,000,000 pounds in 1770, or an annual average of 29,000,000 pounds for the decade.[24] The loss to the colonies of this foregone output is the calculated value of the shaded triangle in Graph 1, which is £64,000 for 1770, or an average of £30,000 for the decade.[25] Thus, the total burden on tobacco amounts to £326,000 for the year 1770, or an average of £207,000 for the period 1763–1772.

The calculation of the encumbrance suffered by rice proceeded in the same manner as the calculation of the burden on tobacco, except that Charleston prices were used instead of Philadelphia prices since South Carolina was the center of colonial rice production. The burden on the price of rice reexports was calculated to be an appreciable 105 per cent. This amounted to £95,000 in 1770, or £110,000 average for the decade 1763–1772.[26]

The indirect loss attributable to the expected increase in rice exports with the increase in price amounted to £25,000 for 1770, or an average of £29,000 for the longer period. In the case of rise, an elasticity of supply of .5 was assumed, due to the limited area of southern marshlands suitable to the cultivation of rice. The whole burden on rice products totaled £120,000 for 1770, or an average of £139,000 for the period 1763–1772.

Tobacco and rice together accounted for the vast bulk of the enumerated products that were reexported and therefore bore most of the burden. If we apply the weighted average of the tobacco and rice burden to the remainder of enumerated reexports, and adjust for the expected increase in supply, we obtain an estimated additional burden of £53,000 for 1770, or an annual average of £35,000 for the ten-year period.

However, to arrive at the total burden on enumerated exports we must allow for the benefits that colonial exports received from preferential duties or bounties. Most enumerated commodities benefited from one or the other: beaver skins, furs, and copper ore appear to be the only exceptions. Enumerated goods consumed in Great Britain amounted to £161,570 in 1770, or an average of £126,716 for the decade. The average preference amounted to 38 per cent of the price of enumerated products consumed in the mother country.[27] Again, assuming an elasticity of supply of one, we find that in the absence of these preferential duties the first-order effects would result in a decline in the amount of these enumerated commodities consumed in England of about £61,000 for 1770, or an average of £48,000 for the decade. The benefit of preferential duties to the colonists is the gain enjoyed by those exports that would have been sent to England in the absence of preferential duties had the colonies been independent (or £38,000 in 1770 and £30,000 average for the decade) plus the gain on the commodities actually sent that would not have been sent to England had the colonies been free. This amounted to £17,000 in 1770, or £9,000 as the annual average between 1763 and 1772. The benefit accruing to the colonies from preferential duties thus totals £55,000 for 1770, or £39,000 for the decade average.

In addition to preferential duties, the Crown annually spent large sums in the form of bounties to promote certain industries. The recorded bounties for the year 1770, for instance, totaled £47,344.[28] These payments were designed to divert resources from more efficient uses into industries where they were employed less efficiently but where, for political purposes, they were thought better occupied. Thus it was better to obtain naval stores in the American colonies at a higher cost than to rely upon foreign imports. Part of the bounty, therefore, was a payment for the inefficient allocation of colonial resources and was no gain to the colonies.

The calculation of the approximate proportion of these payments that exceeded the amount required to pay the cost of the inefficiency is not difficult. Since in every case Great Britain continued to import substantial amounts of these commodities from foreign as well as colonial sources, the demand for bountied goods from the colonies can reasonably be assumed to have been perfectly elastic. That is, the colonies could have sold as much of these goods in England as they desired without lowering the market price. This is shown in Graph 2 as a horizontal demand schedule (D) and OB is the market price of the commodity.

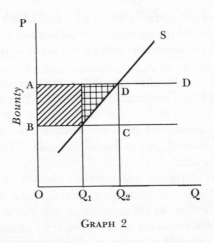

GRAPH 2

The effect of a per-unit bounty is to increase the supply of the commodity; this is shown as an increase in the quantity supplied from Q_1 to Q_2. The net benefit to the colonies of the total bounty (shown on Graph 2 as the area $ABCD$) is the shaded portion of that rectangle. The total bounty payment less the cost of an inefficient use of resources (the unshaded area of the rectangle $ABCD$) gives the net benefit, which must be less than the bounty payment. In order to measure the actual benefit derived by the colonies from the bounty payments we need know only the percentage of the market price represented by the bounty and the elasticity of supply of the commodity.

The export of colonial naval stores was stimulated by bounty payments in significant amounts. The average for the decade 1763–1772 totaled £33,000, and for the year 1770 the payment amounted to £29,803. The average bounty amounted to about 28 per cent of the price; therefore, assuming an elasticity of supply of one, the bounty was responsible for roughly 28 per cent of the exports of naval stores to Great Britain. Figured on this basis, the net gain to the colonists from the bounty on naval stores was 86 per cent of the payment.[29] This amounted to an average of £28,000 for the decade, or £26,000 for the single year 1770.

The second largest bounty payments were for the production of indigo; in 1770 this amounted to £8,732 and for the decade an average of £8,065.[30] Evidently, the indigo bounty not only stimulated increased output but was responsible for the entire output, since the production of indigo in the colonies disappeared after independence. Therefore, the net benefits of the indigo bounty are derived by calculating the value of the triangle as shown in Graph 3. In the absence of the bounty, no indigo would have been

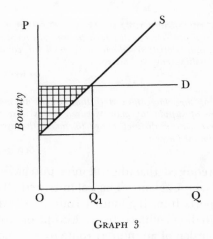

GRAPH 3

exported. The effect of the bounty was to stimulate an export equal to Q_1. The net gain to the colonists from the indigo bounty at best is equal to, and is probably something less than, one half the amount of the bounty. We estimated that 50 per cent of the bounty payment for indigo was gain for indigo producers — gain they would not have enjoyed if the colonies had been independent. This totaled £4,400 in 1770, or £4,000 as the annual average for the decade.[31]

The importation of colonial lumber into Great Britain also received a bounty which, according to Beer, totaled £6,557 in 1769.[32] Sufficient data are not available to allow a calculation of the gain to the colonists from this payment, but it appears that the bounty was just sufficient to pay the added cost of shipping lumber to England. This payment was necessary to divert lumber from the West Indies, which was the colonies' natural market, and to attract it to England. It appears justifiable to assign the entire payment as the cost of a less efficient use of resources. Nevertheless we shall include 50 per cent as a net gain to the colonists, which amounts to £3,300.

The total net gain to the colonies from the bounties paid for colonial products was, therefore, £33,000 in 1770 and an average of £35,000 for the decade. Our analysis of the effect of the Navigation Acts on colonial exports has included the burden on exports, the benefit of the preferential duties, and the net gain from bounty payments. The sum total of these burdens and benefits is a net burden upon exports of £411,000 for 1770.

The average annual burden for the decade 1763–1772 was calculated to be
£307,000.

IV

*The extra expense of importing competitive European products from
England acted as a protective wall which permitted increases in English
prices . . . . Those [statistics] which exist tend to confirm . . . the
theory that trans-shipment was costly.*

                                                              LAWRENCE HARPER [33]

*The clauses of the Navigation Acts that sought to make England
the chief source of supply for manufactured goods were not burden-
some. . . . There was a distinct effort to make the British market
attractive to colonial purchasers.*

                                                              OLIVER DICKERSON [34]

British law required that the colonies purchase their East Indian
and European goods in England. The colonies actually purchased three
quarters of their imports from the mother country, of which about 20 per
cent were goods originally manufactured in Europe or Asia. These imported
goods also bore the burden of an indirect route to the colonies, analogous to
that borne by tobacco destined to be consumed in Europe. This burden was
reflected in higher prices for goods of foreign manufacture in the colonies
than otherwise would have been the case.

Our method for calculating the burden borne by colonial imports
of foreign manufactures is similar to the method used to calculate the cost
of enumeration on colonial goods reexported to Europe. Two commodities,
tea and pepper, for which both colonial and Amsterdam prices are available,
were selected as our sample.[35] Tea and pepper accounted for about 16 per
cent of the value of foreign goods imported into the colonies through
England. The price that would have obtained in the colonies had they been
independent was calculated for these goods exactly as in the case of tobacco.
The alternative prices of these commodities, according to our estimates,
would have averaged 16 per cent lower than they in fact were.[36] Thus, the
colonists paid more for their imports of foreign origin than they would have
paid had they been independent.

The colonies actually imported foreign goods to the average value
of £412,000 for the decade 1763–1772 and of £346,000 for the single year
1770. The burden on the goods, according to our measurement, averaged
£66,000 for the decade, or £55,000 for 1770. However, the burden on imports should not be calculated on the basis of foreign goods alone. The
burden should also be calculated on goods of English manufacture which
were made competitive in the colonial markets by virtue of the artificially
increased cost of foreign goods forced to travel an indirect route to the
colonies.

The bounty laws benefiting English manufactures which were designed to make English goods competitive with those of foreign manufacture
give us a clue to the identity of these English manufactures. If goods of
English manufacture required a bounty to compete with similar foreign
goods suffering the handicap of an indirect shipment, then the colonists, if
independent, would have purchased foreign instead of English goods. Thus,
some English goods actually purchased by the colonists would not have been
purchased if the colonies had been independent.

Linen was the most important of these goods; the list also included
cottons and silks. The colonies thus paid more for most nonwoolen textiles
than they would have if they had existed outside the British Empire. The
additional monetary loss resulting from the purchase of English rather than
foreign goods was calculated to average £73,000 for the decade or £61,000
for 1770 alone.[37] The colonists thus paid a total of £116,000 more in 1770
or £139,000 average for the decade for their imports than they would have
if independent. If we assume, for convenience, a price elasticity of demand
for imports of one, the colonists would have spent the same amount on
imports but they would have received more goods for their money.[38]

The results of this preliminary investigation into the effects of the
Navigation Acts upon the foreign commerce of the American colonies are
found in Table 1. The result is an overall burden for the year 1770 of
£532,000, and an average of £451,000 for the decade.

TABLE 1   NET BURDEN ON COLONIAL FOREIGN COMMERCE

	1770	1763-1772
Exports		
Tobacco	£ 326,000	£ 207,000
Rice	120,000	139,000
Other	53,000	35,000
Burden	499,000	381,000
Preference	55,000	39,000
Bounty	33,000	35,000
Benefit	88,000	74,000
Imports		
Burden	121,000	144,000
Net burden on foreign commerce	£ 532,000	£ 451,000
	or	or
	$ 2,660,000	$ 2,255,000

V

The fact is that colonial shipowners suffered, directly, and colonial shipowners, indirectly, under the Navigation Acts.

LAWRENCE HARPER [39]

Instead of being oppressive the shipping clauses of the Navigation Acts had become an important source of colonial prosperity which was shared by every colony. As a device for launching ships these clauses were more efficient than the fabled beauty of Helen of Troy's face.

OLIVER DICKERSON [40]

The purpose of the various clauses in the Navigation Acts dealing with shipping was to insure that ships built and manned by Englishmen monopolized this aspect of the foreign commerce of the empire. Colonial vessels, for all intents and purposes, were considered English and shared in the benefits of the monopoly.

Calculation of the resultant colonial benefits was hampered by a lack of available data; therefore, the conclusions should be considered tentative. The estimate was constructed in the following manner: an estimated percentage of the total tonnage entering and clearing colonial ports in 1770 that was colonial owned was calculated from the American Inspector General's ledger. Using an estimated average earnings per ton, it was possible to approximate the shipping earnings deriving from the foreign commerce of the American colonies.[41] The total earnings from shipping the foreign commerce of the thirteen colonies were calculated to be £1,228,000, of which 59.4 per cent, or £730,000, was earned by American vessels.

The next question considered was what these earnings would have been had the colonies been independent. Using as a guide what actually did happen between 1789–1792, after the Revolution but before the outbreak of the war in Europe, I found that the colonies' share of the trade carrying their own commerce declined from 59.4 per cent to 53.2 per cent. On this basis, their shipping earnings in 1770 would have been £653,000 instead of £730,000 — a difference of £77,000.

However, as we have seen, had the American colonies been independent their volume of foreign commerce would have been greater. Their ships would have carried a portion of the increased amounts of tobacco, rice, and other exports that would have been shipped, as well as a portion of the larger volume of imports.

My calculations suggest that the volume of shipping required to carry this additional output would have amounted to over 53,000 tons. If American vessels had carried the same percentage of this increased volume as they carried of the total volume in 1789, their earnings in 1770 would have increased to over £742,000 — or a little more than they in fact were during the late colonial period. The composition of the trade, however, would have been different.[42]

Thus, it seems fruitless to do more with the effect of the Navigation Acts upon shipping earnings until we know more about shipping rates before and after the Revolution. The best guess, at this time, is that on balance the colonial shipping industry neither gained nor lost from the Navigation Acts.

VI

Indeed, the question ought not be separated from the larger one of the savings offered Americans by the military and naval protection of the British.

STUART BRUCHEY [43]

The main obligation of the mother country to its colonies in a mercantilist world was to provide protection. In this area lies the significant benefit to the colonies from membership in an empire. The empire of course also performed certain administrative functions for the colonies from which they benefited.

Great Britain in the defense of the empire could provide for the protection of the American colonies at very little additional expense to itself. That is to say that the colonies, if independent, would have had to expend more resources in their own defense than did England, just to maintain the same level of protection. Our estimate of the value of military and naval protection provided by the British to the colonists, since it is based in part upon actual British expenditures, is therefore too low.

The value of British military protection was estimated as follows. Great Britain, before 1762, maintained a standing army in America of 3,000 officers and men. After 1762, the size of this troop complement was increased to 7,500 men.[44] These troops were garrisoned throughout the colonies, including the frontiers where they served as a defensive force against the incursions of hostile Indians. Each man stationed in America cost the mother country an average of £29 a year, or annually a total expense of at least £217,500.[45]

The colonists constantly complained about the quality of the "redcoats" as Indian fighters. Furthermore, they believed the larger standing army in the colonies after 1762 was there not primarily to protect them but for other reasons. However, they found after independence that a standing army of at least 5,000 men was required to replace the British.[46] Thus the benefit to the colonies from the British army stationed in America was conservatively worth at least the cost of 5,000 troops, or £145,000.

Another large colonial benefit stemmed from the protection offered colonial shipping by the British navy, which included the Crown's annual tribute to the Barbary powers. The ability of the British navy to protect its merchant ships from the ravages of pirates far surpassed anything a small independent country could provide. This the colonies learned to their sorrow following the Revolution.

The value of such protection would be reflected in the rise in marine insurance rates for cargoes carried by American vessels after independence. Unfortunately, until research in process is completed, I do not have sufficient data to directly calculate the value of the protection of the British navy in this manner.

However, this benefit can be tentatively measured in an indirect manner. Insurance rates during the 1760's on the West Indies trade one way averaged about 3.5 per cent of the value of the cargo.[47] Rates to England were higher, averaging 7 per cent. These rates on colonial cargoes existed while colonial vessels were protected by the British navy. During the French and Indian War, the risk of seizure increased the rates to the West Indies, which rose steadily until they reached 23 per cent, while rates to England climbed as high as 28 per cent,[48] indicating the influence of risk upon marine insurance rates.

The colonists upon obtaining their independence lost the protection of the British fleet. Insurance rates, as a result, must have increased over the prerevolutionary levels. To estimate the approximate rise in insurance rates, we calculated the percentage decline in insurance rates for American merchant vessels following the launching in 1797 of three frigates which formed the foundation of the small, eighteenth-century American navy.[49]

The percentage difference between the rates on an unprotected merchant marine and those charged on the merchant fleet safeguarded by our small navy was applied to the insurance rates prevailing before the Revolution. The weighted difference in rates between a barely protected merchant marine and a totally unprotected one was slightly over 50 per cent.

Applying this percentage to existing prerevolutionary rates, it appears that the average cargo insurance rate, if the colonies had been independent, would have been at least 8.7 per cent of the value of the cargo instead of 5.4 per cent, a difference in rates of 2.7 per cent. Figuring this increase in insurance charges on the value of colonial cargoes in 1770 gives a low estimate of the value derived from British naval protection of £103,000. Three ships were not the British navy and could not be expected to provide equal protection. Marine insurance rates thus probably increased more than 2.7 per cent. An estimate that rates doubled does not seem unreasonable and would raise the annual value of naval protection to £206,000.

The estimate of the value of British protection of the American colonies is thus made up of the adjusted cost of the army in the colonies,

£145,000, plus the estimated value of naval protection for the merchant marine of £206,000. The estimated total value of the protection afforded the colonies by their membership in the British Empire was thus calculated to be at least £351,000.

By way of a check upon this estimate, the Government of the United States, during its first nine years under the Constitution, found it necessary to spend annually an average of $2,133,000, or £426,600, for national defense.[50] This included the purchase of arms and stores, the fortification of forts and harbors, and the building and manning of a small navy. In addition, an independent America had to bear the expense of conducting an independent foreign policy. The support of ministers to foreign nations, the cost of negotiating and implementing treaties, the payment of tribute to the Barbary nations, all previously provided for by Great Britain, now had to be borne by the independent colonies. These expenses alone cost the United States, during the last decade of the eighteenth century, annually over £60,000.

After achieving independence, the United States found it necessary to spend annually about £487,000 to provide certain functions of government formerly provided by Great Britain. This suggests that our estimate of £351,000 for the value of British protection to the American colonists is too low. It is doubtful, in the light of history, whether the new nation was able to provide this type of governmental services of equal quality to those furnished by the British. If not, even the £487,000 a year understates the value of governmental services supplied by Great Britain to her American colonies.

VII

For reasons which have been explained more fully elsewhere we shall reject Beer's claim that there was no exploitation.
LAWRENCE HARPER [51]

Exploitation . . . by the home country is an economic myth.
OLIVER DICKERSON [52]

My findings with reference to the effect of the Navigation Acts upon the economy of the thirteen colonies indicate a net burden of £532,000, or $2,660,000, in 1770. The average burden for the decade 1763–1772, based upon official values, was somewhat lower — £451,000, or $2,255,000. These estimates are near the lowest estimates made by Harper and seem to strengthen his case that exploitation did exist.[53]

Considering for a moment only the value of the losses on colonial exports and imports, the per capita annual cost to the colonist of being an Englishman instead of an American was $1.24 in 1770. The average per capita cost for the decade based upon official values was a somewhat lower

$1.20. The benefits per capita in 1770 were figured to be 82 cents, and for the decade 94 cents. Subtracting the benefits from the burdens for 1770 shows a per capita loss of 42 cents. The estimate for the decade shows a smaller loss of 26 cents a person. It is unlikely, because of the nature of the estimating procedures employed, that these losses are too low. Conversely it is not at all improbable, and for the same reasons, that the estimated losses are too high.

Suppose that these findings reflect the true magnitude of the cost of the Navigation Acts to the thirteen colonies. The relevant question becomes: How important were these losses? Albert Fishlow stated at last year's meetings that he believed that the average per capita income in the 1780's "could not have been much less than $100." [54] George Rogers Taylor, in his presidential address, hazarded a guess that per capita income did not grow very rapidly, if at all, between 1775 and 1840.[55] Therefore, assuming that average per capita income hovered about $100 between 1763 and 1772, what would it have been had the colonies been independent?

The answer is obvious from Table 2: it would not have been much different. The largest estimated loss on this basis is .54 of 1 per cent of per capita income, or 54 cents on a hundred dollars. Suppose for a moment that my estimates are off by 100 per cent; then, in that case the largest burden would be slightly more than 1 per cent of national income. It is difficult to make a convincing case for exploitation out of these results.

TABLE 2   SUMMARY OF THE RESULTS

	1763–1772	1770
Burdens		
Burden on colonial foreign commerce	£ 451,000	£ 532,000
	or	or
	$ 2,255,000	$ 2,660,000
Burden per capita [a]	$ 1.20	$ 1.24
Benefits		
Benefit of British protection	£ 351,000	£ 351,000
	or	or
	$ 1,775,000	$ 1,775,000
Benefit per capita	$ .94	$ .82
Balance [b]		
Estimate 1	$ −.26	$ −.42

[a] Population for the decade average was figured to be 1,881,000, and for 1770 to be 2,148,000.

[b] The balance was obtained by subtracting the per capita benefits from the per capita burden.

NOTES

Republicanism and Radicalism in the American Revolution,
CECELIA M. KENYON

1 Letter to Hezekiah Niles, Feb. 13, 1818, in Adrienne Koch and William Peden, eds., *The Selected Writings of John and John Quincy Adams* (New York, 1946), 204.

2 Letter to Roger C. Weightman, June 24, 1826, in Paul Leicester Ford, ed., *The Works of Thomas Jefferson* (New York and London, 1904-5), XII, 477.

3 Alexander Hamilton, James Madison, and John Jay, *The Federalist*, ed. Benjamin Fletcher Wright (Cambridge, Mass., 1961): "The first question that offers itself is, whether the general form and aspect of the government be strictly republican? It is evident that no other form would be reconcilable with the genius of the people of America; with the fundamental principles of the Revolution; or with that honorable determination which animates every votary of freedom, to rest all our political experiments on the capacity of mankind for self-government." The Thirty-ninth Essay, p. 280.

4 James Otis, "The Rights of the British Colonies Asserted and Proved" (1764), in Charles F. Mullett, ed., *Some Political Writings of James Otis* (Columbia, Mo., 1929), I, 54: "The necessity of a common, indifferent and impartial judge, makes all men seek one; though few find him in the *sovereign power*, of their respective states or any where else in *subordination to it.*"

5 See the emphatic statement to this effect in Wilson's "On the Legislative Authority of the British Parliament" (1774), in Bird Wilson, ed., *The Works of the Honorable James Wilson, L.L.D.* . . . (Philadelphia, 1804), III, 211: "The interest of the representatives is the same with that of their constituents. Every measure, that is prejudicial to the nation, must be prejudicial to them and their posterity. They cannot betray their electors, without, at the same time, injuring themselves. They must join in bearing the burthen of every oppressive act; and participate in the happy effects of every wise and good law. Influenced by these considerations, they will seriously and with attention examine every measure proposed to them; they will behold it in every light, and extend their views to its most distant consequences."

6 The development of American colonial thought on this subject is reflected in various of the Election Sermons given in New England in the latter part of the 17th century and the first two-thirds of the 18th. Note the variety as well as the similarity of views expressed in these three sermons: "Take heed of any Sinister Aims in whatsover Laws do pass: Laws made to strengthen a particular separate Interest, never did Good, but Hurt to a Body-Politick: that which may serve the present turn, may in a little time prove more Mischievous, than ever it was Advantageous." (Samuel Willard, *The Character of a Good Ruler* . . . [Boston, 1694], 27.) "*Where there are Envyings and Strifes,* Animosities and Divisions, *there is Confusion and every Evil Work.* Where these Govern, if men can but Obtain their particular Ends and Desires, Advance their Party, Confound their Opposers, they are Content, what Prejudices soever the Publick Suffers: Then all the good Offices that make Society Valuable are Intercepted, and Fierceness, and Provocations, and Injuries Succeed." (Timothy Cutler, *The Firm Union of a People Represented* . . . [New-London, 1717], 33.) "Every large community is constituted of a number of little societies, in which there will be different branches of business. These, whatever pains are taken to prevent it, will have their different connections, and form separate interests; it is vastly difficult for those who govern, to keep the balance so exactly poized that neither part may be injured; but much more, to prevent jealousies and suspicions that things are carried

148 NOTES

by favor and affection." (Andrew Eliot, *A Sermon Preached before His Excellency Francis Bernard* . . . [Boston, 1765], 14.)

7 See John Dickinson, *The Political Writings of John Dickinson* . . . (Wilmington, Del., 1801), I, 332, 395.

8 I do not mean to imply that the exclusion of *property* from the Declaration of Independence meant that Americans had ceased to regard it as a natural right to be secured by government. They had not; many of them probably continued to regard it as superior or prior to that of the pursuit of happiness, while the majority saw no conflict between the two. The line of reasoning to which I would call attention is exemplified in John Dickinson's *An Address to the Committee of Correspondence in Barbados* (Philadelphia, 1766), and in his *Letters from a Farmer in Pennsylvania to the Inhabitants of the British Colonies* (Boston, 1768). From the former: "KINGS or parliaments could not *give the rights essential to happiness*, as you confess those invaded by the Stamp Act to be. We claim them from a higher source — from the Kings of kings, and Lord of all the earth. . . . It would be an insult on the divine Majesty to say, that he has given or allowed any man or body of men a *right to make me miserable*. If no man or body of men has *such a right*, I have a *right to be happy*. If there can be no happiness without freedom, I have a *right to be free*. If I cannot enjoy freedom without security of property, I have a *right to be thus secured*," pp. 4–5. From the *Letters from a Farmer*: "Let these truths be indelibly impressed on our minds — that we cannot be happy without being free — that we cannot be free, without being secure in our property — that we cannot be secure in our property, if, without our consent, others may, as by right, take it away — that taxes imposed on us by Parliament, do thus take it away. . . . " p. 137. Dickinson is here clearly placing happiness as a right logically prior to property and even to liberty, which stand in relation to it as means to end. James Wilson also emphasized happiness rather than property, stating that, "the happiness of the society is the *first* law of every government." Wilson, *Works*, III, 206.

By placing the *pursuit of happiness* in the Declaration, and omitting *property*, Jefferson gave official sanction to these views. If the Declaration had lapsed into obscurity, this departure from Locke's trilogy might not have been particularly important, except for the historical record. But the Declaration did not become an historian's document merely. It became an ideological force, and this helped to make Jefferson's substitution operative in actual political life. Of course one may also raise the question whether the Declaration would have had the influence that it has had, if the substitution had not been made. Needless to say, the omission of *property* from the Declaration did not keep it from becoming a dominant, if not the dominant, right during certain periods of United States history.

9 Ford, ed., *Works of Jefferson*, IX, 196.

10 This interpretation is presented at some length in my article, "Men of Little Faith: The Anti-Federalists on the Nature of Representative Government," *Wm. and Mary Qtly.*, 3d Ser., XII (1955), 3–43.

11 Hamilton, Madison, and Jay, *The Federalist*, ed., Wright, 89.

12 In a letter to John Adams in 1814, Jefferson criticized *The Republic* severely and speculated as to the reasons for Plato's reputation. His general estimate of the great philosopher is suggested by these references scattered throughout a lengthy passage: "the whimsies, the puerilities, and unintelligible jargon of this work," "nonsense," "foggy mind"; he also concluded that Plato's dialogues "are libels on Socrates." Jefferson to John Adams, July 5, 1814, in Ford, ed., *Works of Jefferson*, XI, 396–398.

The American Revolution as a Colonial War for Independence,
THOMAS C. BARROW

1 The major statements of the Becker-Beard approach are well known: Carl L. Becker, *The History of Political Parties in the Province of New York, 1760–1776* (Madison, 1909); Charles Beard, *An Economic Interpretation of the Constitution of the United States* (New

York, 1913); J. Franklin Jameson, *The American Revolution Considered as a Social Movement* (Princeton, 1926). Arthur M. Schlesinger's interpretation is summarized in his article, "The American Revolution Reconsidered," *Political Science Quarterly*, XXXIV (1919), 61–78. Jameson's views are re-evaluated in Frederick B. Tolles, "The American Revolution Considered as a Social Movement: A Re-evaluation," *American Historical Review*, LX (1954–55), 1–12. The Becker-Beard approach is currently carried on most sophisticatedly in the work of Merrill Jensen, particularly in *The Articles of Confederation: An Interpretation of the Social-Constitutional History of the American Revolution, 1774–1781* (Madison, 1948). For an interesting later review of his earlier position by Jensen himself see his article, "Democracy and the American Revolution," *Huntington Library Quarterly*, XX (1956–57), 321–341. Elisha P. Douglass, *Rebels and Democrats: The Struggle for Equal Political Rights and Majority Rule During the American Revolution* (Chapel Hill, 1955), summarizes many of the points of controversy and offers his own arguments for an "abortive" internal revolution. On the other side is Clinton L. Rossiter, *Seedtime of the Republic: The Origin of the American Tradition of Political Liberty* (New York, 1953). See also the treatment of the Revolution in Daniel J. Boorstin, *The Genius of American Politics* (Chicago, 1953). But the single work which most directly challenges the Becker-Beard approach is Robert E. Brown, *Middle-Class Democracy and the Revolution in Massachusetts, 1691–1780* (Ithaca, 1955). A convenient summary of the "Brown thesis" is in his article, "Democracy in Colonial Massachusetts," *New England Quarterly*, XXV (1952), 291–313. Bernard Bailyn, "Political Experience and Enlightenment Ideas in Eighteenth-Century America," *Amer. Hist. Rev.*, LXVII (1962–63), 339–351, accepts the argument that there was no internal political or social "revolution" but suggests that the true revolution lay in the Americans' intellectual acceptance of the "revolutionary" implications of their previous experiences concerning government and society. Some recent publications indicate a renewed emphasis on the radical social and political aspects of the American Revolution. See, for example, Gordon S. Wood, "A Note on Mobs in the American Revolution," *William and Mary Quarterly*, 3d Ser., XXIII (1966), 635–642. Of interest, too, is Wood's effort to graft Bernard Bailyn's "intellectual" view of the Revolution onto the older socioeconomic approach in "Rhetoric and Reality in the American Revolution," *ibid.*, 3–32. For another approach, see Jackson T. Main, "Government by the People: The American Revolution and the Democratization of the Legislatures," *ibid.*, 391–407; also Staughton Lynd, *Anti-Federalism in Dutchess County, New York* (Chicago, 1962).

2 The classic statement of the process of "revolution" and its application is Crane Brinton, *The Anatomy of Revolution*, rev. ed. (New York, 1952). See also the formula as worked out in Alfred Meusel, "Revolution and Counter-Revolution," Edwin R. A. Seligman, ed., *Encyclopedia of the Social Sciences* (New York, 1934), XIII, 367–375. But the work that has been most influential in relating the American Revolution to the European revolutionary tradition is Robert R. Palmer, *The Age of the Democratic Revolution: A Political History of Europe and America, 1760–1800*, I (Princeton, 1959).

3 An example of the relationship between colonial status and instability in colonial America is the Regulator movement in South Carolina. As Richard M. Brown points out in *The South Carolina Regulators* (Cambridge, Mass., 1963), the coastal inhabitants were willing to adjust themselves to the needs of the interior sections but were prevented from doing so by English policy decisions and interventions. The result was social and sectional cleavage and controversy. Another more general example, common to all colonies, is that of the currency problem. Any American attempts to solve the riddle of how to obtain and maintain an adequate currency were frustrated by English intervention, so that the problem remained as a continuous source of friction and instability.

4 For example, such has been the course of Ghana during and after Nkrumah, of Algiers during and after Ben Bella, and of Indonesia during and after Sukarno.

5 The best case study of the melting-pot aspect of colonial America is Dietmar Rothermund, *The Layman's Progress* (Philadelphia, 1961). Rothermund's reference to "indirection" as the key to political success is particularly suggestive. *Ibid.*, 93, 134, 140. Interestingly, Rothermund views the Great Awakening as at least partially an effort to use religion to create a bridge, to form a common ground, between the various groups; when religion

failed to accomplish this, logically the next development was the use of "patriotism," a "lay religion" acceptable on rational grounds, to fill the same need. *Ibid.*, 59, 62, 134.

6 Thomas Hutchinson to John Healy Hutchinson, Feb. 14, 1772, Hutchinson Letterbooks (transcripts), XXVII, 296–300, Massachusetts Historical Society, Boston.

7 Hutchinson to Richard Jackson, Apr. 21, 1766, *ibid.*, XXVI, 227–228.

8 Hutchinson to [?], Dec. 30, 1773, *ibid.*, XXVII, 608.

9 "A Dissertation on the Canon and Feudal Law" (1765), John Adams, *Works of John Adams*, ed. Charles F. Adams (Boston, 1850–56), III, 454.

10 "Novanglus," *ibid.*, IV, 131.

11 Bernard Bailyn, *The Ideological Origins of the American Revolution* (Cambridge, Mass., 1967), xi.

12 Speech to Congress, Mar. 4, 1797, Adams, *Works*, ed. Adams, IX, 105. During the Revolution itself Adams had written that "there has been more of this tranquillity and contentment, and fewer riots, insurrections, and seditions throughout the whole war, and in the periods of its greatest distress, than there was for seven years before the war broke out." Letter to Mr. Calkoen, Oct. 26, 1780, *ibid.*, VII, 305.

13 The distinguishing characteristics of "cosmopolitan" and "local" elites as developed by Robert K. Merton, *Social Theory and Social Structure* (Glencoe, 1957), chap. 10, "Patterns of Influence: Local and Cosmopolitan Influentials," are useful. See also, Alvin W. Gouldner, "Cosmopolitans and Locals: Towards an Analysis of Latent Social Roles," *Administrative Science Quarterly*, II (1957–58), 281–306, 444–480.

14 "It is paradoxical that the first constitution formed by democratic processes should be one of the most undemocratic of its time. Although drafted by a convention elected by manhood suffrage, it was not only one of the most aristocratic of the Revolutionary period but also more thoroughly ensured government by the upper classes than the constitution of 1778 rejected by the same electorate." Douglass, *Rebels and Democrats*, 211.

15 Jacob E. Cooke, ed., *The Federalist* (Middletown, Conn., 1961), 56–65. Madison considered the question of the appropriate size for political units further in Federalist 14, *ibid.*. 83–89.

16 Quoted in Cecelia M. Kenyon, *The Antifederalists* (Indianapolis, 1966), xci–xcii. Miss Kenyon's introduction to this collection is an expansion of her provocative article, "Men of Little Faith: The Anti-Federalists on the Nature of Representative Government," *Wm. and Mary Qtly.*, 3d Ser., XII (1955), 2–43. See also Stanley Elkins and Eric McKitrick, "The Founding Fathers: Young Men of the Revolution," *Pol. Sci. Qtly.*, LXXVI (1961), 200–216.

17 Quoted in Kenyon, *Antifederalists*, xcii.

18 Quoted in Edward Handler, *America and Europe in the Political Thought of John Adams* (Cambridge, Mass., 1964), 102.

19 *Ibid.*, 101. Elsewhere Handler comments that "Adams' experience had nothing in common with the concept of revolution as a total renovation of existing institutions previously condemned as denials and perversions of the natural order" and that "nothing affords more certain indication that the Americans underwent a special kind of revolution than the peculiar breed of revolutionary typified by Adams who carried it through." *Ibid.*, 106–107.

20 Speech to Congress, Mar. 4, 1797, Adams, *Works*, ed. Adams, IX, 107.

The Preservation of Colonial Democracy through Revolution,
ROBERT E. BROWN

1 X Adams, The Works of John Adams, 284 (Charles Francis Adams ed., 1850–56).

2 See Robert E. Brown, *Middle-Class Democracy and the Revolution in Massachusetts, 1691–1780* (1955), preface and footnote, p. 2.

3 Id. ch. I.

4 Hector St. John de Crèvecoeur, Letters from an American Farmer, 39–42, 55–58 (1940).

5 Benjamin Franklin, The Writings of Benjamin Franklin, III, 63–65, VIII, 603–13 (Smyth ed. 1907).

6 Id. at 362–63.

7 Hutchinson Papers, Massachusetts Archives, XXV, 207.

8 Id., XXVI, 95–96.

9 Comptroller Weare, "Observations on the British Colonies on the Continent of America," in I Massachusetts Historical Society Collections, 67–82.

10 "Journal of an Officer . . . 1765," Library of Congress Transcripts, British Museum, King's MSS., CCXIII, 126.

11 For economic advantages of poor men in America over the poor of Europe, see William Eddis, Letters from America, Historical and Descriptive, Comprising Occurrences from 1769, to 1777, Inclusive, 109–10 (1792); Thomas to William Preston, May 23, 1773, Preston Papers, Virginia Historical Society; Alexander Spotswood, The Official Letters of Alexander Spotswood, 2 vols. in Collections of the Virginia Historical Society, new series (Richmond, 1882, 1885), I, 3; Virginia Gazette, June 5, 1752; American Archives, ed. by Peter Force, 9 vols. (Washington, 1837–53), 5 Ser., III, 1459; "Thoughts concerning America by Mr. Hassenclever(n)," Shelburne Papers, film, Williamsburg.

12 William Proctor to his brother, July 1739 and November 19, 1742, Amelia County Deed Book 8, pp. 154–65 (VSL).

13 To John Fontaine, June 7, 1754, and to Moses Fontaine, March 30, 1757, Maury Papers, Alderman Library, University of Virginia. See also Eddis, Letters, pp. 142–43.

14 Jonathan Boucher, Reminiscences of an American Loyalist, 1738–1789, pp. 26–27 (Bouchier ed. 1925).

15 Gooch to My Lord Duke, May 2, 1740, and Gooch to ?, August 26, 1746, Gooch Papers, II, 588; III, 865 (Virginia Historical Society).

16 Fauquier to Amherst, c. 1759, Amherst Papers in British Transcripts, Public Record Office, War Office 34, v. 37, Pt. I, p. [38], Library of Congress.

17 Robert Beverley, The History and Present State of Virginia (1705), p. 274, 277–78 (Wright ed. 1947); The Statutes at Large; Being a Collection of all the Laws of Virginia . . . (Hening ed. 1809–23), II, 244; III, 304–29; IV, 37–42, 81–83; V, 424–28; Journals of the House of Burgesses, 1712–26, 65, 67–69, 72–73; Method of taking up land in Virginia, 1753, PRO, CO5, v. 1327, pp. 561–64 (Library of Congress); James Blair to ?, September 23, 1763, "Papers on Quitrents and Customs Confiscations," British Museum, Additional MSS. 38337, film, Alderman Library, U. Va.

18 William Nelson to Lords of Trade, October 18, 1770, House Journals, 1770–72, pp. xxii–xxv; Nelson to Hillsborough, October 15, 1770, PRO, CO5, v. 1348, pp. 198–99 (Library of Congress).

19 Abstracts of all Beverley and Borden deeds, Orange County Deed Books 6–16 and Augusta County Deed Books 1–19 (VSL).

20 William Gooch to Lords of Trade, November 6, 1728. Gooch Papers, I, 75–78 (VHS); William Nelson to Lords of Trade, October 18, 1770. House Journals, 1770–72, pp. xxii–xxv; Nelson to Hillsborough, October 15, 1770, PRO, CO5, v. 1348, pp. 198–99; Dinwiddie to Lords of Trade, June 16, 1753, PRO, CO5, v. 1327, pp. 530–31 (Lib. of Cong.).

21 November 24, 1757, November 8, 1762, and August 3, 1763, Preston Papers (VHS); Carter's Grove Account Book, 1764–86, pp. 42, 48 (VHS); Philip Ludwell Lee to William Lee, April 10, 1770, and July 24, 1772, Lee-Ludwell Papers (VHS); Virginia Gazette (R), December 1, 1768; I George Washington, The Writings of George Washington, 130, 135 (John C. Fitzpatrick ed. 1931); I George Washington, The Diaries of George Washington, 177, 314 (Fitzpatrick ed. 1925); House Journals, 1752–58, p. 380; VII Hening, Statutes, 22–25.

22 Virginia Gazette, August 20 and October 11 and 24, 1751; March 5 and October 12, 1752; July 21, 1768 (R); September 17 and 24, 1772 (P&D); Washington, Diaries, I, 178n., 282, 332; Washington Papers (Lib. of Cong.), XII, 56; Receipts, September 27, 1773, and March 17, April 7, and July 8, 1775, Robert Carter Papers (VHS).

23 Washington to Robert Cary and Company, February 13, 1764, Writings, II, 413–14; Virginia Gazette (P&D), July 23, 1773.

24 Peter to Moses Fontaine, March 30, 1757, Maury Papers (U. Va.).

25 Loudoun County Deed Book B, pp. 184, 192; Book C, pp. 207, 272, 282, 484; Book D, pp. 401, 404, 623; Book E, p. 60; Prince William County Deed Book B, p. 104; Book M, p. 79; Book P, pp. 34, 331; Book Q, pp. 70, 298, 340; Book R, p. 78; Richmond County Deed Book 10, p. 68 (VSL); Francis Jerdone to Captain Hugh Crawford, November 22, 1759, and September 2, 1762, Francis Jerdone Letterbook, 1756–1763, Jerdone Papers (William and Mary College Library); Virginia Gazette, March 5, 1752 and March 3, 1753.

26 Of the men who appear on the tax records as indentured servants, apprentices, overseers, or workers, very few remained in a community to become laborers. Of eighty-six such men on the Norfolk County tax lists in 1751, only fourteen appeared in 1771, and of these, twelve had acquired land or slaves or both. Norfolk County Tithables, 1751, 1771 (Virginia State Library).

27 Andrew Burnaby, Travels Through the Middle Settlements in North-America in the Years 1759 and 1760, p. 150 (1775).

28 IV Adams, Works 359; John Adams, The Familiar Letters of John Adams and his Wife, 120–21 (Adams ed. 1876).

29 The best account of primogeniture and entail is to be found in the excellent but unpublished doctoral dissertation by Clarence Ray Keim, "Influence of Primogeniture and Entail in the development of Virginia" (1926). The author and his wife have confirmed Keim's findings in a work on colonial Virginia which we hope to have in publication soon. For examples of entails that were broken, or in which the younger children were provided for out of the entailed estate, see VI Hening, Statutes 314–16, 321–24; VII, 636–38, 723–30. Eldest son Ralph Wormeley, who inherited all of his father's estate in "taille-male" had to pay his father's debts, £800 to sister Elizabeth; £500 each to sisters Judith, Sarah, and Agatha; keep his sisters until they married or were of age; educate his brother in England; and pay his brother £100 a year for fifteen years. (V Hening, Statutes, 85–89; VII, 628–30).

30 The usual practice of inheritance was a fairly equal division of property among the children. Robert Lewis of Albemarle County, Virginia, was typical except that he had more land than average. Of the sons, John received 1000 acres, including the land he had already received. Nicholas got the 1650 acres where the father lived, Robert received 1865 acres, Charles 1864 acres, and William 1896 acres. Five daughters received 1000 acres each. Albemarle County Will Book 2, p. 204. See also Norfolk County Deed Book H, p. 260; Lancaster County Deed Book 13, pp. 23, 253–54, 279, 301; Book 14, pp. 23, 29–31, 144; Essex County Will Book 11, p. 19. Before he died, Landon Carter expressed pride in the fact that he had maintained a large family, paid off the children's fortunes, and put out three sons with good estates without himself being seriously in debt. Landon Carter Diary, July 19, 1770 (U. Va.).

31 House Journals, 1752–58, p. 100 and passim; I Dinwiddie, The Official Records of Robert Dinwiddie, Lieutenant-Governor of the Colony of Virginia, 1751–1758, 30, in Collections of the Virginia Historical Society, vols. III and IV (1883).

32 Virginia Gazette (P&D), January 12, 1769.

33 Ibid., April 25, 1771.

34 Brown, Middle-Class Democracy, 2n., 38n., 61n.

35 Ibid., Ch. II; II Hening, Statutes 425; III, 26, 53–69, 404–15; IV, 133–34, 475–78; V, 204–07; VI, 261–65. Within the past few years, several books and articles support the thesis that most free adult white men were qualified to vote. See Robert E. Brown, "Democracy in Colonial Massachusetts," XXV New England Quarterly 291–313 (September, 1952); Richard P. McCormick, The History of Voting in New Jersey (1953); Theodore Thayer, Pennsylvania Politics and the Growth of Democracy, 1740–1776 (1953); David S. Lovejoy, Rhode Island Politics and the American Revolution (1958); Milton M. Klein, "Democracy and Politics in Colonial New York," New York History, XL., 221–45 (1959); Chilton Williamson, American Suffrage from Property to Democracy, 1760–1860 (1960); Charles S. Grant, Democracy in the Connecticut Frontier Town of Kent (1961).

36 II Hutchinson, The History of the Colony and Province of Massachusetts-Bay, 299–300 (Mayo ed. 1936).

37 To Israel Williams, May 19, 1749, Israel Williams Papers (Mass. Hist. Soc.).

38 Hutchinson Papers, Massachusetts Archives, XXVII, 339.

39 II Paine, The Complete Writings of Thomas Paine, 287–88 (Foner ed. 1945).

40 I Reed, Life and Correspondence of Joseph Reed, 36–37 (1847).

41 II Spotswood, Letters 1–2; Spotswood's answers to charges by the Assembly, March 25, 1719, PRO, CO5, v. 1318, pp. 576–79 (Lib. of Cong.).

42 Gooch to Lords of Trade, February 22, 1738/9, Gooch Papers, II, 529.

43 Dinwiddie to Lords of Trade, February 23, 1756, PRO, CO5, v. 1328, p. 360.

44 For Catholic voting, see Essex County Deed Book 27, pp. 248–52; Book 29, p. 94 (VSL); House Journals, 1761–65, pp. 126–30. On town voters, see ibid., pp. 88–90. John Fogg, orphan, was apprenticed for six years in 1752 and voted in 1758. William Gillam, aged 17 years, was apprenticed in 1756 until he was twenty-one years old and voted in 1761. Essex County Deed Book 25, p. 318; Book 26, pp. 34, 97; Book 27, pp. 100, 186, 241; election polls, Book 27, pp. 248–52; Book 28, pp. 95–99; Book 29, pp. 1–7; Book 30, pp. 235–42 (VSL). A comparison of Virginia tithable lists, quitrent rolls, deeds, and election polls shows that large numbers of tenants and overseers voted.

45 Brown, Middle-Class Democracy, ch. IV.

46 III Hening, Statutes, 236–45, 414; Virginia Gazette Supplement (P&D). June 14, 1770.

47 House Journals, 1770–72, pp. 187, 197, 268.

48 Ibid., 1712–26. pp. 182–83; 1752–58, pp. 61–62, 240; 1758–61, p. 82; 1761–65, p. 233; 1770–72, pp. 20, 37; William Preston to William Byrd, May 14, 1774, Draper MSS., 3QQ24 (Preston Papers, III, University of Wisconsin); Landon Carter Diary, March 13 and 31, 1752.

49 Brown, "Restriction of Representation in Colonial Massachusetts," XL Mississippi Valley Historical Review (1953); Middle-Class Democracy, Ch. IV; Lords of Trade to King, January 30, 1771, PRO, CO5, v. 1369, p. 40; Order in Council, ibid., v. 1334, p. 31; Royal Instructions to Lord Dunmore, February 7, 1771, Aspinwall Papers, Massachusetts Historical Society Collections, 4 Series, X, 635–36; Edmund Pendleton to William Preston, June 4, 1774, Draper MSS., 3QQ36 (Preston Papers, III).

50 For example, see John C. Miller, Origins of the American Revolution xiii–xix (1959).

51 I Shirley, Correspondence of William Shirley 1731–1760, pp. 88–89 (Lincoln ed. 1912). In most of the colonies, representatives received instructions on how to vote on various issues. When friends of Thomas Hutchinson were instructed to vote against him, Hutchinson wrote: "Instructions to restrain a representative from voting according to his judgment, however popular, always appeared to me unconstitutional and absurd." Hutchinson Papers, Massachusetts Archives, XXVI, 248. In Virginia, "aristocrat" John Robinson, Treasurer and Speaker of the House, argued that representatives were absolutely bound to vote as their constituents directed. Robinson was called "the most popular man in the country, . . . the idol of the people." Landon Carter Diary, October 17, 1754; Francis Fauquier to Lords of Trade, May 12, 1761, PRO, CO5, v. 1330, p. 89. In Virginia, the people could always be heard through a system of petitions that had to be certified to the General Assembly and had to be acted on once there. Most Virginia laws were the direct result of these petitions.

52 Landon Carter Diary, April 1, 1776.

53 More research is needed on representation, especially the economic status of both those who were elected and those whom the voters could have elected but did not. That representatives were not always wealthy men, however, is indicated by the following evidence. Joseph Fry of Andover, Massachusetts, was 243rd. on the tax list when he was representative in 1754, and Joshua Fry, who succeeded him in 1755, was thirty-seventh on the tax list. Andover Tax Lists, 1754, 1755. Oliver Partridge of Hatfield ranked sixteenth in taxes. Hatfield Town Records, I, 182–85. Amelia County, Virginia, elected Thomas Tabb, who rose from a modest holding of six slaves in 1742 to 112 tithable slaves and 11,028 acres of land in 1768. But the county also elected Captain Wood Jones in 1752, a man who paid only four tithes in 1742 and had only nine tithable slaves in 1782, and Edmund Booker in 1758, who owned three tithable slaves in 1742 and thirteen tithable slaves and 568 acres of land in 1768. Amelia Tithables, 1742, 1768, 1782 (VSL).

54 Adams, Familiar Letters, 120–21.

55 III Adams, Works, 456.

56 Id. at 457.

57 V Franklin, Writings, 209; IX, 87–88.

58 Andrew Burnaby noted a charity school "for sixty poor boys and girls" in New York in 1760. Burnaby, Travels, 61–67. Hugh Jones said that in 1724 there were schools in most parishes in Virginia. The Present State of Virginia, ed. by Richard L. Morton (Chapel Hill, 1956), pp. 98, 229n. There were free schools and charity schools in Virginia, in addition to private tutors and tuition schools. Virginia Gazette, January 2 and March 5, 1752, November 29, 1770 (R); Landon Carter Diary, March 12 and May 6, 1772; House Journals, 1752–58, pp. 119, 139, 163–64, 350; VI Hening, Statutes, 309, 389–92. Workers who desired an education could get it from private tutors. One Thomas Brooks, a carpenter who earned £30 a year and keep, paid tutor John Harrower £2 a year for evening and Sunday classes. John Harrower Diary, August 17 and December 6, 1774; January 10, 1775, Williamsburg. Tuition schools charged about £1 a year Virginia money, some four or five days' wages for a carpenter. William Proctor to his brother, November 9, 1742, Amelia County Deed Book, 8, p. 162 (VSL).

59 For example, see I Baldwin, The Stream of American History, 157 (1952).

60 Brown, Middle-Class Democracy, Ch. VI.

61 Burnaby, Travels, 61–67; IV New Jersey Historical Society, Proceedings, 1849–1850, 118–21 (1850).

62 William Robinson to [Bishop of London?], c. 1761, Fulham MSS — Virginia, Box 1, No. 117 (Lib. of Cong.).

63 I Hutchinson, History, 352.

64 Beverley, History, 264. Governor Spotswood told the Bishop of London that yearly agreements between the people and their ministers was the custom and that the people were very sensitive about any interference with their right. In 1719, a convention of the clergy sided with the people over the question of whether the governor or the vestry could select the minister. I Historical Collections Relating to the American Colonial Church, 199–247 (Perry ed. 1870–78). The Reverend Jonathan Boucher stated flatly that the clergy were dependent on "the People, and on them alone." Boucher, American Revolution, xlix–1. Boucher also contended that often several candidates vied for an appointment by preaching the kind of sermons that would appeal to the people. Boucher, Reminiscences, 102–03.

65 House Journals, 1758–61, 85, 104; VII Hening, Statutes, 301; VIII, 432–33; Robert Carter Papers, passim. Governor Gooch lamented in 1735 that "free thinkers multiply very fast having an eminent Layman for their leader." This was probably the Attorney-General, Sir John Randolph. Gooch to Bishop of London, July 8, 1735, Fulham MSS — Virginia, Box 1, No. 68; Gooch Papers, II, 392; Virginia Gazette, May 6, 1737.

66 A Letter from South Carolina . . . Written by a Swiss Gentleman, 23–24 (1718). For a typical picture of the wheels of justice in motion, see Lancaster County (Va) Court Orders, passim. (VSL).

67 Ibid.; Richmond County Order Book 14, p. 376; Richmond Rent Rolls (VSL); Maury to Reverend John Camm, December 12, 1763, House Journals, 1761–65, pp. li–lii; Petition of Archibald Cary to the General Court, June 9, 1756, Archibald Cary Papers, 1756–1785 (VHS).

68 Carl Lotus Becker, The History of Political Parties in the Province of New York, 5, 22 (1909).

69 For example, see James Truslow Adams, Revolutionary New England, 1691–1776 (1923); Arthur M. Schlesinger, The Colonial Merchants and the American Revolution, 1763–1776 (1918), and New Viewpoints in American History (1922); J. Franklin Jameson, The American Revolution Considered as a Social Movement (1926). Of these accounts, Jameson's is the most moderate in its emphasis on class conflict.

70 See such standard texts as John D. Hicks, A Short History of American Democracy 85 (1946) and I Morison and Commager, The Growth of the American Republic 199 (4th ed. 1950). Writers such as Merrill M. Jensen, The Articles of Confederation (1940), and John

C. Miller, Sam Adams, Pioneer in Propaganda (1936), and Origins of the American Revolution (1943) also strongly emphasized the dual revolution.
71 Brown, Middle-Class Democracy, Ch. VII–XV. . . .

The Mechanics in New York Politics, 1774–1788, STAUGHTON LYND

1 Carl L. Becker, The History of Political Parties in the Province of New York, 1760–1776 (Madison, 1909), pp. 5, 11, 22, 256, 275.
2 Specialized studies which confirmed Becker's portrayal of the underprivileged and radical mechanic included Arthur M. Schlesinger, Sr., The Colonial Merchants and the American Revolution, 1763–1776 (New York, 1918); Oscar T. Barck, Jr., New York City During the War for Independence: With Special Reference to the Period of British Occupation (New York, 1931), chap. 1; Herbert Morais, "The Sons of Liberty in New York," The Era of the American Revolution, ed. Richard B. Morris (New York, 1939), pp. 269–289; Eugene P. Link, Democratic-Republican Societies, 1790–1800 (New York, 1942); Richard B. Morris, Government and Labor in Early America (New York, 1946), especially pp. 188–189.
3 See e.g., Milton M. Klein, "Democracy and Politics in Colonial New York," New York History, XL (1959), 221–245, and Walter Hugins, Jacksonian Democracy and the Working Class: A Study of the New York Workingmen's Movement, 1829–1837 (Stanford, 1960).
4 See particularly Robert R. Palmer, "Popular Democracy in the French Revolution: Review Article," French Historical Studies, I (1960), 445–469. According to Georges Lefebvre in revolutionary Paris journeymen and apprentices customarily acted politically with their employers (The Coming of the French Revolution, tr. Robert R. Palmer [Princeton, 1947], p. 98). E. P. Thompson comments that English radicals Thomas Hardy and Francis Place were journeymen at one stage in their careers and master craftsmen at another (The Making of the English Working Class [London, 1963], p. 20).
5 Charles A. Beard, An Economic Interpretation of the Constitution of the United States (New York, 1913), pp. 24–26.
6 Carl Bridenbaugh, The Colonial Craftsman (New York, 1950), p. 155. [For an elaborate discussion of the contemporary meanings of the terms "mechanic," "artisan," and "tradesman" see now Charles S. Olton, "Philadelphia Artisans and the American Revolution" (Doctoral dissertation, University of California at Berkeley, 1967), pp. 3–16. This dissertation on the largest and most radical group of revolutionary artisans confirms the conclusion of the present essay with respect to the mechanics and the suffrage. See pp. 137, 137n., and 367.]
7 For example, William Goforth (one of the mechanics elected to the New York Assembly in 1785) is described in book after book as a "shoemaker" but also sold rum and dry goods (New York Journal, Dec. 2, 1784). William Gilbert, Anthony Post, and Thomas Ivers, three other mechanic politicians, owned property assessed at £5500, £3500, and £2000, respectively ("Tax-Payers of the City and County of New York, 1796," New-York Historical Society).
8 Carl Bridenbaugh, Cities in Revolt: Urban Life in America, 1743–1776 (New York, 1955), p. 283; Benjamin W. Labaree, Patriots and Partisans: The Merchants of Newburyport, 1764–1815 (Cambridge, Mass.; 1962), pp. 4–5.
9 Palmer, "Popular Democracy," p. 453.
10 Esther Forbes, Paul Revere and the World He Lived In (Boston, 1942), pp. 371–373, 396, 400, 416, 458–459.
11 Bridenbaugh, Colonial Craftsman, p. 129; Morris, Government and Labor, p. 42.
12 Barck, New York City, p. 140.
13 Morris, Government and Labor, p. 40. The New York Provincial Convention excused from military duty seventeen men at each furnace for melting iron into pigs; ten anchormakers, four carriers and a bellows-man at the anchor forge in Orange County; two master-workmen and two attendants at each paper mill; and two master-workmen and six laborers at each salt works (New-York Gazette, Aug. 26, 1776).
14 New York Packet, Aug. 5, 1788.

15 See Morris, *Government and Labor*, pp. 150–152, 156–166, 196–201. An illuminating incident occurred in September 1785. Journeymen carpenters employed in building a house for radical leader Isaac Sears publicly thanked him for continuing their wages at the "usual rate" notwithstanding "the ungenerous attempts of the Master-Carpenters to reduce them." In the next issue of the same newspaper the master-carpenters complained of Sears' partiality (*New York Packet*, Sept. 12 and 15, 1785).

16 For characterization of New York City neighborhoods, see T. E. V. Smith, *The City of New York in the Year of Washington's Inauguration, 1789* (New York, 1889), and Frank Monaghan and Marvin Lowenthal, *This Was New York: The Nation's Capital in 1789* (Garden City, N.Y.; 1943).

17 Franklin said of American workmen in the 1780's that they "all demand and obtain much higher wages than any other part of the world would afford them," and Tom Paine stated in *The Crisis*, No. 10, that the "income of a common laborer, who is industrious, is equal to that of the generality of tradesmen in England" (Benjamin Franklin, "The Internal State of America," ed. Verner W. Crane, *William and Mary Quarterly*, third series, XV [1958], 225; *The Complete Writings of Thomas Paine*, ed. Philip Foner [New York, 1945], I, 203). Monaghan and Lowenthal estimate that in 1789, when bread cost three cents a pound and beef three-and-a-half cents, a skilled workman in New York City earned fifty cents a day, an unskilled workman half as much (*This Was New York*, pp. 77, 80). Averages, of course, can be misleading: then as now there was an "other America."

18 Bridenbaugh, *Colonial Craftsman*, p. 169. Franklin testifies to the same effect in "The Internal State of America."

19 Noah Webster, "Description of New York," *New York Directory* (1786), p. xv.

20 *Life, Journals and Correspondence of Rev. Manasseh Cutler, L.L.D.* (Cincinnati, 1888), I, 309.

21 Duc de Francois A. F. Rochefoucauld Liancourt, *Travels Through the United States of America* (London, 1799), II, 672.

22 H. N. Brailsford, *The Levellers and The English Revolution* (London, 1961), p. 128. Franklin, remembering his own beginnings, provided in his will for a loan fund for young tradesmen; similarly Paine, in *Agrarian Justice*, proposed that the state give £15 to every young person reaching the age of twenty-one (Carl Van Doren, *Benjamin Franklin* [New York, 1938], pp. 762–763; *Complete Writings of Paine*, ed. Foner, I, 612–613, 618).

23 *To the Worthy and Industrious Mechanics of this State* [Dec. 1783], broadside, N.-Y.H.S.; *New York Packet*, Feb. 24, 1785.

24 The tax assessments by ward in 1790 are given in *The Iconography of Manhattan Island* ed. Isaac N. Phelps Stokes (six volumes; New York, 1915–1928), V, 1259. The figures for 1793 are comparable: East Ward £837,445; Out Ward £243,728 ("Tax-Payers of the City and County of New York, 1793," N.-Y.H.S.). Voters (by which is here meant persons qualified to vote for state assemblymen) in 1790 are enumerated in the electoral census of that year, *New York Daily Advertiser*, Jan. 15, 1791.

25 See Michael D'Innocenzo, "Voting in Colonial New York" (Master's thesis, Columbia University, 1959), Appendix A, p. 78. We have no electoral census for the colonial era. In 1768, 1924 voters cast ballots in New York City, or 52 per cent of the adult males over 21; in 1769, 1515 or 40 per cent of the adult males voted. Assuming that not all the eligible voters cast ballots, D'Innocenzo concluded that 50 to 60 per cent of the adult men were eligible to vote. [See also Roger J. Champagne, "Liberty Boys and Mechanics of New York City, 1764–1774," *Labor History*, VIII (1967), 123–133, for an analysis of the 1768–1769 poll lists which concludes that two-thirds of the city's adult white males could vote and that one-half of these were mechanics.]

26 See, on the one hand, Becker, *History of Political Parties*, p. 11, and Beard, *Economic Interpretation of the Constitution*, p. 67; and in opposition, Robert E. Brown, *Charles Beard and the Constitution: A Critical Analysis of "An Economic Interpretation of the Constitution"* (Princeton, 1956), pp. 63–64, and Klein, "Democracy and Politics," p. 237.

27 "A Number of Tradesmen," *Pennsylvania Gazette*, Sept. 27, 1770, quoted by Charles H. Lincoln, *The Revolutionary Movement in Pennsylvania, 1760–1776* (Philadelphia, 1901), p. 80n.

28 Roger J. Champagne, "The Sons of Liberty and the Aristocracy in New York Politics" (Doctoral dissertation, University of Wisconsin, 1960), p. 3. In a dissertation on the role of sailors in pre-Revolutionary New York politics, Jesse Lemisch contends that as early as 1765 lower-class elements advocated a distinct "radical" policy of carrying on trade without stamps, while "liberal" merchants espoused non-importation. However, the generalization that workingmen followed mercantile leadership until 1774 is not invalidated if one accepts Lemisch's argument; for he agrees with previous scholars that the Stamp Act mobs followed ship captains such as Isaac Sears and Alexander McDougall. See L. Jesse Lemisch, "Jack Tar vs. John Bull: The Role of New York's Seamen in Precipitating the Revolution" (Doctoral dissertation, Yale University, 1962).

29 Becker, *Political Parties*, p. 120. [See now Bernard Mason, *The Road to Independence: The Revolutionary Movement in New York, 1773–1777* (Lexington, 1966), pp. 15*n.*, 21*n.*, 23*n.*, 27*n.*, for additional evidence that the Mechanics Committee was not simply a continuation of the Sons of Liberty, and represented the assumption by mechanics of a more independent role in politics.]

30 I have found six chairmen of the Committee of Mechanics during 1774–1776: Jonathan Blake, Daniel Dunscomb, Nathan Tylee, Christopher Duyckinck, Lewis Thibou and Malcolm McEwen (Becker, *Political Parties*, pp. 120*n.*, 165*n.*; *New York Journal*, Apr. 11, 1776; *New York Packet*, Apr. 11, 1776; *New-York Gazette*, June 10 and 17, 1776). Duyckinck was a sail-maker and Dunscomb a cooper (*New-York Gazette*, July 23, 1770; *New York Packet*, Aug. 5, 1788). A revolutionary group in Boston on the eve of Independence, the "Loyal Nine," included a printer, a jeweler, two distillers, two braziers, and a master mariner (Bridenbaugh, *The Colonial Craftsman*, p. 175).

31 Isaac Sears and John Lamb had left, Alexander McDougall was absorbed in military duties (see Champagne, "New York Politics and Independence, 1776," *New-York Historical Society Quarterly*, XLVI [1962], 281–282).

32 Becker, *Political Parties*, p. 113*n.*

33 Gouverneur Morris to Mr. Penn, May 20, 1774, *American Archives*, ed. Peter Force, fourth series, I (Washington, D.C.; 1837), 342–343.

34 Champagne, "New York and the Intolerable Acts, 1774," *New-York Historical Society Quarterly*, XLV (1961), 204*n.*

35 Political memorandum of May 20, 1774, Alexander McDougall Papers, New-York Historical Society, quoted in Champagne, "New York and the Intolerable Acts," p. 206.

36 Thomas Young to John Lamb, June 19, 1774, Lamb Papers, N.-Y.H.S.

37 Broadside of July 6, 1774, quoted in Becker, *Political Parties*, p. 123*n.*

38 See *ibid.*, pp. 119–136.

39 Contrast *ibid.*, 118*n.* with Champagne, "New York and the Intolerable Acts," pp. 200–201. Champagne is almost certainly correct; and the point is of some importance, for it indicates that a national government was promoted by radical rather than — as Becker may have wanted to suppose — by conservatives.

40 Schlesinger, Sr., *The Colonial Merchants and the American Revolution*, p. 432.

41 Becker, *Political Parties*, pp. 155–156.

42 *Ibid.*, p. 161*n.*, pp. 162–163.

43 *Ibid.*, pp. 165–168.

44 *Ibid.*, p. 198. The other three were Abraham Brasher, Theophilus Anthony and Jeremiah Platt.

45 In the spring of 1776 the officers of the Committee of Inspection were: chairman, Henry Remsen; deputy chairman, John Broome; secretary, Joshua Winter. The Sub-Committee of Secrecy and Inspection consisted of William Mercier, Daniel Phoenix, Anthony L. Bleecker, Garret Abeel, James Alner, John Stagg (*New-York Gazette*, Feb. 12 and Mar. 11, 1776).

46 Robert R. Palmer, *The Age of the Democratic Revolution: A Political History of Europe and America, 1760–1800*, I (Princeton, 1959), 4–5.

47 Address of the General Committee of Mechanics to the Provincial Congress, May 29, 1776 and address of the General Committee of Mechanics to the Committee of Inspection, Apr. 1, 1776, *New-York Gazette*, June 10 and Apr. 8, 1776.

48 *Ibid.*, Mar. 18, 1776.
49 *Ibid.*, Apr. 8, 1776.
50 *New York Journal*, Apr. 11, 1776.
51 *New York Packet*, Apr. 11, 1776.
52 *New-York Gazette*, June 10, 1776.
53 *Ibid.*, June 17, 1776.
54 Among the political propositions of Paine's *Common Sense* are the following: That representative government is necessary in large societies but should approximate as closely as possible a direct democracy in which each citizen participates; that representatives should be apportioned equally, and rotated by frequent elections; that governments should be limited by written constitutions, providing for the security of persons and property and "above all things, the free exercise of religion." Paine helped to draft the most democratic state constitution of the Revolution, Pennsylvania's. He called it "an open constitution . . . which considers mankind as they came from their maker's hands — *a mere man*, before it can be known what shall be his fortune or his state." (*Complete Writings of Paine*, II, 283, 285). For discussion of these ideas in the New York City press in the spring of 1776, see e.g., "Independent Whig" and "Essex" in the *New York Journal*, Feb. 22, 29, Mar. 7, 14, 28, Apr. 4, 1776; "The Interest of America" in *ibid.*, June 6, 13, 20, 1776; "To the Freeborn Sons of America," "On the Different Kinds of Government," "To the Printer of the New-York Packet," *New York Packet*, Mar. 21, 28, Apr. 18, 1776; and the essays of "Cato" and "Cassandra" in the *New-York Gazette*.
55 *New-York Gazette*, June 10, 1776.
56 *Ibid.*, June 17, 1776.
57 Champagne, "Sons of Liberty," p. 508.
58 As to the axes, see Timothy Pickering to Philip Schuyler, Nov. 18, 1783, Schuyler Papers, New York Public Library.
59 See note 65 below regarding these petitions of 1779.
60 *Votes and Proceedings of the Assembly*, various places and dates, for Mar. 15, 1779; Feb. 4 and Mar. 8, 1780; Mar. 9, 1782; Mar. 3, 1786.
61 [On rural radicalism in New York during the War for Independence, see Essay 2 in Staughton C. Lynd, *Class Conflict, Slavery, and the United States Constitution* (Indianapolis and New York, 1967), 25–61.]
62 It was easier for New York City refugees to advocate heavy taxation while the war was in progress since their own property was behind the British lines and could not be taxed.
63 *Votes and Proceedings of the Assembly* (Fishkill, 1779) for Sept. 18, Oct. 9, 1779.
64 *New York Packet*, Apr. 13, 20, 1780. I am obliged to Mr. Robin Brooks for calling these passages to my attention.
65 *Votes and Proceedings of the Assembly* (Fishkill, 1779) for Oct. 17, 1779.
66 Alexander Hamilton to John Jay [June 26, 1779], *The Papers of Alexander Hamilton*, ed. Harold C. Syrett (New York, 1961–), II, 82.
67 Brutus, *To All Adherents to the British Government and Followers of the British Army Commonly called Tories* . . . (Poughkeepsie, Aug. 15, 1783) and *The Memorial of the Subscribers, in Behalf of Themselves and Others, the Refugee Citizens of New-York* (Newburgh, Sept. 1, 1783), broadsides, N.-Y.H.S. The British officers and Tory inhabitants of New York City, as well as the more well-to-do refugee Whigs, feared during the summer and fall of 1783 that "the lower Classes" would take advantage of the return to the city to seize and plunder property (see chap. VII of my "The Revolution and the Common Man: Farm Tenants and Artisans in New York Politics, 1777–1788" [Doctoral dissertation, Columbia University, 1962]).
68 *Independent New York Gazette*, Nov. 22, 1783.
69 Juvenis, *To the Mechanicks and Free Electors of the City and County of New-York* (Dec. 23, 1783) and A Citizen, *To the Electors of the City of New-York* (Dec. 26, 1783), broadsides, N.-Y.H.S. The nominating meeting of the Committee of Mechanics on Dec. 27 is described in another broadside at N.-Y.H.S. The results of the election, according to the *New York Packet*, Jan. 1, 1784, were:

Marinus Willett	249	Peter V. B. Livingston	35
John Lamb	239	Comfort Sands	31
Henry Rutgers	231	James Beckman	25
Isaac Sears	223	John Morin Scott	17
John Stagg	215	Henry Remsen	11
William Malcolm	212	John Broome	5
Robert Harpur	209	Samuel Broome	5
Peter P. Van Zandt	204	Alexander Hamilton	4
Hugh Hughes	180	Gulien Verplank	3
		Samuel Dodge	2
Daniel Dunscomb	53	John Berrien	2
Evert Bancker	51	Daniel Phoenix	1
Thomas Randall	47	Isaac Stotenburgh	1

The election took place by show of hands at City Hall (*New York Gazetteer*, Dec. 10, 1783). Alexander Hamilton said later that few besides those who had been refugees voted in this election. He also implied that all refugees were permitted to vote upon swearing an oath of loyalty because "if the returning citizens were not at this juncture gratified, tumults were by some apprehended" (*A Second Letter from Phocion to the Considerate Citizens of New-York* [New York, 1784], p. 22).

[70] Meetings of the Committee of Mechanics are reported in *New York Packet*, Jan. 15, 1784; *New York Journal*, Mar. 18, 1784; *Independent Journal*, May 12, 1784; *New York Packet*, May 31, 1784.

[71] *New York Packet*, Apr. 25, 1785 and Apr. 24, 1786; *New York Journal*, Apr. 26, 1787.

[72] *Independent Gazette*, Jan. 29, 1784.

[73] *New Jork Journal*, Feb. 24, 1785.

[74] For the speed with which Tory merchants regained their economic footing after the British evacuation, compare the lists in *Colonial Records of the New York Chamber of Commerce, 1768–1774*, ed. John A. Stevens (New York, 1867), pp. 295, 306, and see Oscar Zeichner, "The Loyalist Problem in New York after the Revolution," *New York History*, XXI (1940), 301. William Seton was the Loyalist Treasurer of the Bank of New York, and Daniel McCormick and Joshua Waddington its Loyalist Directors (*New York Packet*, Mar. 18, 1784). "We never had so much to fear from their arms, as from their influence and wealth," a newspaper correspondent warned. "They hope by their influence in a Bank, to lay the foundation of power, whereby they may not only aid each other in commercial matters, but silence every Whig character who applies to them for aid." (*Independent Gazette*, Mar. 11, 1784). For his role in aiding such Tories, a "Mechanic" attacked Alexander Hamilton in the spring of 1784 as "the confidential or ridiculous earwig of our late worthy General . . . the little, pompose, stripling delegate — the Jack-Daw of public affairs . . . Fox instead of Phocion" (*New York Journal*, Mar. 25, 1784). "Phocion" compounded his sins in mechanic eyes by opposing trade unions as monopolies. *A Letter from Phocion to the Considerate Citizens of New York* (New York, 1784), p. 11.

[75] A Battered Soldier, *To the Whig Mechanicks of the City and County of New-York* (Dec. 27, 1783), broadside, N.-Y.H.S. A Friend to Mechanics replied in kind: "In all countries, it is no uncommon practice for men, grasping at power, to call first upon the Mechanicks, and endeavour to use them as mere Ladders to their ungovernable ambition" (*To the Worthy and Industrious Mechanics of this State*, broadside, N.-Y.H.S.).

[76] *Independent Gazette*, Jan. 24, 1784; *New York Gazetteer*, Mar. 31, 1784.

[77] Petition of Oct. 8, 1784. Papers of the Bank of New York, New York City. The petition observed that before the Revolution the common remedy had been bills of credit, but that after the experiences of the war, bank paper was more likely to command confidence.

[78] Petition of Feb. 10, 1785, Papers of the Bank of New York. There were other reasons for the estrangement between Sears, Lamb, and Willett and their old mechanic followers. Sears had grown wealthy during the war and when he returned to New York City moved into No. 1 Broadway, the home which had been occupied by the British commander, Sir Henry Clinton (Robert J. Christen, "Isaac Sears: Radical in Rebellion" [Master's thesis,

Columbia University, 1953], p. 50). In 1784 Lamb was appointed Collector of Customs for the Port of New York and Willett was appointed Sheriff for the City and County of New York, thus they became, unnaturally for them, duty-bound to oppose riots.

79 The Bank of New York's earliest ledger-book of customers, for 1787–1788, shows the name of such radical merchants as John Broome, Peter Curtenius, David Gelston, Nathaniel Hazard, Isaac Ledyard, Brockholst Livingston, Henry Rutgers, Paschal Smith, [Melancton] Smith and Wyckoff, Marinus Willett and Wynant Van Zandt, but so far as I could tell no prominent mechanics (Papers of the Bank of New York).

80 *New York Journal*, May 13, 1784 and "Mechanic," *ibid.*, Mar. 25, 1784.

81 Lending money was one of the five purposes of the General Society of Mechanics and Tradesmen (*New York Packet*, Feb. 17, 1785). Originally the mechanics asked for a loan fund of £3000; the legislature whittled the sum to £1500 before sending the bill to the Council of Revision, where it was vetoed (Charles Tillinghast to Hugh Hughes, Feb. 26, 1786, Lamb Papers). Nevertheless the General Society went ahead and loaned sums of not less than £100, giving preference to members, on three-fold security in New York City real estate; in December 1787, the minimum loan was lowered to £50 (*Annals of the General Society of Mechanics and Tradesmen of the City of New-York from 1775 to 1880*, ed. Thomas Earle and Charles T. Congdon [New York, 1882], p. 11; minutes of the General Society of Mechanics and Tradesmen, library of the Society, Dec. 14, 1787).

82 *New York Packet*, Feb. 24, 1785.

83 Hugh Hughes to Charles Tillinghast, Mar. 7, 1785, Lamb Papers.

84 *Annals of the General Society*, p. 12.

85 *New York Packet*, Apr. 7, 1785.

86 *Ibid.*, Apr. 14, 1785.

87 The successful Assembly candidates were (*New York Journal*, May 5, 1785):

William Malcolm	666	William Duer	624
William Denning	663	Robert Boyd	623
John Stagg	661	Evert Bancker	623
William Goforth	660	Isaac Sears	574
Robert Troup	641		

With the exception of Troup, all these men had been nominated by the Committee of Mechanics. Interestingly enough, however, the previous year Goforth and another mechanic, Daniel Dunscomb, had run on a conservative slate which triumphed over the Sons of Liberty candidates headed by Sears (for the votes by ward of the 1784 election, see *Independent Journal*, May 1, 1784).

88 *New York Daily Advertiser*, Apr. 1, 1786.

89 *Ibid.*, Apr. 5, 1786.

90 Becker, *Political Parties*, 161n.; *New York Daily Advertiser*, Apr. 14, 1786.

91 *Ibid.*, Apr. 15, 1786.

92 *New York Packet*, Apr. 24, 1786; *Independent Journal*, Apr. 26, 1786.

93 Philip Schuyler wrote to Stephen Van Rensselaer, Apr. 20, 1786: "Colo. Hamilton will serve if elected. The Quakers, Merchants, and some of the Mechanics are for him, but part of the latter averse" (quoted in E. Wilder Spaulding, *New York in the Critical Period, 1783–1789* [New York, 1932], p. 111).

The American Revolution and the Democratization of the Legislatures,
JACKSON TURNER MAIN

1 See Richard Buel, Jr., "Democracy and the American Revolution: A Frame of Reference," *William and Mary Quarterly*, XXI (1964), 165–190.

2 "Z. Y.," Apr. 23, 1764. Other characteristic newspaper articles praising a balanced government and disparaging a democratic one are, "A Son of Liberty," *Providence Gazette, and Country Journal*, Oct. 26, 1771; *Pennsylvania Chronicle, and Universal Advertiser*

(Philadelphia), Aug. 29, Sept. 26, 1768, Aug. 14, 1769; *New-York Gazette: and the Weekly Mercury*, Apr. 23, May 14, 1770; Purdie and Dixon's *Virginia Gazette* (Williamsburg), Oct. 27, 1768; *Connecticut Journal* (New Haven), Mar. 17, 1769; *Newport Mercury*, Nov. 21, 1763.

3 Rind's *Va. Gazette* (Williamsburg), June 9, 1768.

4 Dec. 30, 1768, in *Journal of the Legislative Council of the Colony of New-York . . . 1743 . . . 1775* (Albany, 1861).

5 *Maryland Gazette* (Annapolis), Dec. 3, 1767.

6 *South Carolina Gazette* (Charleston), Sept. 21, 1769.

7 A discussion of the distribution of property and income is contained in Jackson Turner Main, *The Social Structure of Revolutionary America* (Princeton, 1965).

8 Biographical information is reasonably complete for 30 of the 34. Genealogies and town histories were the principal sources. The *New Hampshire Provincial and State Papers* contain much useful information, especially probate records, and the *New England Historical and Genealogical Register* is valuable.

9 Especially important for New York biographies are the volumes of wills included among the *Collections* of the New York Historical Society, and the *New York Biographical Record*.

10 In 1769 four new members were added, and six more were chosen in 1772. The *New Jersey Archives* include several volumes of wills. Tax records, the earliest of which date from 1773, supply data on real estate but not on nonfarm property. They have been microfilmed from originals in the New Jersey State Library, Trenton.

11 The *Maryland Historical Magazine* contains a great deal of biographical data. Essential are the unpublished tax lists in the Maryland State Archives, Annapolis, and the Maryland Historical Society, Baltimore.

12 The 1773 legislature was chosen for study because the tax records of 1782, which are the earliest available, would be most nearly valid in determining the property of the members. The Virginia State Library, Richmond, contains the tax records as well as a remarkable collection of local records on microfilm. E. G. Swem, comp., *Virginia Historical Index* (Roanoke, 1934–36), I–II, is useful.

13 The *South Carolina Historical Magazine* is essential, as is Emily Bellinger Reynolds and Joan Reynolds Faunt, eds., *Biographical Directory of the Senate of South Carolina 1776–1964* (Columbia, 1964). There are some quit rent and probate records in the State Archives building at Columbia.

14 For the development of democratic ideas after 1774, see Merrill Jensen, "Democracy and the American Revolution," *Huntington Library Quarterly*, XX (1957), 321–341. The entrance of many new men into the upper house, and their transformation into more nearly democratic institutions, is emphasized in Main, "Social Origins of a Political Elite: The Upper House in the Revolutionary Era," *ibid.*, XXVII (1964), 147–158. The point will be elaborated in a forthcoming book.

15 Strafford County, which contained the commercial center of Dover, extended north through what are now Belknap and Carroll Counties, then just under settlement.

16 So many men in the 1785 legislature are obscure that the figure cannot be exact, but it is a safe assumption that those who lived in the country and whose occupations are not given in local histories, genealogies, or other published sources, were farmers. Ordinarily men of importance, or business and professional men, are discussed in such sources, so that if one conscientiously searches the published materials, including of course the wills, most of those men who remain unidentified can be confidently termed farmers of moderate property.

17 As far as the fathers of these legislators could be identified, 12 of the prewar 28 were merchants, lawyers, and large landowners, as were 12 or possibly 13 of the postwar 66.

18 Those of unknown property or occupation are excluded.

19 The proportion of self-made men in the House seems to have increased from one fifth to one fourth, but information on the delegates' fathers is too incomplete for precision. Material on land and slave ownership is drawn from manuscript census and tax records as well as from the usual secondary materials. The median acreage declined from

1,400 acres to 1,000 acres; the median number of slaves owned decreased from about 40 to 20. My figures are on two thirds of the men. Charles A. Barker gives 2,400 acres as the average for the 1771 legislature. *The Background of the Revolution in Maryland* (New Haven, 1940), 384.

20 Data for land was obtained on 78 per cent of the 1773 Burgesses and 83 per cent of the delegates in the 1785 house. Percentages for slaves are 70 and 86 respectively. Tax lists beginning in 1782 were the most important source, supplemented by probate records and statements in secondary sources.

21 *Economic status of Mass. Representatives (percentages)*

	1765	*1784 duplicate towns*	*1784 total*
wealthy	17	8	6.5
well-to-do	33	17	15
moderate	40	55	51.5
unknown	10	20	27

Probably most of those whose property is unknown had only moderate incomes. Similarly the proportion of men from prominent old families dropped from 22 per cent to 6 per cent, college educated delegates from 27 per cent to 9 per cent, and representatives whose fathers were well-to-do from 30 per cent to 10 per cent, the change being greatest in the new towns but occurring everywhere.

22 This table analyzes the property of about 900 representatives. The economic status of 85 per cent was discovered with reasonable certainty. Most of the rest were dealt with by informed guesswork. No one was admitted to the wealthy category unless their property was certainly known. Lawyers were assumed to be well-to-do, for almost all of them were. Merchants were also considered well-to-do if they lived in an important urban center, but inland shopkeepers were not. Doctors and judges were distributed on similar principles. Artisans were almost always of moderate property. Farmers and those whose occupation was unknown composed the two largest groups. Those who came from the inland, semi-subsistence communities were almost never well-to-do, the exceptions being conspicuous men, so that if nothing was discovered about them they were almost certainly of moderate means. On the other hand those who lived in the well-developed commercial farm areas were often well-to-do, so they were not assigned to any category unless other information was available. The basis for this procedure was derived from extensive study of property holdings as discussed in my *Social Structure of Revolutionary America*. By such an analysis the proportion of unknowns was reduced to 3 1/3 per cent, most of whom were probably of moderate property. They are eliminated in the table. Percentages for occupation are less accurate, especially those for the post-war South.

23 Illustrations of this antidemocratic bias among Whig spokesmen are numerous, e.g., "A faithful Friend to his Country," *Independent Chronicle* (Boston), Aug. 7, 1777; "The Free Republican," *Boston Magazine*, Aug. 1784, pp. 420–423; "Constitutionalist," *Connecticut Courant* (Hartford), Apr. 10, 1786; "Honestus," *Vermont Gazette* (Bennington), Sept. 18, 1786; "Lycurgus," *Massachusetts Spy* (Worcester), July 12, 26, Aug. 2, 1775; Samuel Chase, *Md. Gazette*, Dec. 11, 1777; "Agricola," *Pennsylvania Packet* (Philadelphia), Feb. 6, 1779; "A Citizen of New Jersey," *New Jersey Gazette* (Trenton), Oct. 10, 1785; and *Falmouth Gazette*, Sept. 17, 1785.

24 *American Herald* (Boston), Dec. 11, 1786.

25 *Gazette of the State of Georgia* (Savannah), Jan. 1, 1789.

26 *Mass. Spy*, July 5, 1775.

27 *Weekly Monitor* (Litchfield), Aug. 6, 1787. For two more examples see "A Watchman," *Pa. Packet*, June 10, 17, 1776; and *Maryland Journal, and Baltimore Advertiser*, Feb. 18, 1777.

28 Jedidiah Morse, *The American Geography* . . . (2d ed., London, 1792), 387.

29 To Samuel Pleasants, Nov. 23, 1776, *Virginia Magazine of History and Biography*, XV (1908), 357.

A Fear of Conspiracy against Liberty, BERNARD BAILYN

1 [Charles F. Adams, ed., *The Works of John Adams*, 10 vols. (Boston, 1850–1856)], III, 477. For characteristic encomiums on the constitution and descriptions of its operating balance, see James Otis, *Rights of the British Colonies* (Boston, 1764: JHL Pamphlet 7), p. 47; [Daniel] Dulaney, *Considerations [on the Propriety of Imposing Taxes in the British Colonies for the Purpose of Raising a revenue* . . . ([Annapolis], 1765)] (JHL Pamphlet 13), p. 15; [Stephen] Johnson, *[Some Important] Observations* [(Newport, 1766)], pp. 27 ff.; [Peter] Whitney, *[The] Transgressions [of a Land* . . . *Two Discourses* . . . (Boston, 1774)], p. 10; [Moses] Mather, *America's Appeal [to an Impartial World* (Hartford, 1775)], pp. 7–8, 34 ff. [JHL Pamphlet refers to the number of the pamphlet in *Pamphlets of the American Revolution.*—Ed.]

2 Adams, *Works*, III, 478–479. . . .

3 *A Letter to the People of Pennsylvania* (Philadelphia, 1760: JHL Pamphlet 2), p. 3; Adams, *Works*, III, 479; Otis, *Rights* (JHL Pamphlet 7), p. 47; Johnson, *Observations*, p. 28.

4 [Robert Carter Nicholas], *Considerations on the Present State of Virginia Examined* ([Williamsburg], 1774), in the Earl G. Swem edition (New York, 1919), p. 40.

5 On the origins of this theory of the English constitution, see Corinne C. Weston, "Beginnings of the Classical Theory of the English Constitution," *Proceedings of the American Philosophical Society*, 100 (1956), 133–144, and the same author's article in the *English Historical Review*, 75 (1960), 410–425. On its popularity in the eighteenth century, see Stanley Pargellis, "The Theory of Balanced Government," in Conyers Read, ed., *The Constitution Reconsidered* (New York, 1938), pp. 37–49. . . .

6 The matching of social powers with powers of government was inadequately worked out even by Montesquieu, though he clearly defined the functions of government as legislative, executive, and judicial. See *Spirit of the Laws* (Franz Neumann, ed., New York, 1949), bk. xi, sec. 6 (especially p. 156; cf. p. lviii). For a detailed account of the intense discussion of Montesquieu and the doctrine of the separation of powers in Massachusetts in 1763, see Ellen E. Brennan, *Plural Office-Holding in Massachusetts 1760–1780* (Chapel Hill, 1945), chap. ii.

7 Mather, *America's Appeal*, p. 8.

8 Adams, *Works*, III, 481; cf. *Four Letters on Interesting Subjects* (Philadelphia, 1776), p. 21.

9 *Letter to the People of Pennsylvania* (JHL Pamphlet 2), pp. 4, 5, 7.

10 Thus Dickinson: ". . . the government here is not only *mixed* but *dependent*, which circumstance occasions *a peculiarity in its form* of a very delicate nature" (*Farmer's Letters*, in [Paul L. Ford, ed., *Writings of John Dickinson* in *Memoirs of the Historical Society of Pennsylvania*, XIV (1895)], p. 386). For an example of the critical importance that, at the height of the crisis, would be attached to the question of how the colonies shared in "the democracy" of the English constitution, see [John] Adams ("Novanglus"), *Novanglus and Massachusettensis* [Boston, 1819], pp. 79 ff. A common assumption, which would evolve into a central point of Revolutionary theory, was that the colonists upon leaving England had "totally disclaim[ed] all *subordination* to and dependence upon the two inferior estates of their mother country" ([William] Hicks, *Nature and Extent of Parliamentary Power* [Philadelphia, 1768], p. 6). Behind the lack of definition of the imperial constitution before 1763 and of the colonies' involvement in it lay the more basic question of the meaning of the British "empire" itself. The concept when applied to the American colonies had only a special and restricted meaning. See Richard Koebner, *Empire* (Cambridge, England, 1961), chap. iii, esp. pp. 77 ff.

11 Levi Hart, *Liberty Described and Recommended* . . . (Hartford, 1775), p. 13 (cf. p. 9); [John Allen], *The Watchman's Alarm* . . . (Salem, 1774), p. [5]. As Allen points out, his definition of liberty — "the true etymology of the word" — was taken from Daniel Fenning's *Royal English Dictionary* (London, 1761). On the antecedents to such definitions of

Montesquieu, Rapin, and Bolingbroke, see Neumann's introduction to *The Spirit of the Laws*, p. xlix–liii.

12 [John Dickinson], *An Address to the Committee of Correspondence in Barbados* . . . (Philadelphia, 1766), in Ford, *Writings*, p. 262; [James Otis], *A Vindication of the British Colonies* (Boston, 1765: JHL Pamphlet 11), p. 8; *Votes and Proceedings of [the Freeholders . . . of . . . Boston* (Boston [1772])], pp. 7–8.

13 Dulany, *Considerations* (JHL Pamphlet 13), p. 30; *Votes and Proceedings of Boston*, p. 8; Otis, *Vindication* (JHL Pamphlet 11), p. 32.

14 Mather, *America's Appeal*, p. 8; [James] Lovell, *Oration* [Boston, 1771], p. 11.

15 Jonathan Mayhew, *Observations on the Charter and Conduct of the Society for the Propagation of the Gospel in Foreign Parts* . . . (Boston, 1763), pp. 103–108.

16 Mayhew, *Observations*, p. 57; Jonathan Mayhew, *Remarks on an Anonymous Tract . . . Being a Second Defence* . . . (Boston, 1764), p. 12; Alden Bradford, *Memoir of the Life and Writings of Rev. Jonathan Mayhew* . . . (Boston, 1838), p. 372. For a full account of "the Anglican Plot," see Carl Bridenbaugh, *Mitre and Sceptre* (New York, 1962), chaps. vii–ix. See also Introduction to [John Aplin], *Verses on Doctor Mayhew's Book of Observations* (Providence, 1763: JHL Pamphlet 3), and pp. 156–158 below.

17 Thus John Adams drew the theme of his *Dissertation on the Canon and Feudal Law* (1765) from the association of the episcopal "plot" and the Stamp Act; see especially the concluding section ("there seems to be a direct and formal design on foot to enslave all America") in *Works*, III, 464. On this association in general, see Bridenbaugh, *Mitre and Sceptre*, chap. ix: "Bishops and Stamps, 1764–1766.". . .

18 For a succinct explanation of the manifest threat of the Stamp Act, see Stephen Hopkins, *Rights of Colonies Examined* (Providence, 1765: JHL Pamphlet 9), pp. 16–17. Adams' almost paranoiac suspicions of Hutchinson's hidden motives run through his *Diary and Autobiography* [ed. Lyman H. Butterfield, *et al.* (Cambridge, Mass., 1961)]; e.g., I, 306; II, 39; III, 430. See also *Novanglus and Massachusettensis* . . . (Boston, 1819), pp. 49–50, 68; *Works*, X, 285–286, 298. It is the generality of such suspicions that accounts for the furor caused by the publication in 1773 of Hutchinson's innocuous letters of 1768 — letters in which, the publishers wrote in the pamphlet's title, "*the Judicious Reader Will Discover the Fatal Source of the Confusion and Bloodshed.*" Josiah Quincy thought he saw the final proof of Hutchinson's conspiratorial efforts in his maneuverings with the North administration in London in 1774 and 1775: "Journal of Josiah Quincy Jun. . . . in England . . . ," *Proceedings of the Massachusetts Historical Society*, 50 (1916–1917), 444, 446, 447, 450, 452. Thacher's suspicions of Hutchinson (whom he called "Summa Potestatis," or "Summa" for short), are traced in the Introduction to his *Sentiments of a British American* (Boston, 1764: JHL Pamphlet 8). Otis' phrase is quoted from his abusive pamphlet, *Brief Remarks on the Defence of the Halifax Libel* . . . (Boston, 1765), p. 5. The charge against Howard appeared in the *Providence Gazette*, Sept. 15, 1764, and is part of the intense antipathy that built up in Providence against the royalist group in Newport. See, in general [Edmund S. Morgan and Helen M. Morgan, *The Stamp Act Crisis* (Chapel Hill, 1953)], chap. iv; and Introduction to Howard's *Letter from a Gentleman at Halifax* (Newport, 1765: JHL Pamphlet 10).

19 *Letters from a Farmer in Pennsylvania* . . . (Philadelphia, 1768), in Paul L. Ford, ed., *Writings of John Dickinson* (*Memoirs of the Historical Society of Pennsylvania*, XIV, Philadelphia, 1895), 382, 383.

20 Dickinson, *Farmer's Letters*, in Ford, *Writings*, p. 380; Albert H. Smyth, ed., *Writings of Benjamin Franklin* (New York, 1905–1907), V, 83. Cf. Verner W. Crane, *Benjamin Franklin's Letters to the Press, 1758–1775* (Chapel Hill, 1950), pp. 106–107, 277.

21 [Silas Downer], *Discourse Delivered in Providence* . . . *at the Dedication of the Tree of Liberty* . . . (Providence, 1768), p. 10; Ebenezer Baldwin, *An Appendix Stating the Heavy Grievances* . . . , published in Samuel Sherwood, *A Sermon Containing Scriptural Instructions to Civil Rulers* . . . (New Haven, [1774]), pp. 52–53; *Observations on Several Acts of Parliament* . . . *and Also on the Conduct of the Officers of the Customs* . . . ([Boston], 1769), p. 15; William Gordon, *Discourse Preached December 15th 1774* . . . (Boston, 1775), p. 11; [James Wilson], *Considerations on the* . . . *Legislative Authority of*

the British Parliament (Philadelphia, 1774), pp. 6–7; Dickinson, Farmer's Letters, in Ford, Writings, pp. 382, 398n, 399–400; Votes and Proceedings of . . . Boston . . . (Boston, [1772]), p. 21. See also, among the voluminous expressions of resentment and fear of petty officeholders in the colonies, [Henry Laurens], Extracts from the Proceedings of the High Court of Vice-Admiralty in Charlestown . . . with . . . Observations on American Custom-House Officers . . . (Charleston, 1769); and A Ministerial Catechise, Suitable To Be Learned by All . . . Pensioners, Placemen . . . (Boston, 1771).

22 For further details on the problem of the judiciary, and for documentation of the paragraphs that follow, see the Introduction and notes to A Letter to the People of Pennsylvania (Philadelphia, 1760: JHL Pamphlet 2).

23 Milton M. Klein, "Prelude to Revolution in New York: Jury Trials and Judicial Tenure," W.M.Q., 3d ser., 17 (1960), 452.

24 [William H. Drayton], A Letter from Freeman of South-Carolina . . . (Charleston, 1774), pp. 10, 20. For other characteristic expressions of the fear of a corrupt judiciary, see [John Allen], An Oration upon the Beauties of Liberty . . . (Boston, 1773), pp. 21 ff.: The Conduct of Cadwallader Colden . . . ([New York], 1767), reprinted in Collections of the New-York Historical Society, X (New York, 1877), 433–467; [John Allen], The American Alarm . . . (Boston, 1773), 1st sec., pp. 17, 20, 27, 28; Votes and Proceedings of Boston, pp. 37–38; Adams, Diary and Autobiography, II, 36, 65–67; III, 297 ff.

25 Votes and Proceedings of Boston, p. 20; Thomas Hutchinson, History of . . . Massachusetts-Bay (Lawrence S. Mayo, ed., Cambridge, 1936), III, 278, 279.

26 Klein, "Prelude to Revolution in New York," pp. 453–459.

27 Carl Ubbelohde, The Vice-Admiralty Courts and the American Revolution (Chapel Hill, 1960), pp. 112, 125–126. For further expressions of antipathy to the admiralty courts, see especially the Laurens pamphlet cited in note 21 above, and also . . . Adams, Works, III, 466–467; Votes and Proceedings of Boston, p. 24.

28 John Adams ("Novanglus"), Novanglus and Massachusettensis, pp. 49–50; Ellen E. Brennan, Plural Office-Holding in Massachusetts 1760–1780 (Chapel Hill, 1945), chaps. i, ii. See also references to Hutchinson, above, note 18.

29 Drayton, Letter from Freeman, pp. 9, 18–19, 32–33; Edward McCrady, The History of South Carolina Under the Royal Government 1719–1776 (New York, 1899), pp. 533–535, 710–713; Adams, Diary and Autobiography, I, 306; II, 39.

30 For a detailed discussion of the Wilkes affair in the context of the present discussion, see Pauline Maier, "John Wilkes and American Disillusionment with Britain," W.M.Q., 3d ser., 20 (1963), 373–395.

31 Boston Sons of Liberty to Wilkes, June 6, 1768, Proceedings of the Massachusetts Historical Society, 47 (1913–1914), 191. The quotation is from Virgil, Eclogues i, 45: "pasture your cattle as of old."

32 William Palfrey to Wilkes, February 21, 1769, Proceedings of the Massachusetts Historical Society, 47 (1913–1914), 197.

33 [Lawrence H. Gipson], The Triumphant Empire (New York, 1961)], X, 200–201, 328–329, 408; cf. Bernhard Knollenberg, Origin of the American Revolution, 1759–1766 (New York, 1960), pp. 87–96.

34 George Rudé, Wilkes and Liberty (Oxford, 1962), pp. 49 ff.; Maier, "Wilkes and American Disillusionment," pp. 386–387.

35 Allen, Oration upon the Beauties of Liberty, p. xiii. [Bowdoin, et al.], Short Narrative of the Horrid Massacre in Boston . . . (Boston, 1770), reprinted within the year three times in Boston, three times in London and once (retitled) in Dublin, appears also in Frederic Kidder, History of the Boston Massacre . . . (Albany, 1870); for the direct association of the Massacre with the problem of standing armies, see Kidder, History, p. 27. The annual Massacre Day orators played up this association in lurid detail: see, for example, Joseph Warren, An Oration . . . (Boston, 1772), pp. 11–12; John Hancock, An Oration . . . (Boston, 1774), pp. 13–15. The view of the Massacre held by John Adams and Josiah Quincy, Jr., the lawyers who successfully defended the soldiers in court, is especially important. Both thought the Massacre was "the strongest of proofs of the danger of standing armies" despite their efforts on the soldiers' behalf; Adams saw nothing incompatible

between the verdict of the jury and his being invited to deliver one of the orations commemorating the Massacre. Josiah Quincy, *Memoir of the Life of Josiah Quincy Jun.* . . . (Boston, 1825), p. 67; Adams, *Diary and Autobiography,* II, 74, 79.

36 *Votes and Proceedings of Boston,* pp. 13–30.

37 [Alexander Hamilton], *A Full Vindication of the Measures of the Congress* . . . (New York, 1774), in H. C. Lodge, ed., *Works* (New York and London, 1904), I, 10; Baldwin, *Appendix,* p. 67; [Samuel Seabury], *A View of the Controversy* . . . (New York, 1774), in Clarence H. Vance, ed., *Letters of a Westchester Farmer* . . . *(1774–1775)* (*Publications of the Westchester County Historical Society,* VIII, White Plains, 1930), p. 123; Oliver Noble, *Some Strictures upon the* . . . *Book of Esther* . . . (Newburyport, 1775), pp. 28, 26; Hancock, *Oration,* p. 9; [Jefferson], *A Summary View* . . . (Williamsburg, 1774), in Paul L. Ford, ed., *Writings of Thomas Jefferson* (New York, 1892–1899), I, 435; on the development of Dickinson's understanding of the cause of the crisis, see Introduction to his *Late Regulations* (Philadelphia, 1765: JHL Pamphlet 14); Quincy, *Observations on the* . . . *Boston Port-Bill with Thoughts on* . . . *Standing Armies* (Boston, 1774), in Quincy, *Memoir,* p. 446 (cf. pp. 464–465); Adams, *Works,* X, 242–243 (for Adams' full elaboration of the ministry's "dark intrigues and wicked machinations" so clearly dovetailed with the Hutchinson clique's maneuverings, see *Novanglus and Massachusettensis,* pp. 15 ff., 49–50, 55, 71–72; *Diary and Autobiography,* II, 80, 90, 119); John C. Miller, *Origins of the American Revolution* (Boston, 1943), p. 332. For other expressions of the fear of "a constant, unremitted, uniform aim to enslave us," see *Votes and Proceedings of Boston,* pp. 30, 37; Allen, *American Alarm,* 1st sec., pp. 8–9, 17, 18, 33; Edmund S. Morgan, *The Gentle Puritan* (New Haven, 1962), pp. 263–265. . . .

38 Allen, *American Alarm,* 1st sec., pp. 18–19; cf. the same author's reference to "*Scotch barbarian troops*" at the St. George's Fields riot, in *Oration upon the Beauties of Liberty,* p. xiii.

39 [Stephen Johnson], *Some Important Observations* . . . (Newport, 1766), p. 15. Jefferson's explanation appeared first as notes he jotted down on reading François Soulé's *Histoire des troubles de l'Amérique anglaise* (London, 1785) at the point where George III's education is mentioned: "The education of the present King was Tory. He gave decisive victories to the Tories. To these were added sundry rich persons sprung up in the E. I. America would have been too formidable a weight in the scale of the Whigs. It was necessary therefore to reduce them by force to concur with the Tories." Later he wrote more formally to Soulé: "The seeds of the war are here traced to their true source. The Tory education of the King was the first preparation for that change in the British government which that party never ceases to wish. This naturally ensured Tory administrations during his life. At the moment he came to the throne and cleared his hands of his enemies by the peace of Paris, the assumptions of unwarrantable right over America commenced; they were so signal, and followed one another so close as to prove they were part of a system either to reduce it under absolute subjection and thereby make it an instrument for attempts on Britain itself, or to sever it from Britain so that it might not be a weight in the Whig scale. This latter alternative however was not considered as the one which would take place. They knew so little of America that they thought it unable to encounter the little finger of Great Britain." *The Papers of Thomas Jefferson* (Julian P. Boyd, ed., Princeton, 1950–), X, 373n2, 369.

40 [Carter Braxton], *An Address to* . . . *Virginia; on the Subject of Government* . . . (Philadelphia, 1776), p. 10.

41 Allen, *American Alarm,* 1st sec., pp. 8–9; Noble, *Some Strictures,* p. 6; Allen, *Oration upon the Beauties of Liberty,* p. 29.

42 Archibald S. Foord, *His Majesty's Opposition, 1714–1830* (Oxford, 1964), pp. 37–38, 51, 53–54, 147–148, 170, 291, 318–319; Noble, *Some Strictures,* pp. 10, 17–18, 12. See also Richard Salter, *A Sermon* . . . (New London, 1768); Johnson, *Some Important Observations,* pp. 39, 55–56; Elisha Fish, *Joy and Gladness* . . . (Providence, 1767).

43 *Four Letters on Interesting Subjects* (Philadelphia, 1776), p. 5.

44 Baldwin, *Appendix,* p. 51, 67–68.

45 Johnson, *Some Important Observations,* p. 20; Thomas Bradbury, *The Ass, or, the*

Serpent . . . (1712: reprinted in Boston, 1768), p. 12n; William Palfrey to Wilkes, February 21 and April 12, 1769, *Proceedings of the Massachusetts Historical Society*, 47 (1913–1914), 197, 199.

[46] [Matthew Robinson-Morris, Lord Rokeby], *Considerations on the Measures Carrying on with Respect to the British Colonies in North America* (2d ed., London, 1774), p. 10. This pamphlet was reprinted three times in Boston, twice in Philadelphia, and once in New York and Hartford in 1774 and 1775. For Abigail Adams' awareness of the identity between Rokeby's views and those of her husband writing as "Novanglus," see her letter of May 22, 1775, in L. H. Butterfield, *et al.*, eds., *Adams Family Correspondence* (Cambridge, 1963), I, 202, 203n11. See also [Joseph Priestley], *An Address to Protestant Dissenters* (Boston, 1774), p. 6; this pamphlet, first published in London in 1773, appeared in three American editions in 1774. And see, in general, Oscar and Mary F. Handlin, "James Burgh and American Revolutionary Theory," *Proceedings of the Massachusetts Historical Society*, 73 (1961), 38–57; H. Trevor Colbourn, "John Dickinson, Historical Revolutionary," *Pa. Mag.*, 83 (1959), 284; Caroline Robbins, *The Eighteenth-Century Commonwealthman* (Cambridge, 1959), chap. ix.

[47] Adams ("Novanglus"), *Novanglus and Massachusettensis*, pp. 25, 22, 43; William Hooper of North Carolina, quoted in Charles F. Mullett, "Classical Influences on the American Revolution," *Classical Journal*, 35 (1939–1940), 103; William H. Drayton, *A Charge on the Rise of the American Empire* . . . (Charleston, 1776), pp. 2–3; Seabury, *A View of the Controversy*, in [Clarence H. Vance, ed., *Letters of a Westchester Farmer*, in *Publications of the Westchester County Historical Society*, VIII (1930)], p. 140.

[48] Samuel Williams, *A Discourse on the Love of Our Country* . . . (Salem, 1775), pp. 21, 22, 23, 25, 26. Cf., e.g., Thomas Coombe, *A Sermon Preached* . . . (Philadelphia, 1775), pp. 19–20; [Richard Wells], *A Few Political Reflections* . . . (Philadelphia, 1774), pp. 38–40, 50.

[49] Adams, *Dissertation*, in *Works*, III, 452n; Jonathan Mayhew, *The Snare Broken* . . . (Boston, 1766), pp. 36, 38.

[50] Rokeby, *Considerations*, p. 148; Ebenezer Baldwin, *The Duty of Rejoicing under Calamities and Afflictions* . . . (New York, 1776), p. 38.

[51] Johnson, *Some Important Observations*, pp. 21, 23; [Robert Carter Nicholas], *Considerations on the Present State of Virginia Examined* ([Williamsburg], 1774), in Earl G. Swem reprint (New York, 1919), pp. 68, 42.

[52] Braxton, *Address*, p. 19; Seabury, *View*, in Vance, *Letters of a Westchester Farmer*, p. 112; Daniel Leonard ("Massachusettensis"), in *Novanglus and Massachusettensis*, p. 185; [Joseph Galloway], *A Candid Examination of the Mutual Claims of Great-Britain and the Colonies* . . . (New York, 1775), p. 31; [Thomas Paine], *Common Sense* . . . (Philadelphia, 1776), in Moncure D. Conway, ed., *The Writings of Thomas Paine* (New York, 1894–1896), I, 68, 84–85, 100–101.

Rhetoric and Reality in the American Revolution, GORDON S. WOOD

[1] This is the title of a recent essay by Edmund S. Morgan in Arthur M. Schlesinger, Jr., and Morton White, eds., *Paths of American Thought* (Boston, 1963), 11–33.

[2] Samuel E. Morison, ed., "William Manning's *The Key of Libberty*," *William and Mary Quarterly*, 3d Ser., XIII (1956), 208.

[3] Edmund S. Morgan, "The American Revolution: Revisions in Need of Revising," *Wm. and Mary Qtly.*, 3d Ser., XIV (1957), 14.

[4] [William Vans Murray], *Political Sketches, Inscribed to His Excellency John Adams* (London, 1787), 21, 48.

[5] [Daniel Leonard], *The Origin of the American Contest with Great-Britain* . . . [by] *Massachusettensis* . . . (New York, 1775), 40; Douglass Adair and John A. Schutz, eds., *Peter Oliver's Origin and Progress of the American Rebellion: A Tory View* (San Marino, 1963), 159.

168 NOTES

6 Simeon Baldwin, *An Oration Pronounced Before the Citizens of New-Haven, July 4th, 1788* . . . (New Haven, 1788), 10; [Murray], *Political Sketches*, 48; David Ramsay, *The History of the American Revolution* (Philadelphia, 1789), I, 350.

7 Thomas Paine, *Letter to the Abbé Raynal* . . . (1782) in Philip S. Foner, ed., *The Complete Writings of Thomas Paine* (New York, 1945), II, 243; John Adams to H. Niles, Feb. 13, 1818, in Charles Francis Adams, ed., *The Works of John Adams* (Boston, 1850–56), X, 282.

8 William Pierce, *An Oration, Delivered at Christ Church, Savannah, on the 4th of July, 1788* . . . (Providence, [1788]), 6; Enos Hitchcock, *An Oration; Delivered July 4th, 1788* . . . (Providence, [1788]), 11.

9 Petition to the King, Oct. 1774, in Worthington C. Ford, ed., *Journals of the Continental Congress, 1774–1789* (Washington, 1904–37), I, 118.

10 Samuel Williams, *The Natural and Civil History of Vermont* . . . (Walpole, New Hamp., 1794), vii, 372–373; Pierce, *Oration* . . . *4th July, 1788*, p. 8.

11 Moses Coit Tyler, *The Literary History of the American Revolution, 1763–1783* (New York, 1897), I, 8–9.

12 For a bald description of the assumptions with which this generation of historians worked see Graham Wallas, *Human Nature in Politics*, 3d ed. (New York, 1921), 5, 45, 48–49, 83, 94, 96, 118, 122, 156.

13 Charles A. Beard, *An Economic Interpretation of the Constitution* (New York, 1935), x, viii.

14 While the Progressive historians were attempting to absorb and use the latest scientific techniques of the day nonbehaviorists in government departments and others with a traditional approach to political theory — men like Andrew C. McLaughlin, Edwin S. Corwin, William S. Carpenter, Charles M. McIlwain, and Benjamin F. Wright — were writing during this same period some of the best work that has ever been done on Revolutionary constitutional and political thought. However, because most of them were not, strictly speaking, historians, they never sought to explain the causes of the Revolution in terms of ideas.

15 Carl L. Becker, *The Declaration of Independence: A Study in the History of Political Ideas* (New York, 1922), 203, 207, 133.

16 Quoted in Philip Davidson, *Propaganda and the American Revolution, 1763–1783* (Chapel Hill, 1941), 141, 373, 150.

17 Arthur M. Schlesinger, *Prelude to Independence: The Newspaper War on Britain, 1764–1776* (New York, 1958), 34. For examples of the scientific work on which the propagandist studies drew, see note one in Sidney I. Pomerantz, "The Patriot Newspaper and the American Revolution," in Richard B. Morris, ed., *The Era of the American Revolution* (New York, 1939), 305.

18 Davidson, *Propaganda*, 59; Schlesinger, *Prelude to Independence*, 20.

19 Davidson, *Propaganda*, xiv, 46.

20 Schlesinger, *Prelude to Independence*, 44; Arthur M. Schlesinger, *New Viewpoints in American History* (New York, 1923), 179.

21 Edmund S. Morgan, "Colonial Ideas of Parliamentary Power, 1764–1766," *Wm. and Mary Qtly.*, 3d Ser., V (1948), 311, 341; Edmund S. and Helen M. Morgan, *The Stamp Act Crisis: Prologue to Revolution*, rev. ed. (New York, 1963), 369–370; Page Smith, "David Ramsay and the Causes of the American Revolution," *Wm. and Mary Qtly.*, 3d Ser., XVII (1960), 70–71.

22 Jack P. Greene, "The Flight From Determinism: A Review of Recent Literature on the Coming of the American Revolution," *South Atlantic Quarterly*, LXI (1962), 257.

23 This revisionist literature of the 1950's is well known. See the listings in Bernard Bailyn, "Political Experience and Enlightenment Ideas in Eighteenth-Century America," *American Historical Review*, LXVII (1961–62), 341n; and in Greene, "Flight From Determinism," 235–259.

24 Greene, "Flight From Determinism," 237, 257; Thad W. Tate, "The Coming of the Revolution in Virginia: Britain's Challenge to Virginia's Ruling Class, 1763–1776," *Wm. and Mary Qtly.*, 3d Ser., XIX (1962), 323–343, esp. 340.

25 Bailyn, "Political Experience and Enlightenment Ideas," 339–351.

26 Bernard Bailyn, ed., assisted by Jane N. Garrett, *Pamphlets of the American Revolution, 1750–1776* (Cambridge, Mass., 1965–), I, viii, 60, x, 20. The 200-page general introduction is entitled, "The Transforming Radicalism of the American Revolution."

27 This is not to say, however, that work on the Revolutionary ideas is in any way finished. For examples of the re-examination of traditional problems in Revolutionary political theory see Richard Buel, Jr., "Democracy and the American Revolution: A Frame of Reference," *Wm. and Mary Qtly.*, 3d Ser., XXI (1964), 165–190; and Bailyn's resolution of James Otis's apparent inconsistency in *Revolutionary Pamphlets*, I, 100–103, 106–107, 121–123, 409–417, 546–552.

28 Smith, "Ramsay and the American Revolution," 72.

29 Morgan, "Revisions in Need of Revising," 13.

30 Adair and Schutz, eds., *Peter Oliver's Origin*, ix. In the present neo-Whig context, Sidney S. Fisher, "The Legendary and Myth-Making Process in Histories of the American Revolution," in American Philosophical Society, *Proceedings*, LI (Philadelphia, 1912), 53–75, takes on a renewed relevance.

31 Bailyn, *Revolutionary Pamphlets*, I, 87, ix.

32 [Moses Mather], *America's Appeal to the Impartial World* . . . (Hartford, 1775), 59; [John Dickinson], *Letters from a Farmer in Pennsylvania to the Inhabitants of the British Colonies* (1768), in Paul L. Ford, ed., *The Life and Writings of John Dickinson* (Historical Society of Pennsylvania, *Memoirs*, XIV [Philadelphia, 1895]), II, 348. Dickinson hinged his entire argument on the ability of the Americans to decipher the "intention" of parliamentary legislation, whether for revenue or for commercial regulation. *Ibid.*, 348, 364.

33 See Herbert Davis, "The Augustan Conception of History," in J. A. Mazzeo, ed., *Reason and the Imagination: Studies in the History of Ideas, 1600–1800* (New York, 1962), 226–228; W. H. Greenleaf, *Order, Empiricism and Politics: Two Traditions of English Political Thought, 1500–1700* (New York, 1964), 166; R. N. Stromberg, "History in the Eighteenth Century," *Journal of the History of Ideas*, XII (1951), 300. It was against this "dominant characteristic of the historical thought of the age," this "tendency to explain events in terms of conscious action by individuals," that the brilliant group of Scottish social scientists writing at the end of the 18th century directed much of their work. Duncan Forbes, " 'Scientific' Whiggism: Adam Smith and John Millar," *Cambridge Journal*, VII (1954), 651, 653–654. While we have had recently several good studies of historical thinking in 17th-century England, virtually nothing has been done on the 18th century. See, however, J. G. A. Pocock, "Burke and the Ancient Constitution — A Problem in the History of Ideas," *The Historical Journal*, III (1960), 125–143; and Stow Persons, "The Cyclical Theory of History in Eighteenth Century America," *American Quarterly*, VI (1954), 147–163.

34 [Dickinson], *Letters from a Farmer*, in Ford, ed., *Writings of Dickinson*, 388.

35 Bailyn has noted that Oliver M. Dickerson, in chap. 7 of his *The Navigation Acts and the American Revolution* (Philadelphia, 1951), "adopts wholesale the contemporary Whig interpretation of the Revolution as the result of a conspiracy of 'King's Friends.' " Bailyn, *Revolutionary Pamphlets*, I, 724.

36 Morgan, "Revisions in Need of Revising," 7, 13, 8; Greene, "Flight From Determinism," 237.

37 Edmund S. Morgan, *The Birth of the Republic, 1763–89* (Chicago, 1956), 51.

38 Greene, "Flight From Determinism," 258; Morgan, *Birth of the Republic*, 3.

39 Bailyn, *Revolutionary Pamphlets*, I, vii, ix.

40 *Ibid.*, vii, viii, 17.

41 J. G. A. Pocock, "Machiavelli, Harrington, and English Political Ideologies in the Eighteenth Century," *Wm. and Mary Qtly.*, 3d Ser., XXII (1965), 550.

42 Sir Lewis Namier, *England in the Age of the American Revolution*, 2d ed. (London, 1961), 131.

43 *Ibid.*, 129.

44 Bailyn, *Revolutionary Pamphlets*, I, 90, x, 169, 140. See Hannah Arendt, *On Revolution* (New York, 1963), 173: "American experience had taught the men of the Revolution

that action, though it may be started in isolation and decided upon by single individuals for very different motives, can be accomplished only by some joint effort in which the motivation of single individuals . . . no longer counts. . . ."

45 See Sir Lewis Namier, *The Structure of Politics at the Accession of George III*, 2d ed. (London, 1961), 16; Sir Lewis Namier, "Human Nature in Politics," in *Personalities and Power: Selected Essays* (New York, 1965), 5–6.

46 Bailyn, *Revolutionary Pamphlets*, I, 22. The French Revolutionaries were using the same group of classical writings to express their estrangement from the *ancien régime* and their hope for the new order. Harold T. Parker, *The Cult of Antiquity and the French Revolutionaries: A Study in the Development of the Revolutionary Spirit* (Chicago, 1937), 22–23.

47 The relation of ideas to social structure is one of the most perplexing and intriguing in the social sciences. For an extensive bibliography on the subject see Norman Birnbaum, "The Sociological Study of Ideology (1940–60)," *Current Sociology*, IX (1960).

48 Jacob Duché, *The American Vine, A Sermon, Preached . . . Before the Honourable Continental Congress, July 20th, 1775 . . .* (Philadelphia, 1775), 29.

49 For recent discussions of French and Puritan revolutionary rhetoric see Peter Gay, "Rhetoric and Politics in the French Revolution," *Amer. Hist. Rev.*, LXVI (1960–61), 664–676; Michael Walzer, "Puritanism as a Revolutionary Ideology," *History and Theory*, III (1963), 59–90. This entire issue of *History and Theory* is devoted to a symposium on the uses of theory in the study of history. In addiiton to the Walzer article, I have found the papers by Samuel H. Beer, "Causal Explanation and Imaginative Re-enactment," and Charles Tilly, "The Analysis of a Counter-Revolution," very stimulating and helpful.

50 Bryan A. Wilson, "Millennialism in Comparative Perspective," *Comparative Studies in Society and History*, VI (1963–64), 108. See also Neil J. Smelser, *Theory of Collective Behaviour* (London, 1962), 83, 120, 383.

51 Tate, "Coming of the Revolution in Virginia," 324–343.

52 Robert E. and B. Katherine Brown, *Virginia, 1705–1786: Democracy or Aristocracy?* (East Lansing, Mich., 1964), 236; Alexander White to Richard Henry Lee, 1758, quoted in J. R. Pole, "Representation and Authority in Virginia from the Revolution to Reform," *The Journal of Southern History*, XXIV (1958), 23.

53 Purdie and Dixon's *Virginia Gazette* (Williamsburg), Apr. 11, 1771; Rind's *Virginia Gazette*, Oct. 31, 1771. See Lester J. Cappon and Stella F. Duff, eds., *Virginia Gazette Index, 1736–1780* (Williamsburg, 1950), I, 351, for entries on the astounding increase in essays on corruption and cost of elections in the late 1760's and early 1770's.

54 *The Defence of Injur'd Merit Unmasked; or, the Scurrilous Piece of Philander Dissected and Exposed to Public View. By a Friend to Merit, wherever found* (n.p., 1771), 10. Robert Carter chose to retire to private life in the early 1770's rather than adjust to the "new system of politicks" that had begun "to prevail generally." Quoted in Louis Morton, *Robert Carter of Nomini Hall: A Virginia Tobacco Planter of the Eighteenth Century* (Williamsburg, 1941), 52.

55 Jay B. Hubbell and Douglass Adair, "Robert Munford's *The Candidates*," *Wm. and Mary Qtly.*, 3d Ser., V (1948), 246, 238. The ambivalence in Munford's attitude toward the representative process is reflected in the different way historians have interpreted his play. Cf. *ibid.*, 223–225, with Brown, *Virginia*, 236–237. Munford's fear of "men who aim at power without merit" was more fully expressed in his later play, *The Patriots*, written in 1775 or 1776. Courtlandt Canby, "Robert Munford's *The Patriots*," *Wm. and Mary Qtly.*, 3d Ser., VI (1949), 437–503, quotation from 450.

56 [John Randolph], *Considerations on the Present State of Virginia* ([Williamsburg], 1774), in Earl G. Swem, ed., *Virginia and the Revolution: Two Pamphlets, 1774* (New York, 1919), 16; Purdie and Dixon's *Virginia Gazette*, Nov. 25, 1773.

57 Rind's *Virginia Gazette*, Sept. 8, 1774; Brown, *Virginia*, 252–254; Morton, *Robert Carter*, 231–250.

58 See George Washington to George Mason, Apr. 5, 1769, in John C. Fitzpatrick, ed., *The Writings of George Washington* (Washington, 1931–44), II, 502; Carl Bridenbaugh, *Myths and Realities: Societies of the Colonial South* (New York, 1963), 5, 10, 14, 16; Emory

G. Evans, "Planter Indebtedness and the Coming of the Revolution in Virginia," *Wm. and Mary Qtly.*, 3d Ser., XIX (1962), 518–519.

59 Rind's *Virginia Gazette*, Aug. 15, 1766. See Carl Bridenbaugh, "Violence and Virtue in Virginia, 1766: or The Importance of the Trivial," Massachusetts Historical Society, *Proceedings*, LXXVI (1964), 3–29.

60 Quoted in Bridenbaugh, *Myths and Realities*, 27. See also Morton, *Robert Carter*, 223–225.

61 John A. Washington to R. H. Lee, June 20, 1778, quoted in Pole, "Representation and Authority in Virginia," 28.

62 Evans, "Planter Indebtedness," 526–527.

63 Julian P. Boyd and others, eds., *The Papers of Thomas Jefferson* (Princeton, 1950–), I, 560. Most of our knowledge of entail and primogeniture in Virginia stems from an unpublished doctoral dissertation, Clarence R. Keim, Influence of Primogeniture and Entail in the Development of Virginia (University of Chicago, 1926). Keim's is a very careful and qualified study and conclusions from his evidence — other than the obvious fact that much land was held in fee simple — are by no means easy to make. See particularly pp. 56, 60–62, 110–114, 122, 195–196.

64 Emory S. Evans, "The Rise and Decline of the Virginia Aristocracy in the Eighteenth Century: The Nelsons," in Darrett B. Rutman, ed., *The Old Dominion: Essays for Thomas Perkins Abernethy* (Charlottesville, 1964), 73–74.

65 Max Farrand, ed., *The Records of the Federal Convention of 1787* (New Haven, 1911), I, 56; Bridenbaugh, *Myths and Realities*, 14, 16.

66 John Adams, "Novanglus," in Charles F. Adams, ed., *The Works of John Adams* (Boston, 1851), IV, 14.

67 Arthur F. Bentley, *The Process of Government: A Study of Social Pressures* (Chicago, 1908), 152.

The Effects of British Imperial Policy upon Colonial Welfare,
ROBERT PAUL THOMAS

1 "Mercantilism and the American Revolution," *Canadian Historical Review*, XXIII (Mar. 1942), 3.

2 *The Navigation Act and the American Revolution* (Philadelphia: University of Pennsylvania Press, 1951), p. 55.

3 "British Mercantilism and the Economic Development of the Thirteen Colonies," *Journal of Economic History*, XII, No. 2 (Spring 1952), 114.

4 The effects of British regulations not considered in this paper will be taken into account in the larger study now in process.

5 The statistics on colonial exports have been adjusted in a manner suggested by James Shepherd and used by him in preparing his balance of payments for the colonial period. Imports, due to a lack of prices, were adjusted by the Schumpeter-Gilboy price index.

6 Quoted in Robert W. Fogel, *Railroads and American Economic Growth* (Baltimore: Johns Hopkins Press, 1964), p. 17.

7 *Journal of Economic History*, XII (1952), 114.

8 In 1790, nearly 80 per cent of the residents of the United States traced their origin, or that of their ancestors, to the British Isles.

9 Bernhard Knollenberg, *Origin of the American Revolution: 1759–1766* (New York: Collier Books, 1961), p. 18.

10 Max Savelle, "The American Balance of Power and European Diplomacy, 1713–78," in Richard B. Morris, ed., *The Era of the American Revolution* (New York: Columbia University Press, 1939), p. 162.

11 Knollenberg, p. 19.

12 This was certainly the case after the American Revolution.

13 "American Economic Growth Before 1840: An Exploratory Essay," *Journal of Economic History*, XXIV, No. 4 (Dec. 1964), 435.

14 B. R. Mitchell, *Abstract of British Historical Statistics* (Cambridge [Engl.]: University Press, 1962), p. 312.

15 The values of imports are the official values f.o.b. Great Britain. For that reason, they are probably approximately 10 to 20 per cent too low. Import figures for 1768 were used because detailed breakdowns for 1770 were unavailable when this paper was written.

16 Sir William Ashley thought the regulations of English mercantilism were pious formulas nullified in the actual world of commerce by fraud and evasion when they existed contrary to national commercial habits. Studies by Lawrence Harper have indicated that the burden of the Navigation Acts was in fact felt in transatlantic commerce.

17 The Molasses Act of 1733 was a law enacted in the interest of the British West Indies. This law taxed foreign molasses sufficiently to make the molasses of the British West Indies competitive. The law was, however, widely evaded.

18 Export commodities shipped to the West Indies were reputed by one source to be worth £275,000 when they left the American colonies and £500,000 when they arrived in the West Indies. The freight factor is thus over 30 per cent. The return trip saw excess cargo capacity and therefore lower rates. The freight factor on the return trip was but 5 per cent. Herbert C. Bell, "West Indian Trade before the Revolution," *American Historical Review*, XXII, No. 2 (Jan. 1917), 273–74.

19 *Canadian Historical Review*, XXIII (1942), 3.

20 Dickerson, p. 33.

21 Since most tobacco was exported, exports for all practical purposes equal output or production.

22 For Philadelphia prices, Anne Bezanson, *et al.*, *Prices and Inflation during the American Revolution: Pennsylvania, 1770–1790* (Philadelphia: University of Pennsylvania Press, 1965). For a European port, Amsterdam prices have been used as found in N. W. Posthumus, *Inquiry into the History of Prices in Holland* (Leiden: E. J. Brill, 1946). For tobacco quantities, see *Historical Statistics of the United States, Colonial Times to 1957* (Washington: U.S. Government Printing Office, 1960), series 230–37, p. 766.

23 Albert Fishlow, discussion of a paper by Gordon Bjork, "The Weaning of the American Economy: Independence, Market Changes, and Economic Development," *Journal of Economic History*, XXIV, No. 4 (Dec. 1964), 565.

24 This amounts to assuming an elasticity of supply of one. This is probably optimistic, since the average exports of tobacco between 1790 and 1793 were 28 per cent greater than the average for the period 1763–72 and 41 per cent greater than for 1770. This suggests on a crude basis an elasticity of supply between .8 and .9. Bjork also found that tobacco prices after the Revolution rose sharply.

25 The indirect burden suffered because of the loss of exports is calculated as the unit burden times the increased output that would have been exported, divided by two.

26 For rice, the prices are to be found in Arthur H. Cole, *Wholesale Commodity Prices in the United States, 1700–1861, Statistical Supplement* (Cambridge: Harvard University Press, 1938). The rice estimate was made on the basis of but one observation in the colonial period (1760). The author considers the rice estimate optimistic.

27 The average preference was figured from statistics presented in tables 2 and 3, found in Lawrence Harper, "The Burden of the Navigation Acts on the Thirteen Colonies" in Morris, ed., *Era of the American Revolution*.

28 Recorded bounty payments for the decade 1763–72 averaged:

Indigo	£ 8,065
Naval stores	32,772
Lumber	6,557
Total	£47,394

29 The gain to the colonists from the bounty payments was figured in the following manner. The gain is in two parts. First, the unit bounty times the quantity that would have been produced without the bounty gives us the clear gain. In order to find that portion of naval stores that would have been produced without the bounty, we assumed

a supply elasticity of one, reckoned the percentage of the price of naval stores that the bounty represented, and thus easily estimated that portion of the supply of naval stores for which the bounty was responsible. The other part would have been produced anyway; on this portion the full amount of the bounty was clear again. On the part stimulated by the bounty, only one half was gain to the colonists.

30 This figure is taken from reports by the London Custom House, retained in Treasury 38, Vol. 363, Public Record Office, London, as originally stated in Dickerson, p. 28, and is accurate. Lawrence Harper "Navigation Acts" (cited in n.27) uses a figure of £23,086. While the Dickerson figure may possibly exclude some payments, the Harper figure is calculated on the basis that all indigo received the bounty, which was not the case. Lewis Grey quotes a British official to the effect that about seven eighths of the indigo exported from South Carolina received the bounty, but much less deserved so, being poor in quality. On this basis the payments could have reached as high as £20,000 a year. Lewis C. Grey, *A History of Southern Agriculture* (Washington: Carnegie Institution, 1933), p. 292.

31 Figured on the basis of an annual bounty of about £20,000. Then around £10,000 would have been the value of the bounty to the producers of indigo.

32 George Louis Beer, *British Colonial Policy, 1754–1765* (New York: Macmillan, 1907), p. 224.

33 "Navigation Acts," p. 36.

34 P. 70.

35 Colonial prices are to be found in Bezanson and Amsterdam prices in Posthumus.

36 Bjork, *Journal of Economic History*, XXIV (1964), 554, found that goods of foreign manufacture (his Index A) fell dramatically in price after the Revolution, while goods in which Britain had a comparative advantage fell little if at all in price (his Index B).

37 This loss was calculated by taking the percentage unit burden on the price of such imports times their total value.

38 The consumer surplus lost to the colonists because of higher import prices could be easily calculated in the Hotelling-Harberger manner.

39 *Canadian Historical Review*, XXIII (1942), 4.

40 P. 32.

41 See James Shepherd, "Colonial Balance of Payments," p. 691, for a discussion of how this estimate was obtained.

42 Colonial vessels probably would have carried relatively less of the trade with the West Indies, assuming that (as happened after the Revolution) they were excluded from the British West Indies. However, they would also presumably have carried relatively more of the transatlantic trade.

43 *Roots of American Economic Growth* (New York: Harper and Row, 1916), p. 74.

44 Knollenberg, p. 34.

45 Great Britain, *House of Commons Journals*, King George III, Vol. XXXII (1768–1770), sessions no. 1768, 1803.

46 *Historical Statistics*, p. 737.

47 Harold E. Gillingham, *Marine Insurance Rates in Philadelphia, 1721–1800* (Philadelphia: Patterson & White, 1933), pp. 18, 64.

48 *Ibid.*

49 Charles Goldsbourgh, *The United States Naval Chronicle* (Washington, 1824), pp. 109–10.

50 U.S. Congress, *American State Papers, Finance*, III, 14th Cong., 1st sess., 63, 69.

51 *Canadian Historical Review*, XXIII (1942) 2.

52 P. xiv.

53 Harper estimated that the burden on tobacco, rice, European goods imported, and the benefits of bounties together added up to a burden of between $2,560,000 and $7,038,000. Harper's estimate of the loss on tobacco and rice really measured the area $(P_1.A.B.P_3)$ in Graph 1 rather than $(P_1.A.E.P_2)$, which is the correct area. However his lower estimate is rather close to ours.

54 *Journal of Economic History*, XXIV (1964), 566.

55 *Ibid.*, p. 429.

SUGGESTIONS FOR FURTHER READING

The amount of historical literature on the American Revolution is enormous because an understanding of the phenomenon is so crucial to understanding American history and character. The student has been introduced to some of this literature in the footnotes of the preceding essays. Because of the many titles on the subject, this guide to further reading will confine itself primarily to classifying the literature of the past decade rather than attempting a full survey of the classics of interpretation and earlier works of scholarship.

Mention of such works as well as the history of the history written about the Revolution may be found in recent surveys of its historiography. Page Smith, "David Ramsay and the Causes of the Revolution," *William and Mary Quarterly*, 3rd series, XVII (Jan., 1960), pp. 51–77, and Merrill Jensen, "Historians and the Nature of the American Revolution," in Ray A. Billington, ed., *The Reinterpretation of Early American History* * (San Marino, Calif.: Henry E. Huntington Library, 1966), pp. 101–128, show the continuity of views on the conflict's causes and nature from then to now but with opposite conclusions. Jack P. Greene's long introduction to his *The Reinterpretation of the American Revolution, 1763–1789* * (New York: Harper and Row, 1968), pp. 2–74, summarizes and expands some of his previous historiographical essays according to an explicit analytical framework. Other valuable surveys of the literature are Edmund S. Morgan, "The American Revolution: Revisions in Need of Revising," *William and Mary Quarterly*, 3rd series, XIV (Jan., 1957), pp. 3–15, and Richard B. Morris, *The American Revolution Reconsidered* * (New York: Harper and Row, 1967), pp. 1–91. An authoritative, classified list of books on all of American history, including the Revolution, has been compiled by Oscar Handlin and others, *Harvard Guide to American History* * (Cambridge, Mass.: Harvard University Press, 1955), scheduled to be revised and up-dated in the early 1970s. Current research and interpretation may be followed in the articles and book reviews of the chief periodical in the field of colonial history, *The William and Mary Quarterly*, 3rd series, published by the Institute of Early American History and Culture at Williamsburg, Virginia. Since so many of the articles listed below were first published in this journal, succeeding citations will be abbreviated as *WMQ*.

General analyses of causation normally take the form of essays or a narrative of the period from the 1760s to the 1780s. Charles McLean Andrews presented the imperial viewpoint in his essays in *The Colonial Background of the American Revolution: An Interpretation* * (New Haven: Yale University Press, 1924), and "The American Revolution: An Interpretation," *American Historical*

---

* An asterisk following a title indicates that it is available in paperback.

175

Review, XXXI (Jan., 1926), pp. 219–232. More recently, Lawrence Gipson summarized his own work according to the same perspective in "The American Revolution as an Aftermath of the Great War for Empire, 1754–1763," *Political Science Quarterly*, LXV (Mar., 1950), pp. 86–104, and at greater length in *The Coming of the Revolution, 1763–1775* * (New York: Harper and Row, 1954). The economic and progressive interpretation found summation at different times in Arthur M. Schlesinger, Sr., "The American Revolution Reconsidered," *Political Science Quarterly*, XXXIV (Mar., 1919), pp. 61–78; Charles A. Beard and Mary R. Beard, *The Rise of American Civilization* (New York: The Macmillan Co., 1927), vol. I, pp. 189–296; Lewis Hacker, *The Triumph of American Capitalism: The Development of Forces in American History to the End of the Nineteenth Century* (New York: Columbia University Press, 1940), pp. 93–195; Merrill Jensen, *The Articles of Confederation: The Interpretation of the Social-Constitutional History of the American Revolution, 1774–1781,* * 3rd printing (Madison: University of Wisconsin Press, 1959), pp. 3–103. Compare Jensen's *The Founding of a Nation: A History of the American Revolution, 1763–1776* (New York: Alfred A. Knopf, 1968) for a recent statement. The so-called consensus school after World War II was first synthesized by Edmund Morgan, *The Birth of the Republic, 1763–89* * (Chicago: University of Chicago Press, 1956). The developing thought of Bernard Bailyn on the role of ideas in the coming of the Revolution may be seen in a comparison of "Political Experience and Enlightenment Ideas in Eighteenth-Century America," *American Historical Review*, LXVII (Jan., 1962), pp. 339–351, with *The Ideological Origins of the American Revolution* (Cambridge, Mass.: Harvard University Press, 1967) and *The Origins of American Politics* (New York: Alfred A. Knopf, 1968). This persuasion has been summarized and extended by Bailyn's student, Gordon Wood, in *The Creation of the American Republic, 1776–1787* (Chapel Hill: University of North Carolina Press, 1969), pp. 1–124. The emerging New Left interpretation may be glimpsed in Jesse Lemisch, "The American Revolution Seen from the Bottom Up," in Barton Bernstein, ed., *Towards a New Past: Dissenting Essays in American History* * (New York: Pantheon Books, 1968), pp. 3–45, and "Jack Tarr in the Streets: Merchant Seamen in the Politics of Revolutionary America," *WMQ*, 3rd series, XXV (July, 1968), pp. 371–407, and in Staughton Lynd, *Class Conflict, Slavery, and the United States Constitution: Ten Essays* (Indianapolis: Bobbs-Merrill Co., 1967), and *Intellectual Origins of American Radicalism* * (New York: Random House, 1968). An interesting amalgamation of recent viewpoints that may illuminate the historiography of the 1970s is the article by Bernard Friedman, "The Shaping of the Radical Consciousness in Provincial New York," *Journal of American History*, LVI (March, 1970), pp. 781–801.

Historians generally agree that the events and issues after 1763 constitute the immediate causes of the war for independence. George Knollenberg would place the date earlier, however, as may be seen in his title, *Origin of the American Revolution, 1759–1766* * (New York: The Macmillan Co., 1960). Edmund Morgan and his wife, Helen, in *The Stamp Act Crisis: Prologue to Revolution* * (Chapel Hill: University of North Carolina Press, 1953), treat the event usually considered the first major one in the series leading to independence. Another significant event is covered by Benjamin W. Labaree, *The Boston Tea Party* * (New York: Oxford University Press, 1964), and the British reaction is the subject of Bernard Donoughue, *British Politics and the American Revolution: The Path to War, 1773–1775* (London and New York: Macmillan and St. Martin's Press, 1964). British army and judicial policy and colonial response may be followed in John Shy, *Toward Lexington: The Role of the British Army and the Coming of the American Revolution* * (Princeton: Princeton University Press, 1965); Carl Ubbelohde, *The Vice-Admiralty Courts and the American Revolution* (Chapel Hill: University of North Carolina Press, 1960); and David Lovejoy, "Rights Imply Equality: The Case against Admiralty Jurisdiction in America, 1764–1776," *WMQ,* 3rd series XVI (Oct., 1959), pp. 459–484. Jack M. Sosin, *Whitehall and the Wilderness: The Middle West in British Colonial Policy, 1760–1775* (Lincoln, Neb.: University of Nebraska Press, 1961) is the latest work on the British government's efforts to regulate the westward expansion of the colonies. Problems over regulating colonial currency are suggested by Jack P. Greene and Richard M. Jellison, "The Currency Act of 1764 in Imperial-Colonial Relations, 1764–1776," *WMQ,* 3rd series, XVIII (Oct., 1961), pp. 485–518; Jack M. Sosin, "Imperial Regulation of Colonial Paper Money, 1764–1773," *Pennsylvania Magazine of History and Biography,* LXXXVIII (April, 1964), pp. 174–198; Joseph Ernst, "Genesis of the Currency Act of 1764: Virginia Paper Money and the Protection of British Investments," *WMQ,* 3rd series, XXII (Jan., 1965), pp. 33–74. The longer view on political differences is taken by Jack Greene in an article "The Role of the Lower Houses of Assembly in Eighteenth-Century Politics," *Journal of Southern History,* XXVII (Nov., 1961), pp. 451–474, and a book, *The Quest for Power: The Lower Houses of Assembly in the Southern Royal Colonies, 1689–1776* (Chapel Hill: University of North Carolina Press, 1963). Carl Bridenbaugh uses the same approach for religious problems in *Mitre and Sceptre: Trans-Atlantic Faiths, Ideas, Personalities, and Politics, 1689–1775* * (New York: Oxford University Press, 1962).

The development of a feeling of a separate identity and a new culture would seem a prerequisite for revolution. Rising nationalism is treated in a series of articles: Max Savelle, "Nationalism and Other Loyalties in the American Revolution," *American History Review,* LXVII (July, 1961), pp. 901–923; Paul Varg, "The Advent of Nationalism, 1758–1776," *American Quarterly,* XVI (Summer, 1964), pp. 160–181; Richard Merritt, "The Emergence of American Nationalism: A Quantitative Approach," *ibid.,* XVII (Summer, 1965), pp. 319–335; John Blassingame, "American Nationalism and Other Loyalties in the Southern Colonies, 1763–1775," *Journal of Southern History,* XXXIV (Feb., 1968), pp. 50–75. Merritt developed his quantitative analysis of self-identity references in newspapers at greater length in *Symbols of Community, 1735–1775* (New Haven: Yale University Press, 1966). The role of the newspapers in fostering the Revolution is related by Arthur M. Schlesinger, Sr., *Prelude to Independence: The Newspaper War on Britain, 1764–1776* * (New York: Alfred A. Knopf, 1957). Max Savelle, *Seeds of Liberty: The Genesis of the American Mind* * (New York: Alfred A. Knopf, 1948) argues for the development of an American culture by the mid-eighteenth century, but see the older work by Michael Kraus, *Intercolonial Aspects of American Culture on* the Eve of the Revolution, With Special Reference to the Northern Towns * (New York: Columbia University Press, 1928), for another view. Alan Heimert explores the relation between revivalism and the transformation of American consciousness as a catalyst for conflict in Religion and the American Mind from the Great Awakening to the Revolution (Cambridge, Mass.: Harvard University Press, 1966).

Unfortunately, the social prerequisites for the Revolution are not as well developed by historians. Suggestive articles of what could be done are P. M. G. Harris, "The Social Origins of American Leaders: The Demographic Foundations," Perspectives in American History, III (1969), 159–346, and Kenneth Lockridge, "Land, Population and the Evolution of New England Society, 1630–1790," Past and Present, no. 39 (1968), pp. 62–80. Both Carl Bridenbaugh, Cities in Revolt: Urban Life in America, 1743–1776 * (New York: Alfred A. Knopf, 1955), and Richard Bushman, From Puritan to Yankee: Character and the Social Order in Connecticut, 1690–1765 (Cambridge, Mass.: Harvard University Press, 1967) tell us more about cultural than social change in the period before the Revolution.

As mentioned in the introduction, one of the important trends of the 1960s was the analysis of the social and political assumptions underlying the polemics used by the contestants. The trend culminated in the previously cited books by Bailyn, Ideological Origins of the American Revolution, and Wood, The Creation of the American Republic. Jack Greene challenges Bailyn's interpretation in "Political Mimesis: A Consideration of the Historical and Cultural Roots of Legislative Behavior in the British Colonies in the Eighteenth Century," American Historical Review, LXXV (December, 1969), pp. 337–360, with comment by Bailyn and reply by Greene following ibid., pp. 361–367. The significance of images of history was argued by H. Trever Colbourn, The Lamp of Experience: Whig History and the Intellectual Origins of the American Revolution (Chapel Hill: University of North Carolina Press, 1965). English sources and background of the ideology are illuminated by, among others, Caroline Robbins, The Eighteenth Century Commonwealthman: Studies in the Transmission, Development, and Circumstances of English Liberal Thought from the Restoration of Charles II until the War with the Thirteen Colonies * (Cambridge, Mass.: Harvard University Press, 1959), and J. G. A. Pocock, "Machiavelli, Harrington, and English Political Ideologies in the Eighteenth Century," WMQ, 3rd series, XXII (Oct., 1965), pp. 549–583. Changing conceptions of empire are delineated in Richard Koebner, Empire * (Cambridge, Eng.: Cambridge University Press, 1961). Perry Miller, "From Covenant to the Revival," in James W. Smith and A. L. Jamieson, eds., The Shaping of American Religion * (Princeton: Princeton University Press, 1961), I, pp. 322–368, and Edmund Morgan, "The Puritan Ethic and The American Revolution," WMQ, 3rd series, XXIV (Jan., 1967), pp. 3–43, explore the psychological and moral tensions beneath the ideology.

A significant word in the turn to semantics is democracy. Besides Bailyn and Wood cited previously, the reader should consult Richard Buel, Jr., "Democracy and the American Revolution: A Frame of Reference," WMQ, 3rd series, XXI (April, 1964), pp. 165–190; and Robert Shoemaker, " 'Democracy' and 'Republic' as Understood in Late Eighteenth Century America," American Speech, XLI (May,

1966), pp. 83–95. Relevant to the meaning as well as the context of the word are Jack R. Pole's article, "Historians and the Problem of Early American Democracy," *American Historical Review*, LXVII (April, 1962), pp. 626–646, and book, *Political Representation in England and the Origins of the American Republic* (London and New York: Macmillan and St. Martin's Press, 1966), as well as Chilton Williamson, *American Suffrage from Property to Democracy** (Princeton: Princeton University Press, 1960).

The semantics and logic of revolution may be examined directly in the sources. Bernard Bailyn will edit four volumes of the polemical literature of which only the first volume has been published: *Pamphlets of the American Revolution, 1750–1776* (Cambridge, Mass.: Harvard University Press, 1965). Merrill Jensen edited a briefer anthology, *Tracts of the American Revolution, 1763–1776* (Indianapolis: Bobbs-Merrill, 1967). A source readings book devoted to ideology is Max Beloff, ed., *The Debate on the American Revolution, 1761–1783** (London: N. Kaye, 1949). The chief document of the Revolution is treated according to different schools of interpretation in Carl Becker, *The Declaration of Independence: A Study in the History of Political Ideas** (New York: Alfred A. Knopf, 1922), and David Hawke, *A Transaction of Free Men: The Birth and Course of the Declaration of Independence* (New York: Charles Scribner's Sons, 1964). Becker's sequence of polemical development is challenged by Edmund Morgan, "Colonial Ideas of Parliamentary Power," *WMQ*, 3rd series, VII (July, 1950), pp. 353–392. A guide to and analysis of another source is provided by Bruce I. Granger, *Political Satire in the American Revolution, 1763–1783* (Ithaca: Cornell University Press, 1960).

George L. Beer's *Origins of The British Colonial System, 1578–1660* (New York: The Macmillan Co., 1908), and *The Old Colonial System, 1660–1754* (New York: The Macmillan Co., 1912) started the modern debate over the operation and fairness of Britain's economic regulations of the colonies. More recently, Oliver M. Dickerson, *The Navigation Acts and the American Revolution** (Philadelphia: University of Pennsylvania Press, 1951), argued that the navigation system was mutually beneficial to the colonies and the mother country, not only in modern retrospect, but also in the colonists' opinion as well, as shown by their lack of protest and evasion before 1763. Lawrence A. Harper, "The Effect of the Navigation Acts on the Thirteen colonies," in Richard B. Morris, ed., *The Era of the American Revolution: Studies Inscribed to Evarts Boutell Greene** (New York: Columbia University Press, 1939), pp. 1–39; Curtis P. Nettels, "British Mercantilism and the Economic Development of the Thirteen Colonies," *Journal of Economic History*, XII (Spring, 1952), pp. 105–114; and Thomas C. Barrow, *Trade and Empire: The British Customs Service in Colonial America, 1660–1775* (Cambridge, Mass.: Harvard University Press, 1967), deny each of these points in turn. Attitudes of specific colonial groups are described in Benjamin Labaree, *Patriots and Partisans: The Merchants of Newburyport, 1764–1815* (Cambridge, Mass.: Harvard University Press, 1962), and Emory G. Evans, "Planter Indebtedness and the Coming of the Revolution in Virginia," *WMQ*, 3rd series, XIX (Oct., 1962), pp. 511–533. The latter's emphasis on the importance of debts in Virginian attitudes toward independence is denied by Thad W. Tate, "The Coming of Revolution in Virginia:

Britain's Challenge to Virginia's Ruling Class, 1763–1776, *ibid.*, pp. 324–343. In an attempt at greater precision, recent analysis has moved to the statistical reconstruction of the balance of trade: Robert P. Thomas, "A Quantitative Approach to the Study of the Effects of British Imperial Policy upon Colonial Welfare: Some Preliminary Findings," *Journal of Economic History*, XXV (Dec., 1965), pp. 615–631, with discussion by Jacob Price, pp. 655–659; Roger L. Ransom, "British Policy and Colonial Growth: Some Implications of the Burden from the Navigation Acts," *ibid.*, XXVIII (Sept., 1968), pp. 427–435, with reply by Robert Thomas, "British Imperial Policy and the Economic Interpretation of the Economic Revolution," *ibid.*, pp. 436–440; James F. Shepherd and Gary Walton, "Estimates of Invisible Earnings in the Balance of Payments of the British North American Colonies, 1768–1772," *ibid.*, XXIX (June, 1969), pp. 230–263; and Peter D. McClelland, "The Cost to America of British Imperial Policy," *American Economic Review*, LIX (May, 1969), pp. 370–381, plus comments by J. R. T. Hughes, *ibid.*, pp. 382–385.

American as well as English historians have been reinterpreting the British side of the story of the events before, during, and after the revolt. Although Lewis B. Namier's two books, *The Structure of Politics at the Accession of George III,* * 2nd ed. (London: Macmillan, 1957), and *England in the Age of The American Revolution,* * 2nd ed. (London: Macmillan, 1961), contain few references to the conflict as such, his methodology has influenced a generation of historians in viewing the nature of English politics at the time. This influence is summarized by Richard Pares, *King George III and the Politicians* * (Oxford, Eng.: Clarendon Press, 1953), and criticized in Herbert Butterfield, *George III and the Historians,* rev. ed. (New York: The Macmillan Co., 1959). Implications of the new work for the interpretation of the Revolution are developed in Eric Robson, *The American Revolution in its Political and Military Aspects, 1763–1783* * (London: Batchworth Press, 1955); Ian R. Christie, *Crisis of Empire: Great Britain and the American Colonies, 1754–1783* * (London and New York: Edward Arnold and W. W. Norton and Co., 1966); and a brief review article by Jack Greene, "The Plunge of the Lemmings: A Consideration of Recent Writings on British Politics and the American Revolution," *South Atlantic Quarterly*, LXVII (Winter, 1968), pp. 141–175. Other significant books in this vein are Charles R. Ritcheson, *British Politics and the American Revolution* (Norman, Okla.: University of Oklahoma Press, 1954); Vincent T. Harlow, *The Founding of the Second British Empire, 1763–1793* (London and New York: Longmans, Green, 1953, 1964); and the fourteen volume *magnum opus* of Lawrence H. Gipson, *The British Empire before the American Revolution* (Caldwell, Ida., and New York: Caxton Printers, Ltd., and Alfred A. Knopf, 1936–1968). Men and policies of colonial administration are the specific subjects of Dora M. Clark, *The Rise of the British Treasury: Colonial Administration in the Eighteenth Century* (New Haven: Yale University Press, 1960), and Franklin Wickwire, *British Subministers and Colonial America, 1763–1783* (Princeton: Princeton University Press, 1966), while Jack M. Sosin, *Agents and Merchants' British Colonial Policy and the Origins of the American Revolution, 1763–1775* (Lincoln, Neb.: University of Nebraska Press, 1965), and Michael Kammen, *A Rope of Sand: The Colonial Agents, British Politics, and the American Revolution* (Ithaca: Cornell

University Press, 1968), add the colonial agents to the mixture of men in interaction in the determination of British policy. A sourcebook on the topic of its title is Charles R. Ritcheson, ed., *The Anglo-American Relation, 1763–1794* * (Reading, Mass.: Addison-Wesley, 1969).

The question of who and how many took the Tory side in the colonies is as problematical as why they did so. The problem of numbers is explored in Wallace Brown, *The King's Friends: The Composition and Motives of American Loyalist Claimants* (Providence: Brown University Press, 1966); Eugene Fingerhut, "Uses and Abuses of the American Loyalist Claims: A Critique of Quantitative Analysis," *WMQ,* 3rd series, XXV (Apr., 1968), pp. 245–258; and Paul Smith, "The American Loyalists: Notes on Their Organization and Numerical Strength," *ibid.,* pp. 259–277. The larger story is the concern of William H. Nelson, *The American Tory* * (New York: Oxford University Press, 1961), and Paul H. Smith, *Loyalists and Redcoats: A Study in British Revolutionary Policy* * (Chapel Hill: University of North Carolina Press, 1964). G. N. D. Evans has edited a book of readings, *Allegiance in America: The Case of the Loyalists* * (Reading, Mass.: Addison-Wesley, 1969).

Who the Whigs were and why is entwined historiographically with the nature of the colonial class structure and power and the economic and political motives of those seeking independence because of the influence of the progressive or economic interpretation. The best summary of that whole interpretation by the man who provided the term "internal revolution" for it is the previously cited Jensen, *The Articles of Confederation,* pp. 3–103. As its long subtitle indicates, Elisha P. Douglass, *Rebels and Democrats: The Struggle for Equal Political Rights and Majority Rule During the American Revolution* * (Chapel Hill: University of North Carolina Press, 1955), is a more recent exploration of this topic. The modern challenge to this whole perspective has been led by Robert E. Brown, *Middle-Class Democracy and the Revolution in Massachusetts, 1691–1780* * (Ithaca: Cornell University Press, 1955), and with his wife, *Virginia, 1705–1786: Democracy and Aristocracy?* (East Lansing, Mich.: Michigan State University Press, 1964). Two recent surveys of the whole debate are Richard B. Morris, *The American Revolution Reconsidered* * (New York: Harper and Row, 1967), pp. 43–91, and Jack Greene, "Changing Interpretations of Early American Politics," in Ray A. Billington, ed., *The Reinterpretation of Early American History* * (San Marino, Calif.: Henry E. Huntington Library, 1966), pp. 151–184. That the debate continues may be seen in recent issues of the *WMQ:* John J. Waters, and John A. Schutz, "Patterns of Massachusetts Colonial Politics: The Writs of Assistance and the Rivalry Between the Otis and Hutchinson Families," *WMQ,* 3rd series, XXIV (Oct., 1967), pp. 543–568; Robert L. Ganyard, "Radicals and Conservatives in Revolutionary North Carolina: A Point at Issue, The October Election, 1776," *ibid.,* pp. 568–587; and Robert M. Weir, " 'The Harmony We Were Famous For': The Interpretation of Pre-Revolutionary South Carolina Politics," *ibid.,* 3rd series, XXVI (Oct., 1969), pp. 473–501. See also David C. Skaggs, "Maryland's Impulse to Social Revolution," *Journal of American History,* LIV (Mar., 1968), pp. 771–786. Gordon Wood contributed "A Note on Mobs in the American Revolution," *WMQ,* 3rd series, XXIII

(Oct., 1966), pp. 635–642, in an attempt to draw the work of European and American historians together on this subject. Jackson T. Main, in *The Social Structure of Revolutionary America* * (Princeton: Princeton University Press, 1965), attempts a preliminary summary of the topic of the title, and in *The Upper House in Revolutionary America, 1763–1788* (Madison, Wisc.: University of Wisconsin Press, 1967), he traces the democratization of a political elite during the transformation of the colonial councils into the state senates. In considering the whole subject of the Whigs' motives and their social and political standing the reader should not neglect the many biographies of Revolutionary personalities available.

The military and diplomatic results of the Revolution are relatively clear compared to other aspects of the conflict. Several recent histories of the Revolution focus on fighting the war in Congress and on the battlefield: John C. Miller, *The Triumph of Freedom, 1775–1783* * (Boston: Little, Brown and Co., 1948); John Alden, *The American Revolution, 1775–1783* * (New York: Harper and Row, 1954); Howard H. Peckham, *The War for Independence, A Military History* * (Chicago: University of Chicago Press, 1958). British historians' views on the military results may be found in the previously cited Robson, *The American Revolution*, and Christie, *Crisis of Empire*, as well as Piers Mackesy, *The War for America, 1775–1783* (Cambridge, Mass.: Harvard University Press, 1964). The war as military history is reviewed by Don Higginbotham, "American Historians and the Military History of the American Revolution," *American Historical Review*, LXX (Oct., 1964), pp. 18–34. The latest books on the diplomacy of the Revolution and the making of peace are Richard Van Alstyne, *Empire and Independence: An International History of the American Revolution* * (New York: John Wiley and Sons, 1965), and Richard B. Morris, *The Peacemakers: The Great Powers and American Independence* (New York: Harper and Row, 1965.) The classic in this field is Samuel F. Bemis, *The Diplomacy of the American Revolution,* * rev. ed. (Bloomington, Ind.: Indiana University Press, 1957).

Less certain than the military and diplomatic outcome are the other results, because they are bound up with the controversy over the very nature of the Revolution considered in its larger sense. Summations of various aspects of the literature up to their date of publication are: Frederick B. Tolles, "The American Revolution as a Social Movement: A Re-evaluation," *American Historical Review*, LIX (Oct., 1954), pp. 1–12, which considers the validity of J. Franklin Jameson's classic of the same title *(Princeton: Princeton University Press, 1926); Clarence Ver Steeg, "The American Revolution Considered as an Economic Movement," *Huntington Library Quarterly*, XX (Aug., 1957), pp. 361–372; and Edmund Morgan, "The American Revolution Considered as an Intellectual Movement," in Morton White and Arthur M. Schlesinger, Jr., eds., *Paths of American Thought* * (Boston: Houghton, Mifflin Co., 1963), pp. 11–33. Since then, besides the articles reprinted here by Kenyon and Barrow, William H. Nelson, "The Revolutionary Character of the American Revolution," *American Historical Review*, LXX (July, 1965), pp. 998–1014, has tried to understand the nature of the Revolution as a total phenomenon. But almost all the books listed in this bibliography bear on this topic, of course. On the nature of political thinking and constitution-making, compare the previously cited works of Bailyn and Wood with Benjamin Wright, *Consensus and Continuity, 1776–1787* * (Boston: Boston University Press, 1958), and with Merrill Jensen, *The Articles of Confederation,* previously mentioned, and *The New Nation: A History of the United States During the Confederation, 1781–1789* (New York: Alfred A. Knopf, 1950). A short statement by Jensen is "Democracy and the American Revolution," *Huntington Library Quarterly,* XX (Aug., 1957), pp. 321–341. A bibliography upon the federal Constitution is provided by another pamphlet in this series. Comparative approaches to the nature of the Revolution are provided by Louis B. Hartz, *The Liberal Tradition in America: An Interpretation of American Political Thought Since the Revolution* * (New York: Harcourt, Brace and World, 1955), pp. 35–86; Robert R. Palmer, *The Age of Democratic Revolution: A Political History of Europe and America, 1760–1800* * (Princeton: Princeton University Press, 1959–1964); Seymour M. Lipset, *The First New Nation: The United States in Historical and Comparative Perspective* * (New York: Basic Books, 1963), especially pp. 13–98; and Hannah Arendt, *On Revolution* * (New York: Viking Press, 1963).

Last, the student should look to theory and evidence himself. A useful survey by a historian of analytical approaches to revolution is Lawrence Stone, "Theories of Revolution," *World Politics,* XVIII (Jan., 1966), pp. 159–176. Contrast the approaches of historians Crane Brinton, *The Anatomy of Revolution,** rev. ed. (Englewood Cliffs, N. J.: Prentice-Hall, 1952), and Louis Gottschalk, "Causes of Revolution," *American Journal of Sociology,* L (July, 1944), pp. 1–8, with those of social scientists, Neil J. Smelser, *Theory of Collective Behavior* (New York: The Free Press, 1963); Harry Eckstein, "On the Etiology of Internal Wars," *History and Theory,* IV (1965), pp. 133–163; and Chalmers Johnson, *Revolutionary Change* * (Boston: Little, Brown and Co., 1966). Besides the sourcebooks listed previously, the student can find collections of documentary evidence in Samuel E. Morison, ed., *Sources and Documents Illustrating the American Revolution, 1764–1788, and the Formation of the Federal Constitution* * (Oxford, Eng.: Oxford University Press, 1923); John Braeman, ed., *The Road to Independence; A Documentary History of the Causes of the American Revolution: 1763–1776* * (New York: G. P. Putnam's Sons, 1963); and Jack P. Greene, ed., *Colonies to Nation, 1763–1789* * (New York: McGraw-Hill Book Co., 1967).